People are not so complicated. Relationships between people are complicated.
—Amos Tversky, quoted in *The Undoing Project* by Michael Lewis

If there is a point to educating people in psychology, it's to make them less judgmental.
—Daniel Kahneman, "#68 Daniel Kahneman: Putting Your Intuition on Ice," *The Knowledge Project* podcast

Contents

Contents

I   The Biased Righteous Mind

Introduction

If we could read the secret history of our enemies, we should find in each man's life sorrow and suffering enough to disarm all hostility.
—Henry Wadsworth Longfellow, *Prose Works of Henry Wadsworth Longfellow*

In 1968, Shirley Chisholm was the first Black woman to be elected to Congress. In 1972, she became the first Black person, and first woman, to run for a major party's nomination for president. A rival in the primary campaign was arch-segregationist Alabama Governor George Wallace. On May 15 of that year, Wallace was shot five times in an assassination attempt, and in early June, Chisholm went to visit him in the hospital. "Shirley Chisholm! What you doing here?" Wallace asked. "I don't want what happened to you to happen to anyone," she replied. Wallace came to tears. When it was time for Chisholm to leave, Wallace did not want to let go of her hand.

The visit might have had a big impact on Wallace. His daughter Peggy said that "Chisholm had the courage to believe that even George Wallace could change. [She] planted a seed of new beginnings in my father's heart." Two years later, Wallace convinced a block of Southern Congressmen to support Chisholm's minimum wage bill, leading to its passage. A few years after that, he publicly renounced racism and asked for forgiveness.

John Lewis said that Wallace's apology was sincere: "I could tell that he was a changed man. He acknowledged his bigotry and assumed responsibility for the harm he had caused. He wanted to be forgiven." Alabama's Black voters agreed too, with over 90 percent voting for him in the 1982 gubernatorial election.[1]

Stranger than Fiction?

This story probably surprised you if you hadn't heard it before. But it probably didn't *shock* you. Redemption stories like this are uncommon but not unheard of. We're all familiar with people who were once at odds with one another overcoming their conflict and recognizing that the other "side" was not as fundamentally and permanently "bad" as they thought.

Misguided conflict is also commonly found in fictional works. It's an effective plot device because it resonates with our experiences—it feels real because it so often is. An example I came across while writing this book occurs in *Cobra Kai*, a streaming television series set in the present day about the characters from the 1980s *Karate Kid* movie series. *Cobra Kai* is primarily about the now middle-aged Johnny Lawrence. Johnny was the villain in the first movie but on the show discovers that he has a good heart after stumbling into becoming a mentor to his teenage neighbor.

Another villain from the movies, John Kreese, is an important character on the show as well. John was the teenage Johnny's karate teacher and became furious at Johnny, and even physically attacked him, after Johnny failed to win a tournament. When the two characters reconnect on the show, Johnny is understandably still upset about this. But he still decides to give John a second chance, knowing firsthand the possibility that people can change. John turns out to be irredeemable, however.

This book is about our bias toward thinking that people with whom we have feuds are true villains like John when they often turn out to be Johnnys: complicated but good at heart. Even Daniel LaRusso—the "Karate Kid," consistently a "good guy" in both the movies and the show—appears to be subject to this bias. Unaware of Johnny's change of heart, Daniel's negative misperceptions of Johnny drive much of the show's plot.

We roll our eyes when we hear someone ask, "Can we disagree without being disagreeable?" (Or even worse, "Why can't we all just get along?") It seems trite to describe a conflict as "just a big misunderstanding." The idea that conflict is typically caused by misperception is literally textbook conflict analysis.[2] Misunderstandings cause conflicts at the smallest and largest scales—misperceptions have even been considered "a central cause of both world wars" (Jervis, 2017, xv).[3]

Yet when we're personally involved in a contentious disagreement—and we all are at various points in our lives—it's clear to us, or so we think, that the fault lies mostly, or even completely, with the other side. We have no doubt that our hostility, and hostile actions, are fully warranted. Often, we even think the other side is an irredeemable bad guy like John, or a bunch of Johns. But Johnnys are out there. They might be even more common in reality than they are on TV.

Partisan Conflict and Misunderstanding

An increasingly intense conflict that most Americans participate in, to various degrees, is the struggle between the two major political parties, the Democrats and the Republicans. It's unclear how much the US has grown apart ideologically over recent decades. Research on this type of polarization, sometimes called *issue polarization* or *ideological polarization*, has yielded relatively mixed results.[4] But it's now widely recognized that *affective polarization*—polarization in how partisans feel about each other (in psychology, *affect* is roughly synonymous with emotion)—has grown steadily over this time and is now at an alarming level.[5]

The standard measure of affective polarization is the difference in survey "feeling thermometer" scores toward a respondent's own party (often called the *in-party* for short) and the opposition party (the *out-party*). Feeling thermometer scores range from zero to one hundred, with zero indicating feelings that are as "cold" as possible and one hundred implying maximally "warm" feelings. Average scores for each presidential election year since 1980 are shown in figure I.1. For partisans on both sides, the gap between in-party and out-party scores has approximately doubled between 1980 and 2020, and the growth in this polarization is almost entirely due to a decline in feelings toward the out-party.

Partisans have grown to feel much more hostility toward both the out-party's voters and (especially) toward out-party politicians and other elites (Druckman and Levendusky, 2019). Both mass partisans (voters) and partisan elites are now highly affectively polarized (Enders, 2021).[6] Since 1980, affective polarization has increased more in the US than other Organisation for Economic Co-operation and Development (OECD) nations with comparable data (Boxell et al., 2020). Some scholars argue that affective polarization is so severe in the US that the term *polarization* is too understated and the conflict should instead be called *political sectarianism* (Finkel et al., 2020).

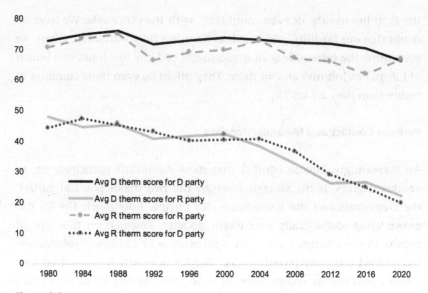

Figure 0.1
Trends in partisan thermometer scores. Source: author's analysis of data from the American National Election Studies, https://electionstudies.org/.

Maybe it's wishful thinking, but I'm going to stick with the milder term *polarization*. Whatever we call it, it's a problem—maybe even America's biggest problem, since it both prevents us from solving other problems and creates new problems in its own right. When we dislike the other side, we become less cooperative, more distrustful, and more likely to act unethically. We politicize issues that are not inherently political, like mask wearing and vaccination during a pandemic. Affective polarization naturally snowballs over time, leading to potentially disastrous threats to democratic norms, institutions, and even violence.[7] The exact negative consequences are unpredictable—but the platitude "divided we fall" has much truth to it.

Affective polarization is obviously a complex phenomenon, with many underlying causes. In this book, I'm going to talk about just one broad category of these causes: misunderstandings. I'll argue that disagreement in US politics—and other political and nonpolitical settings—often leads to what I call *affective polarization bias*: objectively false and overly negative beliefs about the other side's character traits, causing *undue* hostility and even hate. This bias isn't a single cognitive process—I'll discuss how it results from a wide variety of other biases and contextual factors. I'll also talk about why those of us who feel more hostility are likely to be more biased and why undue hostility has likely been exacerbated in US partisan politics over recent decades.

You might think you can't be *objectively* wrong about something as *subjective* as your interpersonal feelings. But you can misjudge another person by your own standards. As a result, you can dislike another person more than you should. This simple point is implied, but not discussed explicitly, in prior literature on affective polarization and clarifies how at least some of our interpersonal hostility is essentially mistaken.

I'm not saying that everyone should get along perfectly well with everyone else. I'm not saying that all, or even most, of our negative feelings toward other individuals or groups are unjustified. I'm just pointing out that we can, of course, misunderstand other people. And since our feelings toward others are influenced by these misunderstandings, we can dislike others more than we should. I'll argue that this "mistaken dislike" tends to result from disagreement in US politics—and a wide range of other contexts.

US Politics, Groups, and One-on-One Relationships

> There is no daylight between divorce court and Congress at this point.
> —Amanda Ripley, "How to Avoid High Conflict," *The Good Fight* podcast

Previous studies and books on US affective polarization have focused on partisan identity and intergroup bias as the explanation for the growth in affective polarization that's occurred here. In a nutshell, the idea is that since evolution has programmed us to favor our in-group "teammates" and demonize the out-group "opposition," as partisanship has become a more important part of our identities for a variety of reasons, partisan warfare, so to speak, has grown.[8]

I don't deny the central importance of group identity effects in partisan politics and affective polarization in the US. But group effects can't be the complete explanation for hostile polarization in general since this type of polarization so often occurs *within* social groups and not just *between* them (as illustrated in figure I.2).[9] We're all familiar with examples from our personal lives and the public sphere: spouses, siblings, friends, neighbors, coworkers, and partners who grew apart, often not so peacefully. Famous

"This will never work, Tom. We're from opposite ends of the same wing of the same political party."

Figure 0.2
An example of within-group affective polarization. Source: Robert Leighton / The New Yorker Collection / The Cartoon Bank.

examples of close friends and partnerships that devolved to the point of bad blood, despite the partners sharing key social identities, include Thomas Jefferson and John Adams, Muhammad Ali and Malcolm X, Betty Friedan and Gloria Steinem, and—founding fathers of behavioral economics, along with Richard Thaler—Daniel Kahneman and Amos Tversky.[10] The bible includes numerous examples of the age-old phenomenon of "sibling rivalry." Even twins sometimes grow apart to the point of not speaking to one another.[11]

The term *affective polarization* hasn't been used in prior academic literature to describe interpersonal hostility in settings other than partisan politics. But it's reasonable to use it in a wide range of contexts. Anytime two "parties" grow apart from each other emotionally, especially due to disagreement, it seems apt to say that affective polarization has occurred.

I'm certainly not the first person to compare American politics to a bad marriage. And if affective polarization can occur within social groups as well as between them, then there must be important causes of affective polarization other than social group differences.

In this book, I'll argue that there are in fact many important causes of affective polarization bias (again, that's undue affective polarization) unrelated to identity effects. So, while I'll focus on political settings throughout the book, and US politics in particular—because of the acute growth in affective polarization that's occurred here and because it's been the focus of my prior research—I'll also discuss examples of the bias occurring in nonpolitical relationships between individuals. These examples both show how widespread affective polarization bias is and serve as useful metaphors for better understanding US politics.

And while I'm well aware of the risks of "bothsides-ism"—discussing problematic behaviors on both sides of a dispute in a way that falsely implies equivalency—I'll mostly avoid the question of "who's to blame" (for polarization in US politics and elsewhere) in this book. I'll elaborate on my reasons for this later. For now, I'll simply note that there's plenty of evidence indicating our trouble-making tendencies are close to universal. Just about all of us are subject to this bias to different degrees, at different points in our lives. Just about all of us unwisely exacerbate conflicts at times— making *ourselves* worse off in the long run—and can do better.

Why Me?

My PhD is in economics, and I've been an economics professor for 15 years now. Why is an economist writing about political feelings? Well, again, this book is about hard feelings being driven by misunderstandings and mistaken beliefs. I'm a behavioral economist, and the study of systematically mistaken beliefs, that is, biased beliefs, is an important part of behavioral economics. Behavioral economics is, broadly speaking, the study of deviations from the "standard" assumptions of economic theory that people are optimal decision makers who use available information as well as possible to form unbiased beliefs when facing uncertainty. Behavioral economists thus seek to understand when economic agents (e.g., investors, entrepreneurs, and consumers) hold unduly positive or negative beliefs about all sorts of outcomes and the implications of these biases.[12]

In my past research, and in new ideas and data presented in this book, I argue that tools from behavioral economics—mathematical models of beliefs and inference, game theoretic interaction and communication, and biases identified and studied primarily in behavioral economics—help enhance our understanding of affective polarization. To be clear, though, while this framework for analyzing affective polarization is new and affective polarization bias is a new concept, I don't claim to be proposing a fundamentally new theory of polarization. I'm far from the first person to suggest that cognitive biases contribute to affective polarization.

Throughout the book I'll be making some new claims, but I'll mainly be extending existing ideas and connecting dots based on research conducted by others, mostly from outside of economics. Two particularly well-known books that mine builds on are *The Righteous Mind*, by psychologist Jonathan Haidt, and *Why We're Polarized*, by journalist Ezra Klein. Both discuss how affective polarization is influenced by cognitive bias and thus imply that affective polarization is often excessive—but never say this directly. Another, quite distinct book that's especially similar in spirit to mine is Buster Benson's *Why Are We Yelling?* Benson discusses how a variety of cognitive biases contribute to hostility in nonpolitical relationships but also doesn't explicitly discuss how hostility itself can be mistaken.

In addition to my general interest in biased beliefs and the importance of affective polarization, there are two other reasons that I'm interested in this topic. The first is directly connected to my being an economist: the sheer inefficiency of undue polarization. Polarization wastes time, money, and effort; prevents mutual gains; and even creates unnecessary harm. Correcting biased beliefs about the other side leading to undue hate is, at least hypothetically, low-hanging fruit for making the world a much better place. Much easier said than done, of course. Still, it's undoubtedly simpler logistically than, say, building a high-speed national rail system or ending a pandemic.

The second reason I'm particularly interested in polarization is personal experience. I admit I've never been politically radical or highly emotive, but I've still experienced my share of unduly hostile polarization. As a kid and teenager, it was mostly as a sports fan. Apparently, I used to have a habit of saying my favorite teams were always "underrated," as my mom made fun of me about this for many years afterward. I also had theories for why players, coaches, and even fans of rival teams were worse *people* for various reasons. (And I was happy to tell you why if you asked and maybe even if you didn't ask.) In my late teens and early twenties, the same went for those with political views I disagreed with.

It felt good to be better than the other side, whether in sports or politics, and to have reasons for why this was the case. I didn't know the term cognitive bias but did "know" the media and refs were biased against my favorite teams and that those teams, and our fans, were even morally superior to the opposition. So, yes, I'd say that I was unduly polarized. I was far from a truth seeker—instead, I believed what I wanted to believe (or thought I wanted to believe) and was naively unaware of doing this. And I'm no rocket scientist, but I'm confident that my self-awareness and logical reasoning skills aren't far below average. My experience made me think that irrational polarization can happen to just about anyone.

In more recent years my personal experience with polarization has often been secondhand with my spouse. (She has fully endorsed this paragraph, by the way.) She happily admits to being prone to many behavioral economics biases—and that there have been many times that she's become unduly polarized toward people she's had disagreements with, mistakenly "assuming the worst" about seemingly bad behavior. Sometimes these are disagreements with acquaintances, friends, and family—and sometimes they're with me. At other times, I've made the same mistake. We've helped each other recognize these tendencies and, at least sometimes, bite our tongues before saying things we'd regret. We've both observed that it's all too easy to fail to recognize our own contributions to conflicts in relationships and to be inclined to write off lost friends and estranged family members as "bad people." If my partner were a more stereotypically "rational" economist, I wouldn't have seen so vividly and frequently how easily we can become unduly inflamed—and, on the plus side, how easily we can forgive and move forward.

Audience and the Rest of This Book

My goal is to write this book in a way that's both readable and informative for students and researchers in a variety of disciplines, and for people outside of academia interested in polarization. I don't assume the reader has any prior knowledge of either polarization or behavioral economics. Readers who are knowledgeable about these topics will be familiar with a fair amount of content. But as an old grad school classmate of mine once said, "repetition is not a bad thing." Experienced instructors know this is almost always the case for students. I think it's surprisingly often the case for seasoned scholars too.

I've written this book in a pretty informal style. That's partly because I hope to have a wide-ranging readership. But it's also because I thought it would be easier for me to write it this way, and easier for you to read, no matter who you are. I've been an academic for a while now, however, and the book is still written accordingly, to some extent—there's a limit to how much I can lighten up. I've tried to be careful to not overstate claims, to provide evidence where necessary, and to note where I am essentially theorizing. There is a little math used sporadically throughout the book—I am an economist, after all. But it's not much, and it's only used to clarify points that might otherwise be muddled.

Before moving ahead, I think it will be helpful to quickly go over the book's organization. Part I consists of this introduction and the first two chapters. In chapter 1, I discuss the general topic of interpersonal dislike as well as how "Bayesian ideal" belief updating can apply to beliefs about character traits. I also propose a more formal definition of affective polarization bias. In chapter 2, I review an array of evidence indicating the existence of affective polarization bias in the US. This is the book's most "meat and potatoes" chapter.

Part II, chapters 3–6, discusses explanations for the bias. Chapter 3 provides my take on some major general biases that affect us in many parts of life, including partisan politics and interpersonal disagreement. Chapters 4–6 are each on a more specific "category" of explanations for affective polarization bias. Each of these chapters also includes some discussion of why the bias would increase over time and how the explanations could also apply to nonpolitical contexts. Chapter 4 covers theories for why we tend to excessively dislike those we disagree with in general, one that is relatively well known and one that is more novel. Chapter 5 discusses why strategic behavior in relationships exacerbates dislike and, in particular, causes dislike to tend to spiral. Chapter 6 is about why we tend to observe, and interpret, information in a way that exacerbates the effects discussed in prior chapters.

Part III is a single chapter, chapter 7, in which I briefly summarize and discuss implications of the prior chapters, considering a wide range of possibilities for short- and long-run impacts. I don't deny the many constraints impeding change, but I think it's still worth thinking through and discussing a variety of options—and maintaining optimism about potential progress. We should certainly strive to avoid a bias toward pessimism and undue certainty that these problems will never be resolved. And whatever the chances are for positive large-scale political change, greater awareness and understanding of affective polarization bias can improve relationships in our everyday lives.

1 Affective Polarization Bias: Theory

The unknowability of one human being to another is an endless subject.
—Anne Enright, "An Interview with Anne Enright," by Conan Putnam

This book is about why we tend to experience too much affective polarization with one another—why disagreements tend to make us dislike other people more than we should—for all types of disagreements but especially when disagreements are overtly political. In this chapter, I'll explain in more detail what I mean by these claims. First, though, let's back up a step and talk about what, in general, causes us to dislike or even hate another person. Sometimes there's something about them that rubs us the wrong way. We're just not that into them, and it's hard to explain why. Usually, however, we have reasons for our feelings. Psychologist Jamil Zaki (2019, 37) writes that "of course, feeling and reason are in constant dialogue. Emotions are built on thought. . . . Emotions reflect not just what happens to us, but how we interpret those things."

Sometimes we dislike another person because we look down upon them—we think they're less capable than they should be in some important way. Dislike can also be driven by our perception that the other person is morally inferior—that they're a "bad guy," so to speak.[1] For our dislike toward someone to grow to become hate, we usually need to think they have "malicious intentions and [are] immoral" (Fischer et al., 2018, 310).

What makes us believe that someone else is a bad guy? What we've seen them do in the past? Yes and no. Consider this thought experiment: your brother Joe was a jerk to you until you were ten. Then, for some reason, he became a great brother, for a full year. You're now turning eleven, and you're confident he's going to be a great brother going forward. So, you probably like Joe now despite the fact that he did a lot more "bad" to you than "good" over the course of your lifetime. (I put the terms "good" and "bad" in quotes here to emphasize that these judgments are subjectively defined—we each have our own criteria for them, and it's hard or perhaps impossible to say which criteria are better than others—but I'll sometimes drop the quotes when I think this meaning is already clear.)

Why do you like Joe now, at age eleven? Because you're convinced that he is now good even though he used to be (or you used to think he was) bad. In other words, our feelings of like and dislike toward Joe and others aren't just based on the sum total of their past actions that we've observed. Instead, these feelings are based on our *beliefs* about who they are now and who they'll be going forward—our beliefs about their deep motives, values, and capabilities, which we expect to be reasonably durable (though maybe impermanent) character traits.[2]

We think people with "good" character traits are more likely to take "good" actions or hold "good" opinions in the future. (A character trait, as I use the term, is just a feature of a person that plays some role in causing their past and future actions.) We thus learn that people are more likely to be good when we observe them do good things in the past.[3] And we feel warmer toward those people because we then expect them to be more likely to do good things going forward.

In economics, we'd call the actions of others that we observe and learn about them from *noisy signals*. A noisy signal is just about anything we observe that provides information about something else we're unsure about without completing resolving the uncertainty. For example, the result from a poll of five hundred likely voters taken one month before the election is a noisy signal for the election outcome. But signals can be much less scientific too. When you run into a friend at the grocery store, their expression and interest in talking to you are signals of how they feel about you. These actions are influenced by many other factors (e.g., their current mood and how busy they are) in addition to this interest—hence the "noise." Interpreting noisy signals is challenging, to say the least.

Still, some signals are clearly more informative than others—a poll of voters taken the night before the election is more informative than the one taken one month earlier. And character traits can change. That's why Joe's most recent behavior is likely more informative about his current character than his actions from the distant past. However, many actions don't tell us much at all about another person's character. And nearly all actions are influenced by circumstances in complex ways that are impossible to account for precisely.

As a result, no actions or words are perfectly informative about another person's character. We can't directly observe any of other people's character traits, so we can't understand any of those traits with certainty. (Even though we might *feel* that we "see" exactly who other people are sometimes. This type of overconfidence turns out to cause a lot of trouble, as I'll later discuss.) We can never perfectly understand *ourselves*, much less other people, about whom we have orders of magnitude less information.

We are sometimes, perhaps usually, wise enough to know that when we see another person take one bad action, it doesn't make them a bad person. If you think Joe's a good guy but he does something that you feel was wrong, you'll be angry with him (especially if you're personally wronged by the action), but you won't immediately dislike him. Anger results from actions perceived to be "wrong" (while dislike and hate result from perceptions of durable characteristics; see Fischer et al., 2018). One bad action is probably only a weak signal about the character traits of someone you know well, and so it probably doesn't have much effect on your beliefs about their traits. But if their bad actions continue, anger can lead to significant changes in your beliefs about their traits and therefore lead to dislike and even hate. Eventually, these signals add up to more information than noise.

An Example

Here's a quantitative example to illustrate the points discussed above and to help take the discussion further. The example is intentionally highly simplistic to be as clear as possible. Suppose you care about just one character trait in other people, generosity, and suppose you think there are just two values of this trait, "generous" or "ungenerous." You think generosity is "good," meaning you like someone more when you believe they are more likely to act generously.

And suppose you consider just two possible actions, giving or not giving money to a charity that you are raising money for. Suppose also that giving is a noisy signal of generosity—if you see someone give, that implies they're more likely to have the generous trait than you would have believed otherwise but doesn't reveal the true value of their trait with certainty. Specifically, let's say you believe that a generous person has a 75 percent probability of giving to your charity (so their probability of not giving is 25 percent) and an ungenerous person has a 10 percent probability of giving (so their probability of not giving is 90 percent).

Finally, suppose you think half of people are generous and half aren't. These are then your *prior beliefs*, often referred to as *priors*, about character traits—what you believe prior to observing new information about someone. If you observe a stranger give, then the mathematically correct way to update beliefs about their probability of being generous is to use *Bayes' rule*, which in this case happens to yield a *posterior* belief (your belief after observing the signal) of an 88 percent chance that the person is generous. Look at this note or figure 1.1 if you're interested in how the 88 percent is computed.[4] But it's also fine to not worry about the details of this calculation for the purposes of this book. If you're unfamiliar with Bayesian updating, you can just think about it as the mathematically correct way to update beliefs with new information given the priors and signal probabilities. It's correct

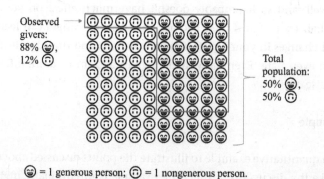

😊 = 1 generous person; 🙁 = 1 nongenerous person.

Figure 1.1
An illustration of Bayesian updating. There are 50 generous people and 50 ungenerous people in total. Since their probabilities of giving to charity are 75 percent and 10 percent, respectively, on average, 37.5 generous people give and 5 ungenerous people give, represented by the people inside the enclosed region. After observing someone give to charity, you know they are inside this region of givers. Eighty-eight percent of this population is generous (37.5/(37.5+5)), and 12 percent is ungenerous. Thus, the Bayesian posterior probability of being generous after being observed giving to charity is 88 percent.

in that if your prior and signal probabilities are correct, then the Bayesian posterior probability will indeed be correct. If you observe a stranger give once, then there's indeed an 88 percent chance the stranger is generous. If you observe a large sample of strangers who give once, approximately 88 percent of them are generous types.

Even though we're not concerned in this book with exactly how the Bayesian posterior is computed, it's worth briefly discussing the intuition of the posterior's value. Many people guess the posterior probability that someone is generous after seeing them give is 75 percent as that's the probability a generous person gives. This would be correct if we'd happened to assume that ungenerous people had a probability of giving of 25 percent. Our Bayesian posterior turns out to be higher than 75 percent though (88 percent) because we assumed ungenerous people are quite unlikely to give (10 percent). This makes giving a stronger signal that the person is generous. If we'd assumed ungenerous people had an even smaller probability of giving, like 2 percent, then the posterior probability of being generous after seeing someone give just once would be even higher (97 percent). If we assumed ungenerous people never gave, then giving just once would prove that the person is generous, so this posterior probability would be 100 percent.

The final assumptions I'll make for this model are on interpersonal feelings. Following the literature on affective polarization, suppose we measure interpersonal feelings with thermometer scores. Let's also assume that the score you give to another person is equal to your perceived probability that they give to charity in the next opportunity they have to give. So, you'll like a stranger more after seeing them give since this makes you think they are more generous, which makes them more likely to give in the future. You dislike a stranger more if you see them not give for analogous reasons.

Comments

Again, this model is highly simplistic, but I don't think it makes any controversial assumptions. It just distills and quantifies key points from the chapter's earlier discussion: you like or dislike other people because of your beliefs about their character trait(s), because these traits affect their probabilities of taking various actions in the future, and you learn about their character trait(s) by observing their actions.

And this example does allow us to demonstrate a basic but crucial point: our beliefs about the character of another person, and thus the degree to which we like or dislike them, can be *objectively* wrong even if character is *subjectively* defined. If you think that someone will give to charity 25 percent of the time but the true probability is 30 percent, then you're just wrong. You'll dislike them too much by your own standards.

Now, yes, it's somewhat unfair to say that you're wrong about someone if you just don't have much information about them. For example, if it's true that half of strangers are generous and half aren't, it would be harsh to say that you're wrong to think that a random stranger has a 50 percent chance of being generous and thus a 42.5 percent chance of giving (a 50/50 average of the two probabilities of giving, 75 percent and 10 percent). Yes, the stranger is either generous or ungenerous, and so they either have a 75 percent or a 10 percent chance of actually giving. In either case your estimate of 42.5 percent is wrong. But your estimate is the best you can do given what you know, so your estimate is right on average. Consequently, given the information you have, you're really doing the best you can.

Similarly, it would be somewhat unfair to say your judgment of someone is wrong if it's based on having seen an action that's unusual for that person, which you just happened to observe due to chance. If you saw an ungenerous person uncharacteristically act generously (give money), and you updated your belief about them being generous upward, then you used your available information appropriately. (Even though your updated beliefs turned out to be less accurate than your prior.)

But if you thought that, say, any person whom you observe give once only had an 80 percent chance of being generous (when the Bayesian probability was 88 percent), then you'd be wrong in a deeper way. Assuming your priors and signal distributions are correct, you would then be wrong on average for the group of one-time givers—your posterior beliefs about their chances of giving in the future would be *biased* in the statistical sense. You'd underestimate their chance of giving in the future. In this contrived example where generosity is the only condition that determines whether you like someone, you'd therefore like the other person less than you should, given the information available to you. (If you're now wondering why one would possibly hold a non-Bayesian belief like this, that's great, exactly the right question to ask. Just hang on—I'll be tackling this question in detail in chapters 3–6.)

The logic here extends to any number of traits or actions. We can systematically misjudge other people's traits, causing us to underestimate or overestimate the probabilities of good or bad actions those people take in the future. This could cause us to like or dislike other people more than we should.

Biased Dislike

I'll now provide a more general definition of the notion of "too much" dislike, given one's available information. My goal is to make this definition as succinct as possible while still being sufficiently precise for the purposes of this book.

> Definition: Person P is subject to *biased dislike* toward person Q if P's thermometer score for Q would increase if P were to hold Bayesian beliefs about Q's action probabilities given P's information and priors.

If holding "correct beliefs" about another person given your information and priors (Bayesian beliefs) would make you like that person better than you currently do, then you are subject to biased dislike toward the person. We could define an analogous positive bias too, but of course the concern of this book is the prevalence and implications of undue dislike. The definition is easily extended to feelings toward groups: you're subject to biased dislike toward a group if you are subject to this bias for a randomly drawn member of the group (based on their group membership). The term *action* in the definition is meant to be interpreted broadly as anything empirically observable, including stated opinions, and to refer to any action or set of actions considered, consciously or unconsciously. The definition refers to a thermometer score as a measure of one person's feelings toward another because it is a concrete and empirically observable measure of interpersonal feelings.

This definition of biased dislike fully allows for subjectivity in criteria for interpersonal feelings. In addition to being agnostic about which actions are better or worse in any given situation, the definition is also agnostic as to how one should weight behavior across different types of situations in determining feelings toward a person, or even how many situations should be considered. The definition works for someone who only cares about giving or not giving to charity. It also works for someone who cares about that plus a million other things—including characteristics that could be unrelated to actions (e.g., aspects of one's appearance)—and we don't have to know anything about the relative importance of each of those things. And the definition doesn't say that having your non-Bayesian beliefs about another person corrected *must* change your feelings toward that person. It just says that biased dislike occurs if having these beliefs corrected *would* improve your feelings.

One might think a weakness to the definition of biased dislike is that not many people—maybe literally no one—typically thinks about other people's potential actions in terms of probabilities. But we do think approximately this way at an unconscious level all the time: we hold beliefs about events being unlikely, expected, likely, very likely, and so on. That's why we feel different degrees of surprise when we observe different events— beforehand we had different (unconscious) beliefs about the probabilities of these events occurring. (We would never feel surprise if we thought all events were equally likely.) If I asked you to, you could estimate probabilities for different actions being taken in different situations for anyone. You might not be confident about your estimates, but you wouldn't make the same estimates for everyone—you'd guess that some people are more likely to take some actions than others.

Another aspect of the definition worth remarking on is that it doesn't refer directly to the way that information is interpreted. The definition refers to current beliefs and does not refer to how one processed information in the past or to how one will process information in the future. I stated the definition this way because doing so is relatively straightforward and transparent and because it's natural to assume biased beliefs reflect bias in past information processing. However, one could also "randomly" mis- interpret information in the past in an overly negative way, which would not imply that the person is generally subject to bias.

An additional issue is that the definition takes available information as given, yet many of us often seek out information that's skewed toward denigrating another person's or group's character traits. This could plausi- bly lead one to hold a negative opinion toward the other person or group that is unbiased given one's available information but overly negative given their true character traits. In this sense, biased dislike as defined above is a conservative definition of undue dislike—this could also occur in other ways.[5] However, Bayesian updating accounts for a general skew in one's information, if one is aware of this skew (and Bayesians generally should be). For example, if I know you want me to like Joe, and so you tell me as many positive things about Joe as possible and no negative things, then telling me just one good thing about Joe probably won't persuade me to like him better. It might even make me dislike him more (you might have "damned him with faint praise"). As a result, skewed information has limited effects on Bayesian beliefs, and generally has larger impacts on non-Bayesians, as I'll discuss in chapter 6.

A final issue with the definition that I'll note is that it might seem to be impractical. Identifying biased dislike between persons P and Q appears to require knowing both P's actual beliefs and P's hypothetical Bayesian beliefs about Q's actions. Eliciting people's beliefs about other people's future actions is hard but often doable. Eliciting the exact Bayesian version of these beliefs is typically downright impossible given that we usually don't know people's priors and private information.

But in situations where an individual doesn't have much information about the other individual or group, *strong* feelings of dislike imply that non-Bayesian overreaction to the limited information has likely occurred. Moreover, in ongoing relationships where the two sides have observed one another extensively, Bayesians are usually expected to hold fairly accurate beliefs about each other. That's because Bayesian beliefs generally converge to true values as more and more information is observed.[6] Substantial inaccuracies in situations like this would therefore suggest non-Bayesian updating. And even if we don't expect any given individual's beliefs about another to be accurate, in the absence of bias we'd expect beliefs across a group of individuals about a group of other individuals to be accurate on average. Systematic inaccuracies in large samples thus imply the presence of systematic bias in the individuals. So, even if we rarely know precisely what a given person's exact Bayesian beliefs should be, we can often use available data to learn about whether groups of people appear to be subject to biased dislike. I'll discuss empirical analysis of biased dislike further in the next chapter.[7]

Affective Polarization Bias

We can now use the definition of biased dislike to formulate a definition of the bias toward excessive affective polarization.

Definition: A person is subject to *affective polarization bias* if they experience biased dislike toward another person, or members of a group, as a direct or indirect result of disagreement with the other person or group.

Affective polarization bias is a specific type of biased dislike. It's biased dislike toward someone, or some group, that you are polarized with, in terms of your opinions—someone you *disagree with*. It's a bias toward interpreting disagreement, in words or actions, as a stronger negative character signal than it really is. So, affective polarization bias is not specific to partisan politics per se since affective polarization is not a phenomenon unique to partisan politics. Affective polarization can happen anytime two groups or individuals disagree. Since biased dislike can conceivably occur anytime two parties (political or otherwise) disagree as well, it makes sense to define affective polarization bias accordingly. Those who are subject to a greater degree of bias will tend to dislike the other side more, so we'd expect the magnitude of this bias to be positively correlated with strength of dislike.

I'm admittedly vague about what constitutes a "disagreement" here. That's intentional to give us some flexibility with how we use the affective polarization bias term going forward. But I'm really just referring to the plain-English definition of disagreement. A disagreement isn't just seeing someone do or say something you don't like—it typically involves some discussion, or at least some shared information, that still fails to result in consensus.

To illustrate with a hypothetical example (there will be plenty of real ones to come), if, say, a disagreement over lawn care between you and your neighbors makes them jump to the conclusion that you're a bad neighbor, which leads them to think that you are more likely to be a downright bad person, and makes them overestimate the chances of you taking (other) bad actions—then they're being influenced by affective polarization bias. Anytime we see someone do something we think they shouldn't, or state an opinion that we disagree with, leading us to excessively demonize them, then we are subject to affective polarization bias. The more you overreact, the more biased your beliefs will be and the more hostility you'll feel.

Again, just because you infer that someone has a bad character trait from something they say or do doesn't mean that you're biased. The bias only occurs when the inference is too strong given the information available to you. This idea of "too strong" is clearly a hard thing to identify, which is why it's so hard to avoid making this mistake in practice. Note, though, that those who are subject to a greater degree of bias will tend to dislike the other side more. Thus, strong feelings of dislike are a clue that bias is relatively likely to have occurred.

Concluding Remarks

The following are key points from this chapter:

- Just about everything we do and say, including our political views, provides a signal to other people about our character traits.
- Our feelings toward others are based on our beliefs about their character traits and corresponding action probabilities. These feelings can be too warm or too cold if our beliefs are incorrect.
- Bayesian beliefs are the standard benchmark for correct beliefs given one's available information. We may or may not hold Bayesian beliefs about other people's character traits, just as we may or may not hold Bayesian beliefs about all unobserved variables.
- Interpreting signals about other people's character traits is hard. Biased dislike occurs when we dislike others more than we should as compared to how we would feel about them if we held Bayesian beliefs. Affective polarization bias is biased dislike toward those we disagree with.

There are a few additional points worth noting before moving ahead. First, to be clear, I am not claiming that affective polarization bias is the main factor driving partisan hostility in the US. As I discuss in the introduction, polarization is incredibly complex, and I definitely don't attempt to offer a complete explanation for it. One undoubtedly important factor in American politics that I mostly neglect in this book is race. While racial issues could contribute to affective polarization bias, they are largely outside of my scope since I am focused on general causes of the bias that apply within and across social identity groups.[8]

Second, affective polarization bias is a new term and concept. We already have plenty of named biases in the behavioral sciences, but I think affective polarization bias is sufficiently distinct that it's worth giving it its own name. One especially closely related existing term is *hostile attribution bias*, which refers to our tendency to interpret ambiguous behaviors by others as having hostile intent.[9] The hostile attribution bias could cause biased dislike and might even result from biased dislike, but the two terms refer to clearly distinct phenomena. Hostile attribution bias refers to a biased interpretation of particular actions, while biased dislike refers to negatively biased perceptions of character traits. Affective polarization bias is even more distinct in that it refers to negative character misperceptions resulting from a particular cause, disagreement. The larger literature on the *fundamental attribution error* is also particularly related, as I discuss further in chapter 3.

Third, I mentioned anger briefly earlier in the chapter but won't discuss it extensively in this book. As noted earlier in the chapter, anger and dislike can be distinguished as feelings caused by bad actions and bad characteristics, respectively. So, an analogous bias for anger could be defined as overestimation of anger-inducing "bad" actions that have occurred in the past. In fact, the hostile attribution bias is an example of this type of bias. Again, such a bias would contribute to biased dislike since, as discussed above, we infer bad traits from bad actions. Anger and dislike are related but distinct; I focus on the latter since affective polarization is normally defined as dislike between the parties, not anger. What's more, dislike is arguably more problematic since pessimistic beliefs about out-party characteristics make cooperation difficult, while anger often spurs productive change (see, e.g., Traister, 2019). But we should stay aware of a possible conflation of these different emotions and corresponding beliefs.[10]

Fourth, as I discuss in the introduction and again in subsequent chapters, social identity theory and strengthened partisan identity are the key explanations for growth in US affective polarization that the literature has focused on, and the causal relationship between identity and affective polarization bias are worth discussing briefly here. This chapter is about how beliefs about character traits can cause dislike. However, identity theory says that identity can cause dislike toward out-groups, which in turn can cause biased beliefs about those groups' character traits. The direction of causality between biased beliefs and dislike thus seems ambiguous. This is not a problem for our purposes, however. If identity causes a person to hold biased beliefs toward the other side that, if "corrected," would not affect feelings of dislike, the person is simply not subject to biased dislike or affective polarization bias, by the definitions of those terms. If dislike would be reduced if the biased beliefs were corrected, then the person is subject to affective polarization bias. The bias can thus be caused by identity-based forces—and by many other factors, as I'll discuss.

The last additional issue that I want to discuss briefly now is asymmetry, alluded to in the introduction. After hearing about affective polarization bias, many of us might suspect it's much more common among people on the other side of the partisan divide. ("I understand them, but they misunderstand me/us.") Perhaps some of these beliefs are mostly or even entirely correct. I certainly am not claiming that the degree of affective polarization bias on both sides of a disagreement must be the same or that responsibility for conflict is generally symmetric. (And I'm certainly not saying this is true for the case of US politics in particular.) But throughout this book, I'll mostly ignore potential asymmetries in the degree of bias across the two sides, in partisan and other settings. I'm doing this partly because of my focus on nearly universal "quirks" in how we think and act. It takes two to tango, and for just about any conflict, both parties bear some responsibility, and both have some room for improvement.[11] Although the magnitudes of these quirks surely aren't equal for all of us, addressing asymmetries would make the analysis much more complicated.

Also, to be frank, part of the reason I'm ignoring asymmetry is to try to maintain credibility with readers on both sides of the spectrum. If this book were about how one side of the US political debate was ten times more biased than the other, I'd probably have trouble maintaining attention and trust from readers from the maligned side—even if I were 100 percent correct. More generally, in conflicts where the parties bear asymmetric responsibility, it's often tactically wise to refrain from accusing one side of being more biased. That's because if the accusation is true, the biased side might be particularly sensitive to the accusation—because of their greater bias! Consider, for example, how it's relatively easy to provide feedback to your wise and easygoing friend who's usually right about things. They don't get worked up about small mistakes or get bent out of shape easily from pushback and even negative feedback. On the other hand, your friend who consistently struggles with his judgment is more likely to fly off the handle if you point out any of his mistakes. His resistance to feedback might in fact be a root cause of the persistence of his bias. As the old saying goes, "do not correct a fool, or he will hate you; correct a wise man, and he will appreciate you."

In the next chapter, I'll discuss evidence of affective polarization bias. It's tricky to show since doing so seems to require knowing 1) what partisans think are good and bad actions, 2) how good or bad we think out-partisans are by these standards, and 3) how good or bad we should think out-partisans actually are by these standards. But there are now many studies reporting that partisans hold overly negative beliefs about out-partisans' character traits in a variety of ways.

2 Affective Polarization Bias: Evidence

I do not conflate moral character with political affiliation.
—John R. Wood, Jr. leader of the antipolarization organization Braver Angels, Twitter, September 24, 2020

The exception proves the rule? Wood's statement is interesting because most of us *do* draw strong inferences about character traits of other people based on their political views. To what extent are these inferences inaccurate, and to what extent do they cause undue dislike?

This chapter is on a few types of research that address this question in different ways. Most of these studies were conducted within just the last few years—which may help explain why affective polarization bias had not been recognized formally before now.

Survey Says

I'll start with some evidence that's relatively ambiguous but still worth discussing briefly: survey responses to questions about Democrats' and Republicans' typical character traits. It's essentially impossible to assess the accuracy of these responses since the traits are defined differently by all of us. Furthermore, talk is cheap: respondents don't have to respond honestly to survey questions, especially when they're not incentivized to do so. They might enjoy overstating the out-party's flaws in surveys or even feel there's a strategic benefit from doing this. So, we can't take these survey responses at face value.

Even when people call the out-party "downright evil"—which 42 percent of survey respondents in both parties did in 2018 (Kalmoe and Mason,

2019)—it's not clear that these responses imply the presence of affective polarization bias. Maybe respondents were referring to specific actions by a subset of out-partisans who they truly (and correctly, given their own criteria) felt were "evil," or maybe they just got a kick out of answering the survey this way but didn't really believe it. Similarly, while several studies have shown that highly affectively polarized partisans on both sides of the aisle dehumanize the opposition, and "dehumanizing evaluations" are "conceptually absurd" if taken literally (Moore-Berg et al., 2020b), again, we don't know how literally these responses are meant.[1] But we can still learn about true beliefs from survey responses if we interpret them carefully, especially when they're compared across questions and over time.

In fact, our willingness to dehumanize the out-party in survey responses has increased sharply over just the last several years. The percentage of American partisans saying out-partisans "lack the traits to be considered fully human" nearly doubled in just three years during the Trump administration, increasing from 18 to 35 percent from 2017 to 2020 (Cassese et al., 2021). There isn't even data on partisan dehumanization questions that dates back much further in time—probably since even these questions would have seemed absurd in prior years. A large change in extreme survey responses like this at least suggests that our beliefs about the out-party's character have changed for the worse. If I claimed that "although our dehumanization of the out-party in surveys doubled over a three-year period, our beliefs about their character traits definitely did not change at all over that period," I doubt you'd buy it. Of course, just because beliefs changed, it wouldn't mean they became more biased. It's even possible beliefs became more accurate over time.

Survey responses on more specific—and more plausible—partisan character traits at different points in time may be more revealing. The Pew Research Center collected this type of data in 2016 and 2019. In both years they asked representative samples of thousands of Americans questions about specific character traits of members of each party. Unsurprisingly, in both years, partisans on both sides generally said they thought out-partisans were relatively likely to have negative traits (see figure 2.1).

What's more interesting is that, for each party in each year, the degree of in-party favoritism varied across the character traits. The results show that most of us don't automatically ascribe all bad qualities to the other side. (We don't just say "they're worse than us at everything.") We're more

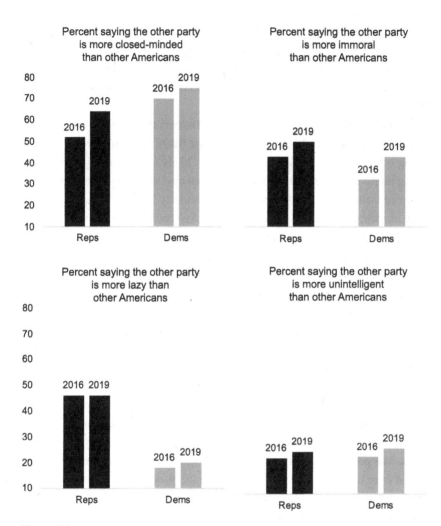

Figure 2.1
Perceptions of partisan character traits. Source: adapted from Pew Research Center (2019) data.

likely to say they have certain bad qualities than others. So, even if these responses are distorted because they're cheap talk, if the distortion is similar across the various traits, then these results imply partisans (on average) truly believe out-partisans are more likely to have some negative traits than others.

Republicans were most likely to say Democrats are relatively closed-minded, immoral, and lazy and were least likely to accuse Democrats of being unintelligent. Democrats were most likely to accuse Republicans of being relatively closed-minded and immoral and were least likely to accuse them of laziness. Yes, *both* sides were particularly likely to accuse the *other* side of being especially closed-minded. Assuming the two sides define closed-mindedness somewhat similarly, this immediately suggests at least one side's perceptions of this trait were skewed.

Moreover, responses changed substantially for some, but not all, traits in just three years between the surveys. Republicans became 8 percentage points more likely to call Democrats relatively immoral between 2016 and 2019 and 12 percentage points more likely to call them more closed-minded. Democrats became 12 percentage points more likely to call Republicans immoral and 5 percentage points more likely to call them closed-minded. Perceptions of laziness, on the other hand, barely budged.

A few years of the Trump era didn't make us more likely to accuse the other side of all bad qualities. But in just three years, we (on both sides) did become more likely to say the other side was worse than ours in particular ways. We probably at least partially believed these accusations were true. (If we were just angrier at the out-party in 2019, we might have been more likely to ascribe all the negative traits to them.) So again, the data strongly suggests real changes in beliefs about particular character traits. Could these changes have been justified?

It's technically possible that our beliefs became more accurate over the three-year period. But both parties had lots of information about each other in both years. It's hard to believe we became significantly better informed about the other side's true character traits in such a short time. It's also possible that the character traits changed over the period. It seems unlikely, though, that deep, underlying traits for a large group of people would change in the same ways this quickly. A final potential justification for changes in survey results is that they were due to the composition of the parties changing. However, the fraction of the electorate identifying with either party didn't change by more than a few percentage points (Pew Research Center, 2020), so this was unlikely to drive such substantial changes in the survey results.

A final explanation for these changes in beliefs is that they were *not* justified and beliefs became more unduly negative—that is, more negatively biased. There was certainly a lot of partisan acrimony over this three-year period that could have exacerbated bias. Among other issues, there was a major investigation into foreign interference in the 2016 election and a presidential impeachment with a nearly 100 percent party-line vote in both chambers of Congress. Citizens on both sides may very well have perceived that the other side took many "bad" actions—and inferred "wow, these people are even worse than I thought." If these inferences were excessive, that would mean that affective polarization bias increased over the period.

"In close relationships and families, there is a trade-off between familiarity and objectivity," according to communications scholar Alan Sillars. In his research, he discusses how misunderstandings in relationships can actually *grow* when we (feel that) we get to know each other better (Sillars, 2002, 2011). Perhaps misunderstanding-driven hostility between partisans has grown over time, even as we have become increasingly familiar with one another in many ways. Again, though, the evidence from these surveys is admittedly just suggestive. The next few sections are on research that more clearly demonstrates biased beliefs.

False Polarization and Other False Partisan Stereotypes

I think President Obama is the most radical president this nation's ever seen.
—Ted Cruz, quoted in "Ted Cruz's Most Provocative Quotes," by Ben Schreckinger

This section discusses evidence that our *perceived polarization* is inaccurate—that we overestimate the extremism of the policy preferences and ideological opinions of those on the other side. This phenomenon is often called *false polarization.* "False" is an overstatement—exaggerated polarization would be more accurate—but "false polarization" is catchy, and it's a standard term, so let's stick with it.

We tend to think that people holding opinions we disagree with have poor character (more on this in chapter 4). So, we're more likely to negatively misjudge the out-party's character when we overestimate our disagreement on the issues and vice versa. In other words, false polarization is an indicator of affective polarization bias. And greater levels of false polarization have indeed been found to be associated with greater affective polarization, suggesting false polarization does in fact cause too much dislike.

False polarization has now been documented repeatedly in the US and around the world.[2] A few examples of it (underestimation of agreement between the parties) are shown in figure 2.2. False polarization in the US has also been shown to be associated with affective polarization and to have increased over time (Bordalo et al., 2020; Enders and Armaly, 2019; Parker et al., 2021). Druckman and colleagues (2022) found evidence of both false polarization and overestimation of out-partisans' political engagement: subjects estimated that 64 percent of out-partisans talk about politics "frequently," while the actual figure was 27 percent. Moreover, when told an out-partisan only discussed politics "rarely" or "occasionally," measured hostility toward the out-partisan declined by 25 percent. These results imply that affective polarization is driven partly by overestimating out-partisans' interest in politics in combination with overestimating their extremism.

Perhaps like survey responses to questions about character traits, some of us exaggerate the extremism of the out-party's positions in survey responses because we have little reason not to. I don't know of any studies of false polarization that provide monetary rewards for accurately answering these questions. (If we received payment for answering questions on the out-party's policy positions accurately, perhaps we'd exaggerate the extremism of these positions less.) Perhaps also those of us who dislike the out-party more are more prone to such exaggeration. I'd guess that such "motivated survey responses" are less relevant to questions about policy positions than character traits, and I think it's very unlikely to be the full explanation for the extensive evidence of false polarization. But this issue is still a caveat to keep in mind when interpreting this research.

False polarization is one type of false stereotyping of the out-party: false stereotypes of their policy views. We also falsely stereotype the *people* in the other party—their demographic characteristics, like age, race, incomes,

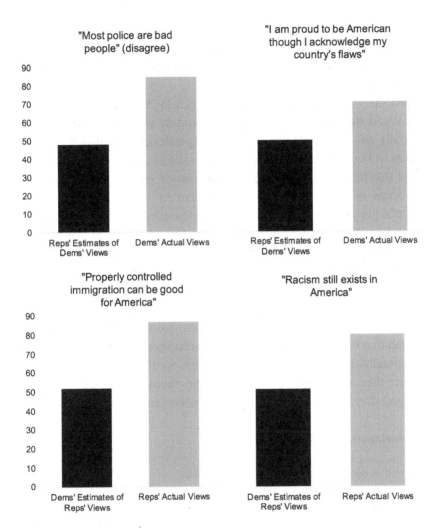

Figure 2.2
Selected gaps between perceived and actual partisan views (graphs show the percentage of respondents who agreed with the given statement except for "most police are bad people," which shows the percentage disagreeing with the statement). Source: adapted from Yudkin et al. (2019).

and where they live. Again, in contrast to unobserved internal character traits, researchers can check the accuracy of these perceptions—and if these beliefs are inaccurate, and correlate with out-party dislike, this would be evidence of affective polarization bias.

False demographic stereotyping was shown by Ahler and Sood (2018), who found that partisans on both sides unduly stereotype both sides— especially the other side. For example, Republicans estimated that 35.7 percent of Democrats identify as atheist or agnostic, while Democrats estimated this figure to be 24.5 percent (the correct figure was 8.7 percent). Democrats estimated that over 44.1 percent of Republicans earn over $250,000 per year, while Republicans estimated this to be 33.3 percent. The correct figure here was 2.2 percent. Ahler and Sood showed that these errors are robust to providing respondents with monetary incentives for accuracy and that respondents who make larger errors tend to feel greater negative affect toward the out-party.

It's worth noting that false demographic stereotypes could contribute to false (issue) polarization and perhaps even vice versa. I'm not aware of research that cleanly distinguishes these mechanisms. Regardless, these are conceptually distinct ways that we can misjudge the out-party. The data indicate that we inaccurately stereotype the opposition in both of these ways and they both contribute to affective polarization bias.

False Metaperceptions

> Hatred of liberals is all that's left of conservatism.
> —headline of Paul Waldman's 2020 *Washington Post* article

Another key way misperceptions drive hostility is that partisans overestimate the hostility *they* feel toward *us*, and as a result we feel too much hostility toward *them*. Beliefs that people hold about other peoples' beliefs are usually called second-order beliefs in economics and metaperceptions in psychology. Biased metaperceptions can cause biased dislike. The basic logic is it that if we think the out-party dislikes us, we'll interpret this as a signal of poor character on their part given that we tend to think of ourselves as pretty good people. So, overestimating their hostility toward us leads us to feel undue hostility toward them. Again, the causality could go the other direction as well, in which case biased metaperceptions would still indicate biased dislike.

The existence of large negative biases in metaperceptions, and the partially self-fulfilling nature of these biases, became widely recognized in the literature starting in two papers published in 2020. Moore-Berg and colleagues (2020a) reported that "Democrats and Republicans assumed that the levels of prejudice and dehumanization held by the other side (i.e., meta-prejudice and meta-dehumanization) were 50–300% [!] higher than what was actually expressed by a representative sample of outgroup political partisans." They also showed that negative metaperceptions were associated with greater enmity toward the out-party.

The second of these two papers, Lees and Cikara (2020), showed that partisans on both sides of the aisle overestimated the negativity of the out-party's perceptions of hypothetical in-party political actions, like requiring a sitting governor of the opposing party to disclose their taxes. For example, in one of their studies, on a scale of dislike of an action ranging from zero to one hundred (one hundred equals strongest dislike), actual dislike felt by the out-party was on average in the forties, but the in-party's perceived out-group dislike was nearly double this, in the eighties.

The robustness of this finding was quickly rigorously tested when Ruggeri and colleagues (2021) employed a global network of over eighty researchers to conduct extensive replications of Lees and Cikara's work. The replications occurred across twenty-six countries and included over ten thousand participants. Ruggeri's team defined "in-groups," "out-groups," and relevant actions carefully so as to be appropriate for each country. They found that for twenty-five of the twenty-six countries, in-groups overestimated perceived negativity felt by the out-group toward them. Like false polarization, biased metaperceptions appear to be a nearly ubiquitous phenomenon in partisan politics, and not unique to the US, implying that this bias is prevalent in most partisan contexts.[3]

Ruggeri and colleagues' studies didn't incentivize responses for accuracy. However, they did replicate another of Lees and Cikara's findings, which indirectly demonstrate the validity of the main results: that informing respondents about true out-group perceptions reduced negative judgments toward the out-group. Negative judgments in the US were reduced, on average, from about sixty to just over fifty (on a scale of zero to one hundred) for respondents informed about true out-group judgments. The declines were about the same size or even larger in almost all of the ten other countries where this additional test was conducted.

The reduction in hostility resulting from *corrections* to biased metaperceptions implies that false metaperceptions were indeed a cause of affective polarization bias. If metaperceptions hadn't contributed to hostility, then correcting these metaperceptions wouldn't have reduced hostility. Furthermore, if metaperceptions were just exaggerated survey responses, then having them corrected shouldn't have affected feelings toward the out-group (since there'd be nothing to truly correct). So, the positive effect of corrections to metaperceptions supports both the idea that metaperceptions contribute to driving hostility and the validity of the main measures of metaperceptions.

False Beliefs about Behavior

I'll next talk about research showing that we have unduly negative beliefs about actual choices made by out-partisans. This includes some new analysis I've done for this book, and it's arguably the most direct evidence available of affective polarization bias, so this section will be a bit more detailed than the previous ones.[4]

The first of these studies was conducted by Tappin and McKay (2019). The authors recruited over one thousand participants online in the summer of 2016 to play an economic game in groups of six, with each group including three Democrats and three Republicans. All six participants in each group were faced with three options: 1) $5 for yourself and nothing for others in the group (in their paper, Tappin and McKay call this the "self-interest" action), 2) $2.50 for yourself and your copartisans only (the "out-party hostility" action), and 3) $2.50 for everyone in the group (the "collective interest" action).

Tappin and McKay found that, on average, choices were nearly identical across the two parties and most participants in both parties played collective interest, cutting their own payoff in half to help all of their group mates, even the out-partisans. For Democrats, 60 percent played collective interest, while only 26 percent played self-interest, and 14 percent played out-party hostility. For Republicans, 59 percent played collective interest, 26 percent played self-interest, and just 15 percent played out-party hostility.

Tappin and McKay also asked participants how they thought others from both parties would play the game but didn't analyze this data, so I looked at this myself.[5] I found that, first, Republicans were actually more optimistic about Democrats playing collective interest than about their copartisans doing so: on average, Republicans guessed 43 percent of Democrats would choose this action and just 37 percent of other Republicans would. Democrats thought 47 percent of their copartisans would play collective interest but thought just 30 percent of out-partisans would do so. (These results and others are summarized in table 2.1.)

Partisans on both sides underestimated the chance of out-partisans playing the most prosocial action by over 10 percentage points. Democrats underestimated this much more than they underestimated their copartisans' chances of taking this action. But remember, part of the criteria for affective polarization bias is that you judge people whom you disagree with as less likely to take the "good" action given your own definition of good. And who knows, maybe some subjects thought that "collective interest" was not the morally best action. Perhaps those with a moral rule that it's best to "look out for your own" thought the "out-party hostility" action was best. Some might even have thought that maximizing self-interest was the right thing to do.

Tappin and McKay didn't ask participants to comment on which action they thought was morally best. However, since subjects had both individual and partisan incentives to make choices other than collective interest, the most plausible reason that a subject would actually choose collective interest is that they believed it was the "right thing to do." If you're taking an action not because it most benefits yourself or even your team, you must think the action is "good." And if you're willing to make a personal sacrifice to do the right thing, it seems clear you'd want people on the other side to do the same. (By contrast, you might have chosen "self-interest" to benefit yourself despite not thinking it was morally ideal.)

So, suppose participants who chose collective interest perceived that this action was the "best" action—the strongest signal of good character. Republicans who made this choice thought 59 percent of copartisans would make the same choice, almost exactly the correct figure. But these Republicans also thought just 49 percent of Democrats would make this choice. Democrats who chose collective interest thought 69 percent of copartisans would make the same choice—and only 35 percent of Republicans! Democrats thus underestimated Republicans' chances of playing collective interest relative to that of Democrats by over 30 percentage points.

Tappin and McKay also asked participants detailed questions about perceptions of moral traits for typical voters in each party and which traits they considered most important. They then used these responses to compute a "weighted moral polarization index" reflecting the degree to which subjects felt their own party is morally superior to the out-party *in the ways that matter most to those same subjects*. In other words, they constructed a variable measuring how morally superior each subject felt the in-party was as compared to the out-party, accounting for subjectivity in the relative importance of different moral values. For example, if a respondent said altruism and honesty were the only two traits that mattered for her, then the index would be the average of her perception of the in-party's advantage for these two traits.

I looked at the subset of participants who chose collective interest themselves *and* were relatively morally polarized (in the top half of their party's moral polarization distribution). This subset of Democrats thought their copartisans were more than 40 percentage points more likely than outpartisans to choose the collective interest action! This implies a bias of over 40 percentage points given that the two parties were actually about equally likely to take the action. Analogous Republicans thought their copartisans were more than 30 percentage points more likely than out-partisans to do this, nearly as large a bias.

These results imply that participants on both sides were subject to affective polarization bias. Participants on both sides underestimated out-partisans' chances of taking the "best" action (by the participants' own standards, as implied by their own choices). And participants who perceived that out-partisans' character traits were worse (by the participants' own standards) had the most overly negative beliefs about the out-party's behavior.

A caveat for these results is that Tappin and McKay didn't incentivize participants to report beliefs about other subjects' behavior accurately. A related study by behavioral economist Eugen Dimant did provide these incentives. Dimant (2021) presents results from several experiments with thousands of subjects, but I'll focus on the one where he collected data on the behavior and beliefs about out-party behavior. In this experiment, conducted in 2020, nearly six hundred subjects were paired up to play

Table 2.1
Average beliefs about the percentage of other participants playing collective interest
for different participant groups. Actual percentages of Democrats and Republicans
playing collective interest were 59.5 percent and 59.4 percent, respectively.

	All Democratic or Republican participants	Participants who played collective interest themselves	Participants who played collective interest themselves and were morally polarized
Democratic participants' beliefs about other Democrats' choices	47.3%	69.2%	71.1%
Democratic participants' beliefs about Republicans' choices	29.6%	35.4%	28.9%
Republican participants' beliefs about other Republicans' choices	37.3%	58.6%	70.1%
Republican participants' beliefs about Democrats' choices	42.9%	49.3%	38.7%

Source: author's analysis of data from Tappin and McKay (2019).

a simultaneous public good game: each subject was given $10 with the option to contribute any or all of this to "produce a public good." Any dollar contributed to the public good turned into $1.50 to be shared. However, since the two players split the resulting public good 50/50, the contributor only received $0.75 from each $1 she contributed. Thus, public good contributions help your partner at a small cost to yourself, so stronger prosocial motives should have led to larger contributions.

Dimant asked subjects about their feelings about President Trump and classified subjects as Trump "lovers," Trump "haters," or indifferent. The haters contributed, on average, just under $5 to the public good when told they were paired with Trump lovers and a bit over $6.50 when paired with fellow haters. Trump lovers contributed around $5 when paired with haters and just over $6 when paired with fellow lovers. Once again, nearly identical behavior was observed across the two groups, and this behavior was substantially prosocial even when subjects were paired with political opponents.

Dimant also asked subjects to guess what their counterparts would contribute, with bonus payments for accurate guesses. Trump lovers' guesses were close, on average, to the actual contributions made by Trump haters when they were paired together. Trump haters' guesses were too low when paired with lovers: haters guessed lovers would contribute under $4 on average (again, the actual average was $5), consistent with biased dislike.

Moreover, both lovers and haters who had the most polarized feelings underestimated the contributions by subjects who held a contrary view of Trump.[6] These same subjects did *not* underestimate average contributions by those with aligned opinions about Trump, so they did not simply underestimate contributions in general, only those made by people with opposing political views. Dimant's sample is smaller than Tappin and McKay's and is not large enough to split the analysis by the contribution size, feelings toward Trump, and polarized feelings. So, we're not able to focus on polarized subjects who made high contributions themselves. Still, it seems safe to assume that higher contributions were generally considered indicators of better character since they entailed individual sacrifice to grow the total pie. Given this assumption, these results imply that the most polarized participants on both sides underestimated the probability of the other side taking "good" actions and thus were subject to affective polarization bias.

A third paper that reports beliefs about out-party behavior in games with financial incentives is Whitt and colleagues (2021). They conducted several experiments in 2019, and in the simplest of these, the *dictator game*, the experimenters also asked participants for their beliefs about out-partisan behavior. In the dictator game, one player is given some amount of money (in this case, $10) to unilaterally allocate between themselves and another player. For example, the dictator could choose to either allocate $5 to each player, keep $9 for herself and give away just $1, or keep all $10. (Yes, it's really not much of a "game.") The authors didn't incentivize belief accuracy, and unlike the games studied by Tappin and McKay and Dimant, there's no action in the dictator game that involves making a self-sacrifice that yields a larger benefit to other player(s) (an action that "grows the pie"). As a result, identifying subjectively "good" actions is less clear—for example, it's plausible that partisans thought making a small contribution is "good" when one's own side does this (because the other side does not deserve more) but "bad" when the other side does this (since one's own side deserves better). For these reasons, let's take these results with an additional grain of salt.

Whitt and colleagues found that, on average, Democrats actually over-estimated Republican contributions (Democrats expected $2.67 on average, while Republicans only gave $2.35). Republicans did underestimate Democratic contributions, receiving $2.91 on average from them but only expecting $2.43. And members of both parties who said they felt least close with the out-party underestimated contributions by the out-party, consistent with affective polarization bias, assuming larger contributions were considered "good." The 136 Democrats who said they felt least close with Republicans expected, on average, a contribution of $1.94, and the 102 analogous Republicans expected just $1.26 (both lower than the average contributions they received of $2.35 and $2.91, respectively).

Summing up, across three papers, partisans usually had overly negative beliefs about out-party actions, and these beliefs were especially negatively biased for the most polarized partisans.[7] I'll discuss the interpretation of these results further below, but I first want to talk about one more study examining beliefs about out-partisan behavior in a setting with more intense, though hypothetical, stakes.

Political scientists Michael Barber and Ryan Davis asked survey respondents in 2018 to consider the classic philosophical thought experiment called the trolley problem, but with a partisan twist. In the trolley problem, you're told a train is heading down a track and bound to kill five people, but you can flip a switch to make the train go down a side track, which would kill just one person. Barber and Davis (2019) were interested in whether knowing the partisan identities of the people on each track would affect whether we flip the switch.

Just over 90 percent of respondents from both parties said they'd flip the switch without knowing the partisan identities of the people on each track. When told the single person on the side-track was a copartisan and that the five on the main track were out-partisans, willingness to make the sacrifice declined. However, average choices were still around the same for respondents in both parties: approximately 60 percent of both Democratic and Republican respondents said they'd flip the switch to save five out-partisans.

Barber and Davis didn't ask subjects about their perceptions of out-partisans' choices, so I conducted a preregistered study to assess the accuracy of these perceptions myself. In an incentivized survey conducted in October 2020, I used the research website Prolific to ask approximately one hundred members of each party to guess the percentage of members of each party that said they would sacrifice a copartisan to save five out-partisans, with relatively large bonus payments for correct answers. I paid $1 for each guess that was within 10 percentage points of the correct number and $0.50 for guesses within 10–15 percentage points of correct, on top of a flat $1.50 participation fee, for those who passed an attention check. The study took approximately five minutes. I also offered to share the original research that their bonus payments were based on to confirm their bonus payments were correct. (I ended up sharing this with all participants, not just those who asked to see it.)

Democratic respondents, on average, guessed 58.8 percent of Democrats would make the copartisan sacrifice to save the five out-partisans but that only 48.2 percent of Republicans would do this (versus a true value of 60 percent). Republican respondents guessed around 52.5 percent of Republicans would make the copartisan sacrifice but that just 48.6 percent Democrats would do this (versus a true value of 58 percent). So, members of both parties underestimated the percentage of out-partisans who said they'd make the copartisan sacrifice, and they overestimated the difference between copartisan and out-partisan chances of making the life-saving sacrifice.

I also solicited the standard measure of affective polarization for respondents via thermometer scores of both parties and checked behavior specifically for those respondents in the top half of the polarization distribution who also said they'd make the sacrifice themselves, indicating they agreed this was the morally best choice. Republicans in this group guessed that 64 percent of fellow Republicans would make the sacrifice but only 53 percent of Democrats would do so. Democrats in this group guessed 66 percent of Democrats would make the sacrifice but just 53 percent of Republicans. Again, members of both parties were approximately equally likely to make the in-party sacrifice.

These results provide additional confirmation that partisans, especially when more affectively polarized, typically hold unduly negative beliefs about out-partisan behavior. In most cases in these studies, the magnitude of bias was large for the most polarized subjects. The results for average party members are more inconsistent, but they are still indicative of affective polarization bias more often than not (for six of eight cases across the two parties and four studies).

Further Remarks on the Experiments

What else might explain the results from these experiments besides affective polarization bias? Maybe there was some aspect of this group of experiments that made evidence of the bias unusually likely to appear in them? The experiments were reasonably distinct from one another, however. The games and surveys differed in various ways though they did all use online subject pools. The results could also be unique to these four studies due to sheer randomness, but that's unlikely given the reasonably large sample sizes.

Perhaps affective polarization bias is more likely to appear to exist in contrived experiments like these in general, and less likely in natural settings, and so evidence of the bias in experiments is weak evidence of the bias existing outside the lab? I think this is unlikely though. Even if behavior is relatively "good" in research experiments, why wouldn't subjects account for this when stating beliefs about how they expect other subjects to behave in these games? In other words, if Democrats are jerks in general but behave well in games played for research, then shouldn't Republican research participants have said they expected Democrats to behave well in experiments? Especially when those participants were paid more for being correct about this? I think it's just as plausible, if not more so, that our beliefs about out-party behavior are *less* unduly biased in experiments like these than in natural settings—that we overestimate "bad" actions more in the wild, when there is less structure, and a number of other forces contributing to bias (which I'll be discussing) are more salient.

Still, to be clear, I can't rule this alternative explanation out. And for all of these analyses, causality likely runs in both directions: beliefs affect feelings and feelings affect beliefs. (We dislike "them" because we think they have certain poor character traits and, as a result, think they also have other poor character traits.) But the logic of the first effect—that beliefs about character drive feelings—is especially clear and supported by relevant literature, as discussed in chapter 1. Overall, these results complement the research discussed in the previous sections of this chapter, providing reasonably strong evidence that partisans are influenced by affective polarization bias, especially those who are most affectively polarized.

Concluding Remarks

In this chapter, I've reviewed a few types of evidence of affective polarization bias in US partisan politics:

- survey responses implying beliefs about some (and not all) negative character traits for out-partisans growing worse over time;
- overestimation of out-party ideological extremism (false polarization);
- overestimation of differences in demographic characteristics between the parties (false partisan stereotypes);
- overestimation of hostility felt by out-partisans toward the in-party (false metaperceptions);
- and overestimation of the propensity for out-partisans to take "bad" actions in incentivized experiments.

These results generally apply to partisans on both sides of the aisle. Those of us with the most negative feelings toward the out-party tend to have the least accurate beliefs, consistent with greater inaccuracy (bias) causing more dislike, and there is some evidence of inaccuracy increasing over time. None of the individual pieces of evidence is remotely conclusive, but together they provide solid confirmation of the existence and importance of affective polarization bias. I haven't cherry-picked—I've reported the limited contradictory evidence that I'm aware of.

These studies don't directly show that any given individual has interpreted their private information in a non-Bayesian way. However, as noted in chapter 1, the prevalence of false beliefs in large samples implies the prevalence of bias—especially in conjunction with the vast literature on relevant cognitive biases, which I'll discuss in subsequent chapters. The model and definitions of chapter 1 are theoretical benchmarks, intended to clarify what mistaken dislike means, and I hope future research can bring them to data more directly.

A limitation to the studies discussed in this chapter is that they only address the accuracy of voter beliefs about other voters and not whether voters hold false beliefs about politicians—or whether politicians hold false beliefs about other politicians. I'd guess that both mistakes do occur given the especially strong negative feelings directed toward politicians from both voters and politicians themselves and the general association between extreme negative feelings and bias. But we lack the data to test for this type of bias directly, as far as I know. And I won't deny that politicians might have worse traits than voters in various ways.[8] (Narcissism is one that comes to mind.) It's even possible that politicians' traits have become "worse" over time due to institutional changes leading to different types of people being selected into politics (Hall, 2019).

Many studies have also found evidence of biases contributing to conflict in interpersonal relationships outside of politics. For example, Sillars and Parry (1982, 203) write that "it is typical for parties involved in conflicts to overattribute responsibility to one another and to underestimate the effects of self in causing conflicts. This tendency has been observed in married couples, executives [in the workplace], and college roommates."[9] Further-more, as discussed in the introduction, we all know from personal experi-ence and examples from history and fiction how easy it is for disagreements to become unnecessarily disagreeable in a variety of contexts.

On the other hand, a crucial difference between many interpersonal relationships and partisan politics is that people often choose to be in their nonpolitical relationships (such as a marriage) and thus tend to have a much stronger preference for the relationship to be congenial. As a result, *positive* misperceptions are much more likely to occur in nonpolitical rela-tionships, and the general correlation between misperceptions and rela-tionship quality is consequently noisier.[10] In politics, "motivated biases" are much more likely to be negative. I'll discuss this topic, and the general causes of biased perceptions in relationships, in depth in the next chapter.

II   Explanations

3   Overarching Biases

Don't believe everything you think.
—title of Thomas Kida's 2006 book

In this chapter I'll discuss a handful of fundamental biases that contribute to affective polarization bias in a wide range of situations. These biases have been covered extensively elsewhere, and many of them will already be familiar to some readers. So, I'll keep most of this discussion pretty brief, but I will add some new commentary and new examples for familiar topics and will also discuss some biases that haven't gotten much attention in the polarization literature before now.

Groups and Identity: An Economical Take

Our politics is groupish, not selfish.
—Jonathan Haidt, *The Righteous Mind*

As noted in the introduction, strengthened partisan identity is the explanation for growth in affective polarization in US politics that's received the most attention from the prior scholarly and popular literature. Since it's been covered elsewhere extensively, I'll keep my discussion of this topic especially concise. I'll start by borrowing the nice summary provided by Finkel and colleagues (2020, 534):

> In recent decades, the nation's major political parties have sorted in terms of ideological identity and demography. Whereas self-identified liberals and conservatives used to be distributed broadly between the two parties, today the former are

overwhelmingly Democrats and the latter are overwhelmingly Republicans. The parties also have sorted along racial, religious, educational, and geographic lines. Although far from absolute, such alignment of ideological identities and demography transforms political orientation into a mega-identity that renders opposing partisans different from, even incomprehensible to, one another.

Sorting and mega-identity are key terms here. Our political views, and many of our other characteristics and behaviors, have been sorted into being aligned with one side or the other. Liberal Republicans and conservative Democrats were once common—and are now practically extinct. Even rural Democrats and urban Republicans are much rarer than they once were. Are you a "Prius or pickup"? Which one you own says a lot about your mega-identity—your cultural tastes, education, where you live—and your political views.[1] We obviously don't all identify completely with one political side or the other. But many aspects of our identities are much more aligned with our voting habits than they were a few decades ago.[2]

Strengthened partisan identity means people take political disputes more personally—we think of our political affiliations and beliefs as more important parts of who we are. As a result, we've become both more loyal to our political "teammates" and more hostile to the opposition team. We've evolved to fight for our groups since this helps them to survive and thrive and thus also helps perpetuate our own genes. We heuristically apply this instinct to all groups we identify with, however they're defined, and fight harder for groups that are more important parts of our identities. Fighting for our groups can entail intergroup bias: valorizing our teammates and demonizing the opposition simply because of their group identities.[3] Since negative judgments can be excessive, intergroup bias can cause affective polarization bias.

Demonization of the out-group happens for several reasons. We unconsciously prefer consistency in our beliefs (more on this below) and therefore process negative information about the out-group much more fluently than positive information. Our minds automatically link similar ideas, so we unconsciously associate them with other negative concepts. People generally "act up" (behave less ethically and more aggressively) more often in groups (see, e.g., Meier and Hinsz, 2004); when we see out-group members doing this, it gives us fodder for the demonization.

Perhaps most importantly, group identities also make us want to demonize the out-party. We might even "love to hate" the other side. As a result, we use *motivated reasoning* to unconsciously disparage the out-group's character. Motivated reasoning might appear to be a straightforward concept, but it's surprisingly subtle and complex as I discuss in this next section.

Motivated Reasoning

> It is difficult to get a man to understand something when his salary depends upon his not understanding it.
> —Upton Sinclair, *I, Candidate for Governor, and How I Got Licked*

Motivated reasoning is referred to frequently in polarization literature but is not often discussed in-depth. It's a topic that warrants a fairly careful discussion for the purposes of this book, however, because it so often contributes to affective polarization bias.[4] Motivated reasoning is the technical term for wishful thinking, constrained, at least somewhat, by the bounds of plausibility. It involves *some* reasoning. It's not pure delusion, but it's not reasoning in search of truth; it's reasoning in support of an agenda. Gilovich (1991) provides a clear and succinct description: motivated reasoning makes us ask ourselves (unconsciously) "can I believe it?" for claims we wish to be true and "must I believe it?" for claims we wish to be untrue.

Like intergroup bias, motivated reasoning is both highly intuitive—and even more pervasive and subtle than most of us realize. We are often aware of other people's thoughts being influenced by wishful thinking. But we're usually oblivious when motivated reasoning affects our own beliefs. Disproportionate awareness of other people's belief biases is a well-documented phenomenon called the *bias blind spot*: we see many cognitive biases in other people, but we're blind to our own (see, e.g., West et al., 2012). The bias blind spot is an example of a motivated cognition in its own right: we notice others' biases and not our own in large part because we're motivated to think of ourselves as unbiased. That is to say, motivated reasoning contributes to our lack of awareness of our own motivated reasoning.

It's well known that motivated reasoning often plays a role when people make risky decisions and that entrepreneurs in particular tend to be motivated to overestimate their chances of success (Kahneman, 2011). But motivated reasoning occurs in much more subtle ways too. For example, Islam (2021) ran an experiment during the COVID-19 pandemic in which he randomly gave some people restaurant gift cards, and found that this caused people to believe that going to those restaurants entailed less risk. Motivated reasoning can even contribute to excessive caution. For instance, people unhappy with their jobs might be averse to the effort, fear, and stress from making a change and can thus "motivatedly" convince themselves that sticking with the status quo is best.

Motivated reasoning also insidiously affects our mundane everyday decisions. Suppose you need to be at work at 9:00 a.m. It's 7:00 a.m. and you think you only need thirty minutes to get ready, plus thirty minutes to commute, and therefore you stay in bed until 8:00. But you end up needing forty minutes of prep time after getting out of bed, so you don't leave until 8:40, and the commute takes thirty-five minutes, and so you end up fifteen minutes late. Your error in planning was probably due partly to thinking wishfully about how much time you needed to get ready—you were motivated to underestimate this because it allowed you to lounge in bed longer. However, we often don't recognize this error, even in retrospect, or at least don't remember it, so it's easily repeated.

Motivated reasoning is likely also more common than we realize because it can occur in more ways than we realize. We rehearse information that we hope is true (*congenial information*) in our minds relatively often—we think about this information and discuss it with others, relatively frequently— keeping it at the front of our minds where it is less likely to be forgotten. By contrast, we give less attention to uncongenial information; if we know it, we're more likely to forget it, and if it's new, we're less likely to pay attention to it. We're also too credulous of congenial information that's uncertain or unverified. When confronted with mixed evidence, we ignore the uncongenial parts and pay more attention to congenial aspects. When presented with just uncongenial information, we discount it as likely wrong or anomalous and forget it relatively quickly. We internally and externally search for strong arguments to support congenial opinions. And we seek out new sources of congenial information and avoid sources of information likely to be uncongenial. (Some of these points are explored further in chapter 6.)[5]

So, if we want to demonize the out-party (consciously or unconsciously), motivated reasoning easily helps to make this happen, typically without our awareness.[6] This motivated reasoning offers both intrinsic and extrinsic benefits. The primary intrinsic benefit from (excessive) demonization of the out-party is that it can make us feel good about ourselves and our identities by confirming or enhancing our beliefs about our good judgment and moral righteousness. In two-party competition, the worse *they* are, the better *we* are by comparison. Demonizing the out-party can also make us think the in-party is more likely to prevail in future elections and policy choices, which is a pleasant thought. And it might simply be fun to talk to politically like-minded friends about the horrors of the other side. (Our friends are indeed usually like-minded; more on this also in chapter 6.)

Demonizing the out-party can also be motivated by extrinsic benefits—real consequences, outside of your head—for multiple reasons. Hostility toward the out-party can benefit the in-party via improved political motivation and engagement. "Motivated reasoning to improve motivation" might sound circular, but it's not since these are different types of motivation. Telling yourself and your team "we're gonna win!" can make you and your teammates exert more effort and indeed become more likely to win.

Out-party hostility can benefit individual partisans, beyond just helping them to feel good, by allowing them to signal their loyalty and contributions to the in-group (Petersen et al., 2020; Williams, 2020; Connors, 2021). If your Facebook or real-world friends indeed share your political preferences, in addition to enjoying discussing the latest outrageous thing out-partisans have done, you might also truly bond with others over this. Out-group hostility can be morally valued—disliking the out-group can actually cause the in-group to consider you to be a morally better person (Cohen et al., 2006). You might also impress your friends by sharing interesting facts or clever opinions about the other side's hypocrisy. On the other hand, complaining about—or even just acknowledging—flaws in the in-party's leaders or proposed policies might not go over so well and could even cause real harm to your relationships. We have a "preference for belief consonance" (Golman et al., 2016)—we want our beliefs to align with those around us.

Politically motivated reasoning can also provide real extrinsic benefits to your side by making you a more powerful advocate for that side. *Seinfeld's* George Costanza famously said, "It's not a lie if you believe it." Research has shown that people are indeed more persuasive when they believe their own arguments. We're unlikely to swing elections with our arguments, but we might win smaller-scale debates with friends and family, or at least win over other people watching the debates. Winning these debates can yield real benefits for ourselves, contributing to the general *evolutionary adaptiveness* of motivated reasoning—why a tendency to engage in motivated reasoning would emerge from natural selection—which then occurs even in settings where our personal voices are less impactful (like politics). Some argue that this extrinsic benefit of motivated reasoning—its usefulness for winning arguments and impressing audiences—is the key evolutionary explanation for the broad prevalence of motivated reasoning.[7]

There's a plethora of evidence that motivated reasoning affects how voters and politicians think about politics and partisanship.[8] Much of this evidence implies motivated excessive demonization of the out-party. For instance, Everett and colleagues (2021) show that partisans evaluate the exact same act as less moral when it's performed by an out-partisan (versus a copartisan). More generally, in a metastudy of nineteen other studies, Hewstone's (1990) results imply the *ultimate attribution error* is influenced by motivated reasoning. The ultimate attribution error extends the *fundamental attribution error*—our tendency to overattribute other people's actions to character traits instead of circumstances, which can cause biased dislike—to groups. (Yes, both errors have quite grandiose names.) Hewstone's metastudy implies that this tendency is "motivatedly" asymmetric: we attribute positive acts by in-groups to character traits and negative acts to bad luck and vice versa for out-groups.

Motivated reasoning can also contribute to within-group conflicts, however, and even to conflict in one-on-one relationships. Even romantic partners jockey for status with one another and are therefore each motivated to overestimate how often they're correct and how often their partner is wrong. When relationships run into trouble, we're motivated to blame the other side and not ourselves.

On the other hand, partners are, as I note at the end of chapter 2, much more likely to be motivated to think positively about each other than competing social groups. Spouses, friends, business partners, and neighbors usually want to get along and even to hold high opinions of each other. (Though, yes, even in these relationships, hating the other side might sometimes hold some appeal.) As a result, motivated reasoning is less likely to cause undue hostility in one-on-one relationships as compared to partisan politics. However, the other overarching biases that contribute to affective polarization bias, which I'll discuss next, are more likely to affect relationships between both individuals and groups.

Confirmation Bias and Myside Bias

> The human understanding when it has once adopted an opinion draws all things
> else to support and agree with it.
>
> —Francis Bacon, *Novum Organum*

The next bias I'll talk about is one that's now especially well known: *confirmation bias*, our tendency to seek and interpret new information to confirm what we already believe. We are drawn to information that supports our preexisting beliefs (our priors) and to ignore conflicting information. Tell someone a reason they're right about a strongly held belief, and they're all ears. Tell them a reason they're wrong, and it's in one ear and out the other.

Confirmation bias can be influenced by motivated reasoning. (Some of the examples of motivated reasoning discussed in the previous section are also examples of confirmation bias.) Often our priors are beliefs that we wish to be true, and therefore we're motivated to confirm their truthfulness. This type of confirmation bias is also sometimes called *desirability bias* (Tappin et al., 2017; Grant, 2021).

Confirmation bias can also be motivated by a desire to maintain consistency in our beliefs—to prove that we weren't wrong in the past (to others and to ourselves) and to avoid looking wishy-washy. (We are more likely to refuse to admit we're wrong when we lack *intellectual humility*; more on this later in the chapter.) The longer we've held a belief, the more unpleasant it might seem to change it—the worse we'll look (or fear we'll look) if we admit to being wrong, both to others and ourselves—and therefore the more motivated we'll be to confirm the belief. For instance, Dunn (2021) reports that a senior astrophysicist at Harvard said about a mysterious extraterrestrial entity, "This object is so weird—I wish it never existed." It might seem he wished the object didn't exist just because it was puzzling and hard to explain. However, he might have also "wish[ed the new object] never existed" because it called into question the validity of his earlier work or posed a threat to his reputation.

But confirmation bias can be unmotivated as well—that is, it can cause us to confirm beliefs that we are indifferent about or even wish to be untrue. This distinction between motivated and unmotivated confirmation bias was first made, to my knowledge, by Nickerson (1998) in a highly cited survey paper. *Unmotivated* is a term that comes up occasionally in academic literature, though not often, but I think it's a very useful one. Other terminology is sometimes used to make this type of distinction; for example, Pennycook and Rand (2019b) refer to motivated reasoning versus *classical reasoning*. Unmotivated versus motivated seems clearer to me though. And psychology and neuroscience research has repeatedly shown that we indeed see what we expect to see even when we don't wish to see it.[9] For example, recently when I saw an email that opened by saying "Almost the end of the week!," I at first read it as saying "Almost the end of the world!" (Maybe I was in a pessimistic mood at the time.)

The *Bayesian brain* hypothesis in neuroscience helps to explain why we experience unmotivated confirmation bias. The hypothesis, in a nutshell, is that the brain is constantly developing a stream of predictions for what will happen in the near future and interpreting sensory input in light of these predictions because relying on just the input would be inefficient. The way I read the email referred to above was an example of an attempt at this type of efficiency. I read "Almost the end of the w__!" and guessed the "w" word was "world." If that hadn't surprised me, I wouldn't have double-checked it and would have simply incorrectly seen what I expected to see and never known I'd made a mistake.

When our brains make guesses about what we're seeing based on our priors, it causes us to be more likely to neglect information that's inconsistent with our priors and sometimes completely ignore it (Yon, 2019). The Bayesian brain hypothesis doesn't claim that our brains always precisely implement Bayes' rule, just that our brains incorporate priors (in addition to signals) in determining perception (Clark, 2015). (Recall that Bayes' rule is the mathematically correct way to update prior beliefs given new information.) "Non-Bayesian brain" perception would neglect your priors and be based entirely on the external input.

Most of the time our guesses are right. When you read "guess," you might indeed correctly guess that the word is "guess" after just seeing "gu__s" and noting the context and spare yourself the mental effort of processing all five letters. The problem is that often we don't realize the guesses are wrong until it's too late—or we never realize this.

For another example of unmotivated confirmation bias, consider the picture below, a famous "reversible figure" that can be interpreted as depicting either a duck or a rabbit. You might have just seen one of these at

Figure 3.1
The rabbit-duck illusion, first published in *Fliegende Blätter* (1892).

first, but after hearing about the alternative interpretation, you probably can see that one as well. Nevertheless, try just thinking about one of these terms repeatedly in your head while looking at the picture. For example, say "duck, duck, duck" repeatedly (keep going—seriously, try it and don't stop—while looking at figure 3.1), and I suspect you'll just see the duck or at least find it unpleasant to see the rabbit interpretation. It's a nice example of how we often see what we expect to see and ignore complexity and ambiguity (Kahneman calls this the "coherence-seeking" nature of our automatic minds). We even sometimes hear what we expect to hear. (For a neat example of this, google "green needle brainstorm" and take your pick of the first few links that pop up; see also Locker, 2020.)

What I'm calling motivated confirmation bias is also very similar to *myside bias*, defined by the cognitive psychologist Keith Stanovich (2021, ix) as the (motivated) tendency to "evaluate evidence, generate evidence, and test hypotheses in a manner biased toward their own prior beliefs, opinions, and attitudes."[10] I recommend Stanovich's book, *The Bias That Divides Us*, for a deep discussion of this topic. It points out that myside bias is uncorrelated with our other cognitive or demographic characteristics, making it more ubiquitous than just about any other bias. Stanovich's book doesn't cover unmotivated confirmation bias, but he's told me he agrees it's a useful term.

Earlier in this chapter, I discussed reasons that motivated reasoning can contribute to affective polarization bias, which apply to myside bias and motivated confirmation bias as well. Unmotivated confirmation bias can also contribute to affective polarization bias, both inside and outside of politics. If our brains "align our experience with our expectations" (Yon, 2019)—and our expectations are distorted toward overestimating the degree to which the out-party is "bad"—unmotivated confirmation bias will cause this distortion to persist and maybe even grow (perhaps in conjunction with motivated confirmation bias).

Unmotivated confirmation bias is also naturally more relevant to conflict than the motivated version in settings where we're motivated to like, not dislike, the other side (friends, colleagues, spouses). If we feel slighted by the other side and develop a grudge, this can be hard to overcome due to our tendency to continue to see evidence confirming its legitimacy and to be blind to the signs that our beliefs are invalid, even when we'd truly be better off seeing these signs clearly. But since friends and lovers are motivated to "win" disputes (for the sake of ego and perhaps to enhance one's power in future joint decisions), myside bias is also relevant to these conflicts.

Overprecision

> It ain't what you don't know that gets you into trouble. It's what you know for sure that just ain't so.
> —credited to Mark Twain

"Will Mindik be a good leader? She is intelligent and strong." Daniel Kahneman asks the reader to consider this question in his magnum opus, *Thinking, Fast and Slow* (2011, 86). For most people, our first instinct is to simply answer yes. We don't think about the information we are not provided with that's also relevant to the correct answer, like whether Mindik is cruel or kind. Better answers than "yes" include "maybe" and "I need to know more."

In *Thinking, Fast and Slow*, Kahneman dubs this type of thinking— jumping to conclusions without full information and failing to consider what's not known—WYSIATI: "what you see is all there is." (Kahneman pronounces it "whiz-ee-ah-tee.") He writes that "jumping to conclusions on the basis of limited evidence is so important to an understanding of intuitive thinking, and comes up so often in this book, that I will use a cumbersome abbreviation for it" (86). Maybe Kahneman thought WYSI-ATI would catch on despite being a "cumbersome abbreviation" because the phenomenon it refers to is sufficiently common and important. That's apparently been the case: Google scholar reports just six works referred to WYSIATI in 2011, and over one hundred per year have done so in most years since 2015.[11]

The idea behind WYSIATI—that we fail to think carefully about the information we *don't* see and reality tends to be more complicated than it seems—of course wasn't novel in 2011. But the specific term is still very useful for identifying this important, common phenomenon. Moreover, the term WYSIATI captures an extreme form of several previously existing concepts, including the behavioral economics term *overinference* (excessive belief updating in response to a signal), our tendency to think in terms of causal stories rather than probabilistic possibilities (Shiller, 2017), the fundamental attribution error (referred to above), and the closely related *correspondence bias* (overinference about a person's traits based on observed actions; see Ross and Nisbett, 1991). Eminent political psychologist Philip Tetlock even calls WYSIATI "the mother of all cognitive illusions" in his book *Superforecasting* (2015).

I'll return to this claim at the end of the chapter. For now, I'll say that I agree WYSIATI is an important cause of another particularly ubiquitous bias, *overprecision*: overconfidence in the precision of our knowledge and beliefs.[12] Behavioral economists now typically distinguish between two main types of overconfidence: overprecision—overconfidence in the precision of our knowledge and beliefs—and *overoptimism*—overconfidence in something we wish to be true, a consequence of motivated reasoning (see, e.g., Grubb, 2015). There is some connection between these two biases, but they are distinct. One can hold overly precise beliefs about something one wishes were not true. (For example, a student who thinks "I'll never figure out the answer to this math problem, no matter how hard I try.")

Overoptimism is widespread—but overprecision is likely even more common. The psychologist Don Moore, who specializes in the study of various forms of overconfidence (and wrote a book on the topic, *Perfectly Confident*), has called overprecision "the most robust type of overconfidence" (Haran et al., 2010, 467). While people are actually sometimes too pessimistic about some outcomes or aspects of their own, or their group's, abilities, Moore (2020, 8) writes in his book that "unlike [overoptimism], reversals of overprecision are vanishingly rare."

Ortoleva and Snowberg (2015) report that a general tendency to hold overly precise beliefs correlates with ideological extremism (see also Ahrens et al., 2021, and the literature on *cognitive rigidity* and extremism such as Zmigrod et al., 2020). Ortoleva and Snowberg measure overprecision by looking at overconfidence in knowledge about various facts such as the date Shakespeare was born—gaps between people's expressed confidence in this knowledge and their actual knowledge. Using Ortoleva and Snowberg's data, I found that overprecision also predicts greater levels of affective polarization, holding fixed ideological extremism, partisan identity, and even a measure of motivated reasoning (Stone, 2019). Overprecision can lead to persistent undue hostility by exacerbating the effects of other biases. Once we jump to the conclusion that a news item indicates the outparty is "bad," WYSIATI and overprecision make us overconfident in this information and more likely to see (both motivated and unmotivated) confirmatory evidence in the future. See also Barker and colleagues (2021), who study *epistemic hubris*, a concept very similar to overprecision, and report that it's associated with stronger partisanship on both sides of the aisle.

It's also straightforward to see how overprecision can exacerbate conflict and hostility in nonpolitical relationships. I'm not aware of research studying overprecision per se in these contexts. However, Daks and Rogge (2020, 215) conduct a metastudy of 174 studies of an inversely related construct, *psychological flexibility* ("a set of skills that individuals engage when presented with difficult or challenging thoughts, feelings, emotions, or experiences"). They show that flexibility is linked to several positive outcomes in relationships, such as better family cohesion and higher relationship satisfaction for couples.

Despite the ubiquity and broad implications of WYSIATI and overprecision, these terms have received very little attention from the psychology and political science polarization literatures. A related term that comes up occasionally, but also not often in the polarization literatures, is *naive realism*: overestimating one's own objectivity and lack of bias (Robinson et al., 1995).[13] Naive realism has been called a particularly underappreciated source of interpersonal conflict and distrust (Lieberman, 2022; Ross, 2018). It contributes to overprecision and likely results, at least partly, from WYSIATI—thinking "what you see is all there is" will make you overestimate your own objectivity. I'll be talking about naive realism's contributions to affective polarization bias much more in chapter 4.

An additional related concept whose implications for affective polarization have been studied more extensively is *intellectual humility*. Science journalist Brian Resnick defines this term as "the characteristic that allows for admission of wrongness" (Resnick, 2019). Lack of intellectual humility could both cause, and be caused by, overprecision, and several studies have indeed found that intellectual humility is associated directly with (lower) partisan hostility and indirectly via lower myside bias (Bowes et al., 2020; Krumrei-Mancuso and Newman, 2020; Stanley et al., 2020).

Overprecision also encompasses our tendency to think about complex issues in overly simplistic categories, a phenomenon called *coarse thinking* or *categorical thinking* (McHugh et al., 2021). Ignoring complexity is another type of overprecision in beliefs.[14] Often, we boil things down to just two categories, reducing complexity to a false binary, and are hence subject to a *binary bias* (Fisher and Keil, 2018). A related phenomenon that you've probably heard of is the *halo effect*—that we exaggerate the consistency of positive attributes in people that we like; if we like a person for one reason, we'll tend to think they're good in other ways as well (Kahneman, 2011). The *horns effect* is analogous (Rowley and Namasamy, 2016). If you dislike party X, candidate X, or person X, you'll have trouble giving them credit for anything positive they've done or for even having any positive attribute. This could, of course, cause your perception of the poor quality of their character to be exaggerated. A Manichean ("good versus evil") view of the world is a particularly clear way that overly precise binary thinking could contribute to undue hostility, and even hatred, in politics.

Concluding Remarks

To summarize, I'll quickly review these biases and discuss how they relate to one another. Figure 3.2 provides an illustration of my view of key causal relationships between the major factors and biases discussed.

Although it's a term that's rarely been used in prior literature on polarization, all roads lead to overprecision—overconfidence in what we know. One type of overly precise beliefs worth highlighting is our tendency to think in false binaries, and good versus evil in particular. And overprecision has numerous causes. The first shown on the graph (starting on the top left) is our tendency to see what we expect to see whether or not we wish to see it (unmotivated confirmation bias). In turn, as our beliefs are strengthened and become more precise, they become more likely to color our interpretation of new information. Next is WYSIATI—our tendency to jump to conclusions due to failure to recognize when we only have limited information. After that comes naive realism (caused at least partly by

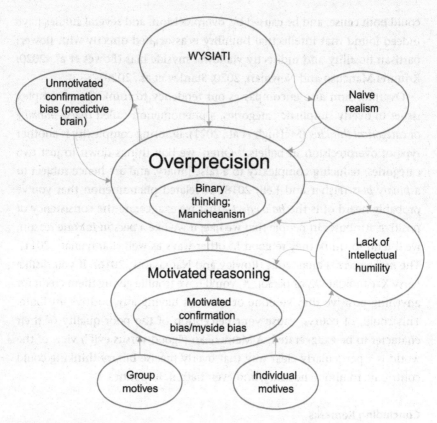

Figure 3.2
Directed graph illustrating the relationships between the main biases covered in this chapter.

WYSIATI), our tendency to overestimate our own objectivity and underestimate our own biases.

The large node below overprecision is indeed a major cause of overprecision: motivated reasoning, including myside bias (motivated search for, and interpretation of, evidence) and, more general, motivated cognition. We often believe what we wish to believe and interpret and search for evidence that confirms these beliefs. Our motives are driven by our group identities, which can be a stronger force when these identities are aligned and constitute a mega-identity, and are also driven by individual factors.

We may also be motivated to prove we're right and to avoid admitting we're wrong; that is, motivated reasoning can make us lack intellectual humility. Lack of intellectual humility can in turn cause us to be more likely to engage in motivated reasoning to defend opinions we wish to be true due to ego, identity, and reputation-protective motives. Our aversion to admitting uncertainty and error (our lack of intellectual humility) also contributes to overprecision, and overprecision in turn makes us less prone to admitting our own errors.

Tetlock called WYSIATI the mother of all cognitive illusions. But WYSI-ATI doesn't incorporate motivated reasoning, another fundamental driver of bias. A small extension of the term to *WYSWIATI*—what you see *or want* is all there is—perhaps does capture the root cause of most of our misperceptions.

I'll continue to discuss how these biases contribute to affective polarization bias in subsequent chapters. In the next chapter I'll focus on naive realism and also introduce a related important bias, the false consensus effect. Neither of these biases have received a lot of attention in other literature on polarization, and false consensus has been particularly neglected. But I'll argue both help to explain how disagreement often leads to undue hostility in politics and can lead to affective polarization bias in just about any relationship.

4 Tastes and Truth

De gustibus non est disputandum.
("There's no disputing tastes," Latin phrase)

And you say to me, friends, there is no disputing over tastes and tasting? But all of life is a dispute over taste and tasting!
—Friedrich Nietzsche, *Thus Spake Zarathustra*

According to the definition of affective polarization bias I've proposed, you can't be wrong about *what* to judge people on. You can only be wrong about *how* you correspondingly judge them. Maybe there are criteria that we objectively should or shouldn't use to make character judgments. But I don't claim to know what these are. As a result, my definition of this bias could be "conservative" in the sense that it only captures some, and not all, ways that we may mistakenly dislike other people.

Distinguishing the subjective from the objective is often practically impossible. Perhaps that's why we sometimes say "de gustibus non est disputandum" ("there's no disputing tastes"). In the second epigraph quote above, Nietzsche points out that this phrase is empirically inaccurate—that we often do dispute tastes. But de gustibus is, I think, more usefully thought of as suggestion than description: when we disagree on matters of taste, we typically won't be able to figure out whose tastes are "better," so there's often no sense in fighting about it. (My definition of affective polarization bias follows this advice.)

On the other hand, it's certainly true, as Nietzsche notes, that many of us don't shy away from disputing tastes. This chapter discusses two theories for why such disputes over tastes can in fact often cause undue hostility.

Moral Taste Buds

Jonathan Haidt's book on polarization, *The Righteous Mind*, is already widely considered seminal, though it was published just a decade ago. One of Haidt's key points is that Democrats and Republicans typically prioritize different moral values, or what he calls *moral foundations*. He discusses five main foundations in the book: fairness, care, loyalty, authority, and purity. Liberals value the first two higher than the others, and conservatives place approximately equal weight on all five. See figure 4.1 for a depiction of how the importance of each foundation corresponds to ideology.

Haidt famously compares moral foundations to taste buds. He argues that, in the same way that cuisines vary across cultures, preferences for different moral foundations vary systematically by culture. But just as cuisines must all please some of the same taste receptors that all humans share, moral codes must please at least some of our shared moral foundations.

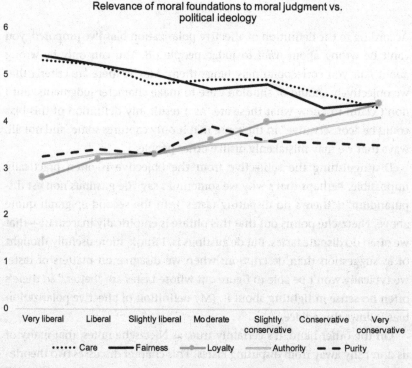

Figure 4.1
Moral foundations versus ideology. Source: adapted from Haidt (2007).

Moral foundations theory has received a lot of attention and a fair amount of criticism since Haidt's book was published (see, e.g., Hatemi et al., 2019; Curry, 2019). But the basic concept—that members of the two major parties tend to have different basic moral values and these values are as much a part of us as are our tastes in food and are thus nearly immutable for the near-term future—makes sense to most of us intuitively and has been supported by subsequent research (Kivikangas et al., 2021; Isler et al., 2021).

An important piece of support for moral foundations theory comes from behavioral economist Ben Enke (2020a) in his paper "Moral Values and Voting." Enke argues that, consistent with Haidt's work, moral values are a key difference between Democrats and Republicans and this difference has indeed grown over recent decades. However, contra *The Righteous Mind*, Enke argues these differences largely boil down to a single moral dimension, universalism versus communitarianism. He defines universalism as "an ethic of universal human concern . . . irrespective of the context or identity of the people involved," whereas communitarianism is "loyalty to the local community . . . tied to certain relationships or groups" (3680). Enke conducts a text analysis of congressional and presidential candidates' speeches since the 1960s and finds that Democrats use more universalist language than Republicans, to an increasingly greater degree over time. He also presents survey results indicating voters who embraced more universalist values were more likely to vote Democrat.

For the purposes of this chapter, the number of moral foundations doesn't matter as much as the metaphor comparing moral values to tastes. The expression "there's no disputing tastes," interpreted as advice, then implies that we should tone down our culture wars and related political fights. But, again, the fact that we need to be *advised* not to dispute tastes underscores the fact that we so often *do* dispute them. Sometimes we even dispute literal matters of tastes—which types of food taste better than others. And these disputes can go beyond friendly debates, evoking real character judgments and even dislike. Why?

Naive Realism and False Consensus

Haidt doesn't explicitly answer this question in his book. Much of the book is ultimately about undue dislike—after all, its subtitle is "Why Good People Are Divided by Politics and Religion"—but he doesn't directly discuss mechanisms for why having different moral taste buds would make us dislike other people more than we should. Similarly, some strands of the political science literature argue that policy disagreements and differences in moral convictions contribute to affective polarization, in addition to group identity differences. However, these papers also typically don't discuss underlying cognitive mechanisms.[1] It's very intuitive that such disagreements tend to be disagreeable (as I've already noted more than once in this book), so maybe that's why the topic isn't often analyzed explicitly. However, it's a fundamental underlying issue, so it's worth digging into to try to understand more clearly.

Before proceeding, it will be helpful to first provide a more precise definition of *subjective* versus *objective* for the context of this chapter. Definitions of these terms might be controversial in some disciplines (see, e.g., Gaukroger, 2012), but in economics there's a straightforward distinction between two closely related terms, *horizontal* and *vertical product characteristics*. Horizontal characteristics are those for which fully informed consumers have different preferences—some consumers like those characteristics in a good and some dislike them. Vertical characteristics are things that consumers all prefer more of. Location is a canonical example of a horizontal characteristic; consumers who live on the east side of town prefer firms located on the east side, all else equal, and consumers on the west side prefer firms on the west side. Durability is a vertical characteristic; we all agree that goods that last longer before breaking are better.

Like our moral taste buds, our horizontal preferences are part of who we are, at least for the immediate future. A disagreement between two consumers about which good is "better" driven solely by the two consumers having different horizontal preferences is thus not something that can be resolved via discussion or debate. There's no sense in arguing about which store is "better," east or west, if location is the only difference between them (hypothetically) and store preferences are based just on location. No one is right or wrong; the consumers' preferences are just different. Therefore it's often wise to avoid disputing tastes—there's not really any point to it.

On the other hand, differences in opinion over vertical characteristics of goods (or other subjects) can *only* be driven by differences in beliefs about factual matters. These differences in opinion must be due to at least one of the two disputants being uninformed, misinformed, or downright wrong in some way. As a result, it very well might be productive to debate the point and try to hash this out. Let's return to the example of durability as a vertical characteristic: in reality, we usually don't know for sure if, say, brand X or Y is more durable. If I think X is more durable and you think Y is, one of us is right and the other is wrong. It is reasonable for us to talk about this as discussion might allow us to improve the accuracy of one or both of our beliefs.

Thus, in this chapter when I say something is a "subjective" issue, I mean that differences in opinion for the issue are like differences in preferences for horizontal characteristics of a good, a matter of differing tastes. Analogously, when I say an issue is objective, I mean that we all share the same tastes for it, so it's akin to a vertical feature of a good. By the way, these definitions are consistent with how I've used the terms earlier in the book: we can have subjective preferences for different character traits in other people, while it's objectively better to have more accurate beliefs about other people's traits and future action probabilities. I'm just spelling things out a little more carefully here.

Now to return to undue hostility: this can arise in a few ways, all of which result in part, or entirely, from naive realism. Recall that naive realism, discussed briefly in chapter 3, is an overestimation of how objectively we see the world. Naive realism often refers to the overconfidence of the objectivity of our beliefs, causing overprecision. If others disagree with us on "vertical" issues and we're overconfident in our beliefs, we'll likely then overinfer that others' beliefs are mistaken and influenced by bias and poor judgment. Our mistaken inferences about others could then naturally lead to biased dislike toward them. For example, if you and I disagree on which headache medication works best, I might think you were brainwashed by ads for your favored brand or that you stubbornly ignore other valid evidence indicating you're wrong. Both beliefs could make me like you less— and dislike you too much if I'm overconfident in how correct my beliefs are.

Naive realism can also make us overestimate the objectivity of our *preferences*. If we think that if we like salads better than burgers, then salads must simply be (objectively) *better* than burgers, then we'll think that people who choose burgers are simply *wrong* and not just different. That is, naive realism can make us mistakenly think that horizontal issues are vertical ones. This type of naive realism in tastes contributes to why, for example, parents of each generation often think the music their kids like isn't as good as the music they grew up with. (We typically like this music best mainly because we're more familiar with it and have positive nostalgic associations.[2])

Naive realism in tastes also helps explain why we tend to debate matters of taste more than we should. We think our disagreements aren't intractable differences in taste buds but instead are actually simply matters of conflicting beliefs that can potentially be resolved via debate. This is, of course, *sometimes* true. I sometimes debate with my spouse what to make for dinner, and she turns out to be right—I'll later agree that what she wanted was better than what I had suggested. However, if we're biased toward overestimating our own objectivity (and we are!), then we'll overestimate how often these debates can be productive—how often our perceived preferences are driven by objective traits versus subjective ones.

Misperceiving our tastes as objective truths can then also naturally lead to undue dislike. The reasons are similar to why undue dislike can result from overconfidence in beliefs on truly vertical issues. For example, suppose feelings toward, say, some genre of music are driven largely by horizontal characteristics, but I think "I like this music; therefore it's high quality" (e.g., "jazz music from the 1920s is the *best* music of all time"). This would naturally lead me to have overly negative beliefs about people who disagree with me about this music. I'll overinfer that those who dislike it assessed its vertical characteristics incorrectly—that they simply don't realize how *good* it is, and so their judgment, and perhaps even intelligence, is worse than I would have thought otherwise. As a result, my confusion about matters of taste would cause me to hold unduly negative beliefs about their character traits (and corresponding action probabilities) and thus cause me to feel undue dislike toward them, that is, be subject to affective polarization bias ("If you don't like jazz from the 20s, there's something wrong with you"). See Ross (2018) for a more general discussion of these ideas and related research.

But why might disagreeing with other people on matters of tastes—even literal tastes for different types of food—affect, and even skew, our beliefs about other people's moral character? This is perhaps more puzzling. In my prior research (Stone, 2020a), I've proposed an explanation using an additional factor on the psychology of tastes: our tendency to overestimate the similarity of others' tastes and beliefs with our own. This phenomenon, called the *false consensus effect*, is also an extremely well-established empirical regularity in social psychology (see, e.g., Mullen et al., 1985). It's closely

Table 4.1
Examples of the false consensus effect (N = 122)

Item	Percentage of endorsers	Average endorser estimated percentage of endorsers	Average nonendorser estimated percentage of endorsers
1. I sweat very easily even on cool days	21%	44.5%	29.2%
2. My conduct is largely controlled by the behavior of those around me	28%	60.1%	49.4%
3. My hardest battles are with myself	73%	62.8%	46.2%
Total (for all 40 MMPI-2 items reported in the paper)	49.9%	55.6%	44.4%

Source: adapted from Krueger and Clement (1994).

related to naive realism and may often result from naive realism, but the two phenomena are distinct, as I'll explain. Table 4.1 shows some examples of false consensus: for statements from the Minnesota Multiphasic Personality Inventory (MMPI-2), people who endorse statements themselves tend to overestimate the percentage of others endorsing the statement, while people who don't endorse the statement tend to underestimate the total percentage of endorsers.

The false consensus effect is a simple and intuitive phenomenon. It makes sense that we'd use available information—our own tastes—to judge the prevalence of such tastes in others. The problem is we put too much weight on what we know about ourselves and systematically underestimate the degree to which other people differ from us in all sorts of ways. We are, again, too prone to think "what [we] see is all there is." Overprecision exacerbates the problem by making us excessively confident in our (biased) beliefs about others' tastes and beliefs.

The false consensus effect doesn't always cause problems in relationships. Overestimating your similarity with your partner is usually a positive sign for the quality of the relationship (Montoya et al., 2008). But I argue that, perhaps counterintuitively, overestimating the extent to which we share tastes with other people can also cause undue dislike. That's because if, say, Jill believes she shares the same tastes with Jane, then it's logical for Jill to interpret differences in her and Jane's *expressed opinions* as signals of differences in *moral character*. If Jill overestimates the degree to which she and Jane share the same true tastes, and sees Jill espousing an opinion inconsistent with these tastes, it's natural for Jill to think Jane has a hidden ulterior motive for what she says. Hidden motives are usually bad ones, and being disingenuous is usually a sign of bad character too. As a result, Jill would be subject to undue hostility toward Jane.

For instance, when Jill and Jane debate where to get dinner and Jane suggests the taco place because it's "the best" but Jill thinks the pizza place is the best, Jill might think Jane secretly agrees but has a hidden, self-serving motive for suggesting the taco place (perhaps it's more convenient for Jane). Moreover, if we observe others with different tastes from our own making such inferences and becoming more hostile toward us, and we don't understand the role of false consensus in their thinking, we may falsely attribute their behavior to poor character as well. (It's worth noting that the false consensus effect has not typically been found to apply to our own vertically differentiated characteristics, like competence and judgment—we don't overestimate how much we have these in common with other people.)

Naive realism and the false consensus effect can cause unduly negative character inferences in a wide range of settings. This may be most likely to happen when two people don't know each other well at all and so are especially likely to misunderstand each other's preferences. For example, consider a person who typically reclines his airplane seat sitting in front of, and reclining toward, someone who thinks reclining is rude. The recliner probably reclines without asking first because he thinks it's his right to do so and also thinks that this right is universally understood, due to overestimating his objectivity and falsely thinking there is a consensus about it ("That's why the buttons for reclining are there, right?").

The "antirecliner" thinks it's obvious that reclining is an invasion of another person's space and should only be done when you sit in front of an empty seat; if you must recline toward another person, "everyone knows" you should ask first ("and anyone who reclines without at least asking first is a jerk"). Do a web search for "airplane seat recline fight video" if you want to see examples of what can happen next. It's worth noting that this is a situation where motivated reasoning would likely exacerbate the false consensus effect for both individuals—if I want to recline, I'll be motivated to believe this is a widely accepted legitimate thing to do, and if I don't want the person in front of me to recline, I'll be motivated to think it's widely accepted that one shouldn't do this without at least asking first.

However, people who are intimately familiar with one another can be subject to a false consensus effect as well—and therefore also be subject to false consensus-driven undue conflict. Even friends, family, and spouses can be subject to false consensus with each other, and, again, while this can have positive implications, it can also cause disagreement that leads to undue conflict. Here's an illustrative example. Spouse A loves flowers (and getting a gift of flowers), but spouse B doesn't. Spouse B knows that A likes flowers better than B. But because of the false consensus effect, B underappreciates the difference in their tastes: B underestimates ("even after all these years") how much more A likes flowers than B. So B decides it's not worth bothering to get flowers often. Spouse A takes this as evidence that B does not care that much about A or is simply lazy or inconsiderate. You can see how undue hostility between A and B—and undue hostility given their misunderstanding of one another—might easily ensue.

Back to Politics

How do naive realism and the false consensus bias help connect Haidt's moral foundations theory to political hostility? Well, of course we *don't* have false consensus about support for many of the policies that we fight over. We more often have the opposite problem: we underestimate common ground in our views about specific policies. That's the problem of false polarization discussed in chapter 2.

We're well aware of real and perceived disagreements on many policy and related moral issues. When these disagreements are driven by different beliefs about the effectiveness of various policies, overconfidence in our own beliefs (overprecision, driven by naive realism among other factors) will make us overinfer others are mistaken in their beliefs and make us unduly judge others negatively.

Moreover, moral foundations theory implies many of these disagreements are ultimately subjective, at least for practical purposes. Again, naive realism makes us confuse the subjective with the objective, and this confusion seems to in fact be especially pronounced for our beliefs about moral values. People indeed think their values are objective truths. For example, Skitka and colleagues (2021, 352) state this point clearly in their review article on the psychology of moral convictions: "People tend to perceive their morally convicted attitudes as objectively true facts that are grounded in fundamental truths about reality."

It's important to note that even if someone is *wrong* about the universality of their moral convictions, disliking another person because they fail to embrace the same morals does not necessarily cause affective polarization bias. Suppose you think fairness is always more important than other moral considerations and that everyone should think this. And suppose your brother Joe doesn't care about fairness, and you know this about him and dislike him for this reason. Then you're not misjudging him by your standards and are thus not subject to biased dislike. But if you think everyone, including Joe, *should* share your moral values, then you'll probably dislike him further. You'll think the fact that he doesn't share the value signals something deeper that's wrong with him.[3] And naive realism will naturally lead us to misjudge how often our values should be shared.

For example, suppose (just for the sake of example!) that views on abortion are akin to Haidt's moral tastes and are thus subjective as I've defined the term above. Suppose also, in the interest of simplicity, there are just two possible views on the issue, "pro-choice" or "pro-life," and suppose I'm pro-choice and subject to naive realism. I thus think being pro-choice is objectively "correct." If you're pro-life and I know you're pro-life and dislike you accordingly, that's not affective polarization bias; I am judging you correctly by my standards. But if I incorrectly think we *should* share a view on this issue, and think you have the wrong view on the issue, I may then overinfer that you have other "bad" traits that caused you to have this wrong view. I'd then overestimate the probability of you taking other "bad" actions, leading me to dislike you more than I should (given my other preferences and values). Naive realism can make me think you're a "bad" person in general, and not just for this one issue, more than I should.

Perhaps some (or even all) moral issues that moral foundations theory implies are "subjective" truly are "objective." I'm not a moral philosopher and certainly won't make any definitive claims here. But perhaps no one can know for sure. And knowing that we perhaps can't know for sure, and that we have a general bias toward interpreting our personal tastes as universal truths, should temper our judgments. Even if we could somehow be sure that aspects of morality are "objective," knowing we tend to be overconfident in our beliefs on these issues should also temper our judgment of those who disagree. Moreover, if our differences on moral foundations are *practically* irreconcilable, at least for the immediate future, then our different opinions on these issues are essentially subjective, for practical purposes. If naive realism makes us overestimate the degree to which these differences can be reconciled, we'll still end up judging others with different moral values and different value-driven policy preferences too negatively.

Undue Suspicion

> Politics is the art of making your selfish desires seem like the national interest.
> —Thomas Sowell, "They're Baaack: Random Thoughts"

The false consensus bias can also cause political disagreement to yield undue dislike via suspicion that the other side is disingenuous about the reasons they support the policies they advocate. As Sowell alludes to in the quote just above, this suspicion is widespread. We often think others overstate the social benefits of policies they personally benefit from and sometimes even realize we do this ourselves. For instance, we might make arguments that lower or higher tax rates benefit society overall while truly being motivated by more personally relevant effects.

On the other hand, Sowell's quote is, of course, too cynical: often we do argue for policies that we feel are best for the country (due to a combination of our "tastes" broadly defined, beliefs, and some mixture of the two that we usually don't fully understand). The false consensus effect would then make us overestimate others' agreement that these policies are best. When we then observe out-partisans arguing for different policies, we'll logically infer their arguments are disingenuous or made in "bad faith."[4] Or if we see someone take a political action (with "political" broadly defined) that "they know isn't right," we'll assume they have a bad motive. Bad faith and bad motives signal bad character, and, again, excessive inference of bad character yields affective polarization bias.

For example, suppose Democrats overestimate the similarity in their true views on the benefits of higher tax rates and level of government spending with Republicans: Democrats assume Republicans (silently) agree about the societal benefits of taxing and spending more than they really do. Suppose Democrats then observe Republicans vocally objecting to increased tax and spending. Democrats would then logically look for an alternative explanation for this vocal opposition by Republicans (such as wealthy members of the party benefiting being personally worse off from tax hikes) and suspect Republicans of being disingenuous when they make claims about the general benefits of tax cuts and harms of tax increases.

Or to return to abortion, suppose you're pro-life and subject to false consensus about pro-life being widely understood to be morally correct. Then if you see someone else support pro-choice policies, or even get an abortion themselves, you'll naturally assume they must have a bad motive. Perhaps you think they benefit from pro-choice policies leading to other political gains, or you think their choice to get an abortion reflects on some moral failing that they're aware of but don't have the strength of will to overcome. Again, judging them for taking an action that you think is "bad" would not imply affective polarization bias. The bias would come from your false assumption that "they know it's bad and they're doing it anyway," and false consensus is likely to make you think this.

Since the false consensus effect applies to both tastes and beliefs, it can cause undue suspicion regardless of whether policy disagreements are driven by tastes or beliefs. Democrats' and Republicans' disagreements on optimal tax policy might be due to different tastes for the "size" of government and different beliefs about the effects of tax policy on economic growth and the distribution of income. Either way, overestimating the underlying agreement logically causes overinference of the chance of the other side having an ulterior motive for claiming to disagree.

For another example, consider hostile disagreement over Trump's "America First" foreign policy. (For simplicity, let's ignore the phrase's unsavory historical associations.) This disagreement could be driven by differences in "moral tastes" (we may disagree over to what extent Americans should make sacrifices to help people around the world) and by differences in beliefs over how to best achieve the shared value of taking actions that serve America's interests (we may also disagree over to what extent supporting allies ultimately benefits Americans). Overestimating the similarity of either our values or beliefs, or both, implies excessive inference of bad motives for those with different views. If I think that supporting allies does not benefit Americans much and I see that you do favor more support for allies (or so-called allies), I'm likely to think you might be disloyal, naive, or perhaps even personally or politically benefit from helping those other nations.

A Formal Example

Here's a simplified version of the model of false consensus-driven undue hostility from Stone (2020a) that I think provides additional clarity. Suppose there are two parties, left and right, and you're on the right. You want to know how "unselfish" or not someone on the left is. Suppose this character trait is denoted by C, and assume $0 < C < 1$, and you think each value is equally likely. So, on average, you expect C to be 0.5. Suppose you dislike selfishness, so you dislike someone more when you think their C value is lower.

You don't observe the out-party's (average) C directly, but you do observe a signal of it: a public policy that they support, which can be represented by a number greater than 0. This policy, call it X, affects society overall, and can provide "partisan benefits"—it can make members of the out-party better off, at society's expense. Now suppose that X represents the "size of government" and higher values of X yield greater partisan benefits for the left—for example, provide more government services, subsidies, and jobs for their constituents. So higher values of X might signal higher selfishness for the left. But the left also has a "taste parameter," T: a value of X that they feel is best for society, which is any number greater than or equal to zero. (This parameter could be driven by either direct preferences or beliefs about the extent to which higher values of X are good for society since false consensus can apply to either.)

Assume the left chooses X based on a combination of tastes and selfishness in a simple way:

$$X = T + \frac{1}{C} - 1.$$

If the left is fully unselfish and $C = 1$, they'd choose a value of X equal to T. If $C = 1/2$, then $X = T + 1$. If the left is more selfish with, say, $C = 1/3$, then X becomes larger ($X = T + 2$).

So, if you are on the right, you can infer the C value of someone on the left directly from X if you know their taste for the size of government, T. Rearranging the equation for X, the correct inference is $C = 1/(X + 1 - T)$. (Note that by assumption, $X \geq T$.)

Now suppose you think you know their T, but you are influenced by false consensus. Since you lean right, your taste is lower than theirs. Suppose you think their taste is t, with $t = T - b$, so b is your bias (the amount you under-estimate how high their value of T is, because your value is smaller and you are subject to false consensus). Then your inferred C from observing their X, C^I, is determined as follows:

$$C^I = \frac{1}{X+1-t} = \frac{1}{X+1-T+b}.$$

Using the original definition of C to substitute $1/C$ for $X + 1 - T$ in the right-hand-side denominator, we can then show that

$$C^I = C/(1+bC).$$

This is strictly less than C if $b > 0$. In other words, the false consensus bias makes you underestimate the other side's character.

Moreover, the larger the bias (b), the more you underestimate their C. For example, suppose that since you lean right, your taste for government size is low, say, a 2, and suppose the left's taste is symmetric (around the midpoint of 5), so it is equal to 8. And suppose you know they lean left, but you're subject to a false consensus effect, so you perceive their taste is less than 8; let's say 6 (so your $b = 2$).

Then, if you see them choose $X = 8$, you should infer their $C = 1$, but you'll actually infer $C = 1/3$. If you see them choose $X = 10$, you should infer $C = 1/3$, but you'll infer $C = 1/5$. See figure 4.2 for an illustration; the gaps between inferred and actual character (affective polarization bias) are greater for larger values of character and larger values of b.

The details don't matter; as long as you experience false consensus bias (and your taste parameter is less than theirs), you'll always underestimate their C after observing their choice of X and thus experience biased dis-like. If you observe them defending a high value of X that they chose by arguing that large X is optimal (i.e., large T), you'll think they're being disingenuous—that they actually agree with you that small T is better.

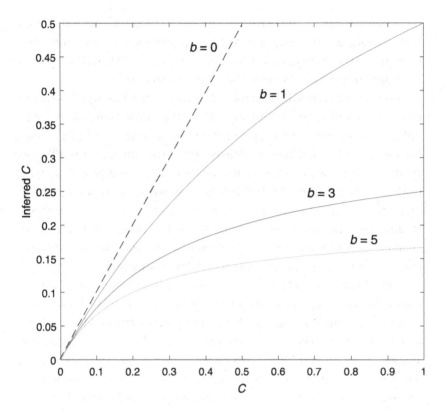

Figure 4.2
Inferred versus actual character (C) for different levels of false consensus bias (b). C minus inferred C is the underestimation of character due to false consensus bias.

Concluding Remarks

> The worst offence . . . which can be committed by a polemic is to stigmatize those who hold the contrary opinion as bad and immoral men.
>
> —J. S. Mill, *On Liberty*

Tough love or comforting attachment? Free-range or sheltered? Parents make these types of choices every day when deciding how much autonomy to grant their children and how to react when they struggle. There's usually no obviously optimal choice, just tradeoffs: more freedom generally means more learning but also more painful mistakes.[5] The good news is that there is also usually a wide range of reasonable options for how to balance these objectives. Even if it's unclear which option is precisely best, it's also clear most options are basically fine—they're good enough.

Many parents generally lean toward a single "parenting style"—and I've observed that many of us also, at least quietly, judge those whose styles differ from our own. This judgment is unlikely to lead to outright conflict between parents of different children but can do so. (My spouse is still upset about a stranger who once gave her advice on how to deal with a crying baby in a grocery store.) Explicit conflict over parenting styles is probably more likely to occur between members of different generations within a family: teens and parents most obviously but also parents and their grown children (over how the grown children were raised) and parents and grand-parents (over how to raise the new generation of children).

Many disputes in politics today boil down to a similar question: to what extent should the government protect or push its citizens? Government is, of course, not literally a parental figure, and voters aren't children. Still, we look to it to play many of a parent's roles—to provide safety, protection, and guidance. It's possible for government to err in the direction of either too much or too little "protection," broadly defined. This chapter is about why we unduly infer bad traits in those whose political opinions differ from our own. Just as we tend to dislike parents who we think are too strict—and those we think are too lax—we do the same for our fellow citizens who have different beliefs about various aspects of public policy.

I argue that we overinfer negative character traits in those who disagree with us due to naive realism and the related false consensus effect. A summary of these biases, and the mechanisms by which they can lead to biased dislike, is as follows:

- Naive realism is the overestimation of objective truth in our tastes or beliefs. This causes affective polarization bias by making us overinfer that actions or opinions that differ from our own ideals are flawed, and therefore that people who take those actions or have those opinions have "bad" character traits.

- The false consensus bias, which can result from naive realism, is the overestimation of the similarity of others' tastes or beliefs to our own. This causes affective polarization bias by making us falsely infer that people who take actions or make statements inconsistent with our own tastes or beliefs have "bad" motives for those actions or statements, which we interpret as signals for generally "bad" character traits.

The arguments made in this chapter for why these general biases would cause biased dislike are applications of what's sometimes called economic signaling theory. But the basic logic is straightforward: if we observe people taking opinions that differ from our own and underestimate the legitimate causes of differences in our opinions, we'll overattribute these differences to negative factors.

It's also straightforward to see how the mechanisms discussed here could have contributed to growth in biased dislike between the parties during the period partisan affective polarization has grown in the US. As the parties have sorted, they've grown to disagree more, in principle and in practice, and expressed moral values have diverged. Since larger disagreements imply larger errors due to the mechanisms discussed in this chapter, growth in disagreement implies growth in biased dislike.

The theories discussed in this chapter are logical extensions of the empirically well-established naive realism and false consensus effects. Prior literature has discussed naive realism as a cause of social conflict and polarization, though I would say to a surprisingly limited extent. Since the ideas of biased dislike and affective polarization bias are newly proposed in this book, there hasn't been prior work explicitly arguing that these are implications of naive realism. My own prior theory work on false consensus and affective polarization is the only work that I'm aware of making this argument. And I'm not aware of direct evidence of either of these specific biases leading to biased character judgments. Constructing studies that directly examine the effects of naive realism and false consensus on undue dislike would be difficult but I'm sure not impossible. I hope future researchers are up for this challenge.

5 Strategy and Repeated Interactions

When someone attacks me, I always attack back . . . except 100x more.
—Donald J. Trump, Twitter, November 11, 2012

The last chapter was on polarization and conflict being driven by true differences in opinion. However, sometimes we clash with other people for *strategic* reasons: we take actions that create or exacerbate conflict as a response to what other people have done in the past, or to try to influence what others do in the future. In chapter 1, I talked about how our words and actions signal our character traits, but imperfectly, and how difficult it usually is to interpret these signals. Strategic influences on other people's actions are often subtle and ambiguous, which can make interpretation of these actions even more challenging.

In this chapter, I'll discuss why strategic behavior and thinking, in conjunction with our cognitive biases, can indeed contribute to affective polarization bias. Strategic behavior actually hasn't been studied extensively in formal research on affective polarization in politics, though I've done some work in this area. But most of the ideas I'll discuss here aren't novel— they've come up in more informal analyses of political polarization or have been studied in other disciplines, such as conflict analysis and relationship psychology. And like in chapter 4, I'll be making some claims that are straightforward extensions of prior research, but still conjectural, and I hope will be investigated further in future work.

As usual, I won't be doing any complicated math but will use concepts and jargon from game theory, the standard tool used by economists, behavioral or otherwise, to study strategic interaction. I'll review the basics of game theory in the next section, with some commentary on behavioral issues that are often overlooked. Throughout the chapter, I'll focus on one specific game—the repeated prisoner's dilemma—as a benchmark model. This game captures a fundamental feature of most ongoing relationships: the potential for mutual gains from cooperation in tension with a clear immediate conflict of interest. Nonetheless, it's a simple model and is thus far from being a perfect model of any relationship. In fact, I'll argue the greater complexity of the real world is itself a major cause of biased dislike.

Game Theory and the Prisoner's Dilemma 101: A Behavioral Take

In game theory, a *game* is any situation with two or more people or groups (the *players*) whose outcomes depend on both their own choices and other players' choices. Each player chooses a *strategy* (an action or plan of actions), and outcomes (quantified as *payoffs*) result from the combination of strategies played. The simplest game structure is "2x2," meaning two players each choose one of two strategies before knowing the other's choice. These games can be fully represented with a *payoff matrix*: a table whose rows represent one player's strategies, columns represent the other player's strategies, and cells show the payoffs for each player resulting from the corresponding strategies.

The *prisoner's dilemma* is the first game taught in most introductions to game theory, for good reason.[1] Here's a brief description for any readers who might find this useful. Two prisoners are separately questioned about a crime. If neither confesses, then there is a lack of evidence against them and both get a relatively mild punishment. If just one prisoner confesses, he gets a lighter sentence as a reward for this and the other prisoner gets the worst possible sentence. If both confess, they both avoid the worst sentence but receive longer sentences than they would if neither confessed. Table 5.1 shows an example payoff matrix. For each prisoner, confession is a *dominant strategy*: it's optimal for yourself no matter what the other player does.

The prisoner's dilemma is so renowned because it's the simplest and clearest demonstration of how the famed *invisible hand* theory of economics—the idea that doing what's best for yourself also yields an outcome best for the group, as if you were guided by an invisible hand—can fail. When a prisoner chooses to confess, she chooses what's good for herself but bad for the "group." The point that self-interest can harm the

Table 5.1
A payoff matrix for a prisoner's dilemma game

	Prisoner 2 doesn't confess	Prisoner 2 confesses
Prisoner 1 doesn't confess	P1's jail term = 1 year P2's jail term = 1 year (No one snitches)	P1's jail term = 3 years P2's jail term = 0 years (Only P2 snitches)
Prisoner 1 confesses	P1's jail term = 0 years P2's jail term = 3 years (Only P1 snitches)	P1's jail term = 2 years P2's jail term = 2 years (Both snitch)

group is made so clearly and powerfully in the prisoner's dilemma that the term has become synonymous with this general phenomenon. Anytime two players each have a dominant strategy that, if played by both, makes them both worse off, we can say the two are in a prisoner's dilemma. For example, consider two countries in an arms race: both have incentives to build more weapons to gain an advantage over the other, but when both do this, neither gains the advantage and they're both worse off than before. Or consider two roommates deciding how much effort to put into cleaning a shared kitchen: both might prefer to shirk on this, but again, when both do this, they're both worse off than they would be if they both did some cleaning.

In the general form of a prisoner's dilemma, each player is said to choose between cooperation (C) and defection (D). (Cooperation with the other player, that is, so for the original context, this means *not* confessing.) Table 5.2 presents a general payoff matrix. For this to be a prisoner's dilemma, three conditions must hold: 1) $Y > W$, 2) $Z > X$, and 3) $W > Z$. The term W refers to each player's payoff when both players cooperate, Y is a player's payoff when she defects and the other cooperates, Z is each player's payoff when both defect, and X is one's payoff from cooperating when the other defects. The first two conditions imply defecting is a dominant strategy. The last condition implies defection by both players is (socially) *inefficient*: worse for both players than cooperation by both players.

Now, you might think decent roommates, especially if friends with one another, would clean up the kitchen just because it's the right thing to do, even if shirking on clean-up appears to be a dominant strategy. And of course roommates usually do help clean shared spaces in reality. In fact, even strangers sometimes cooperate in prisoner's dilemmas. Some of the

Table 5.2
The general form of a prisoner's dilemma (if 1) Y > W, 2) Z > X, and 3) W > Z), with player 1's payoff written first

	Player 2 cooperates	Player 2 defects
Player 1 cooperates	W, W	X, Y
Player 1 defects	Y, X	Z, Z

Table 5.3
The *Golden Balls* payoff matrix

	Player 2 splits	Player 2 steals
Player 1 splits	Both players get half the prize	P1 gets 0 P2 gets the whole prize
Player 1 steals	P1 gets the whole prize P2 gets 0	Both get 0

games discussed in chapter 2 were variants of prisoner's dilemmas, and participants indeed often cooperated. There was actually even an entire game show based on the premise that strangers might cooperate in a prisoner's dilemma called *Golden Balls* (plenty of clips are easily found online). Two players simultaneously choose "split" (cooperate) or "steal" (defect)—table 5.3 shows the payoff matrix. Only about half of participants chose to steal, even in the last round (van den Assem et al., 2012).

Some players cooperate in prisoner's dilemmas because they truly don't want to take an action making themselves better off at another person's expense. Others cooperate mainly because they're being watched. Reputation and image effects loom especially large on a televised version of the game. The payoffs shown in the payoff matrices above are thus incomplete. These are supposed to show the *total* payoff for each player after each pair of strategies is played, so the written payoffs should reflect these social factors if they are relevant. But prisoner's dilemma payoff matrices are rarely written this way—we almost always just write the *explicit* (observable) payoffs, like jail terms or monetary payoffs, and omit unobserved factors, like preferences for the other player's well-being or reputation effects.

Certain character traits can make us do what's best for the group—for example, cooperate in a prisoner's dilemma—even if this is not immediately

Table 5.4
Player 1's total payoff for one outcome of a prisoner's dilemma; Y is the explicit payoff referred to in table 5.2

	Player 2 cooperates
Player 1 defects	P1's total payoff = Y + payoff from altruism or spite toward P2 + payoff from reputation effects + payoff from failure to reciprocate P2's cooperation + any other implicit or psychological factors

best for ourselves. Our desire to have a reputation for having these character traits can also make us do this. (The importance of our perceptions of the character of others is, of course, the raison d'etre for this book.) In fact, it's only the existence of these other, more ambiguous concerns that make each prisoner's choice a *dilemma*. If either player just looked at the explicit payoffs for herself, the choice is easy: given that you have a dominant strategy to defect, you should obviously defect. Table 5.4 presents a single payoff from one cell from a payoff matrix incorporating these additional intangible payoffs. You can see why payoffs aren't typically written out this way.[2]

What's more, even in the absence of prosociality or reputation concerns— that is, even with purely self-interested players who are happy for it to be publicly known that they are purely self-interested—cooperation by both players in a prisoner's dilemma can be attained if the same players play this game again in the future. Even purely selfish players will cooperate if they think they will be sufficiently rewarded in the future by the other player (as alluded to in figure 5.1). This simple point is implied by the fact that we have regulatory agencies dedicated to preventing fundamentally self-interested actors—corporations (by law, required to take actions in the best interest of their shareholders)—from cooperating, that is, colluding. (Collusion is of course illegal because although it can benefit firms, the cost to consumers or workers is greater.)

The details of the math can get a little tricky here, but the basic concept of why repeated interaction can yield self-serving cooperation can be made clear with a simple example. Suppose the players indefinitely repeat the game shown in table 5.5. Also suppose player 1 (the row player) thinks that player 2 will start off cooperating and then switches to defect forever as punishment if player 1 ever defects. Then, if player 1 cooperates in each

Figure 5.1
Repeated interactions can yield sustained cooperation. Source: Zach Weinersmith, *SMBC (Saturday Morning Breakfast Cereal)*, https://www.smbc-comics.com/comic/dilemma-2.

Table 5.5
Explicit payoffs for a prisoner's dilemma

	Cooperate	Defect
Cooperate	2, 2	0, 3
Defect	3, 0	0.5, 0.5

of the first two *stage games* (rounds of play), she expects to receive a total payoff of 2 + 2 = 4. If player 1 defected in period 1, she'd receive a payoff of 3 in the first round and then a payoff of 0.5 in each later round (since player 2 will be defecting, player 1 maximizes her payoff by defecting also, yielding a payoff of 0.5), for a total payoff of 3.5. Since 4 > 3.5, cooperation maximizes player 1's total payoff for the first two rounds. Cooperation also yields higher payoffs in all later rounds (2 instead of 0.5). Thus, cooperation maximizes the total sum of player 1's stage game payoffs. The same logic applies to player 2.

There are countless strategies for repeated prisoner's dilemmas: plans for what to do in any round of play given the history of play in prior rounds. For example, you could start off defecting and then cooperate if and only if the other player cooperates for the first two or three periods. You could also experiment with defection and cooperation in the first few periods; there are all sorts of possibilities. And there are countless outcomes to the repeated games that can occur in reality—and even countless equilibrium strategy pairs in which neither player has an incentive to change her strategy, holding fixed the other player's strategy. There's an equilibrium in which both players insist on always defecting (if I think you're going to do this, I might as well do the same), and there are many different strategies in which the players could reach an equilibrium outcome in which they both cooperate forever.

But one especially simple strategy that research has found to be surprisingly effective in repeated prisoner's dilemmas is called, appropriately, *tit for tat*: cooperate in round one and then in each future round play whatever action the other player played in the prior period. If your partner cooperated last round, then you cooperate this round, and if your partner defected last round, you defect this round. Your memory is effectively limited to whatever single action your counterpart took most recently, and your strategy is effectively direct reciprocation. Tit for tat is certainly simple. And it's easy to see that tit for tat, if played without error by both players, leads to consistent cooperation by both players. Both cooperate in round 1 and then reciprocate each other's cooperation forever after.

Famously, in 1980, the first repeated prisoner's dilemma computer "tournament" was held, run by political scientist Robert Axelrod. Fourteen strategies were submitted by professional game theorists, and each strategy was pitted against each of the others for two hundred rounds of play. Tit for tat was the simplest strategy submitted, requiring the fewest lines of code—and it was the most successful, yielding the highest total payoff. In a follow-up tournament attracting more competition (sixty-two strategies from six countries) and refined so that the end of the game was randomly determined instead of known to be reached after two hundred rounds, again, tit for tat was the simplest submission—and again it was the tournament's champion (despite entrants knowing tit for tat won the first tournament)![3]

After this success, tit for tat gained a reputation for being a robustly effective strategy in repeated prisoner's dilemmas. It is also certainly very intuitive—people (and other animals) naturally engage in direct reciprocity with those we repeatedly interact with—and is therefore widely considered to be an evolutionarily adaptive behavior (see, e.g., Christakis, 2019). Tit for tat neatly addresses two human needs: one backward-looking and emotional (exacting justice for the other player's past sins) and the other forward-looking and practical (deterrence of future sins). Tit for tat seems to both work in theory and be ingrained in our nature. But, as I'll soon discuss, there are many reasons why tit for tat can be problematic in the more complex games we play in reality.

Back to Politics

Are Republicans and Democrats players in a repeated prisoner's dilemma? Yes and no. Yes, members of both parties repeatedly choose between actions that are relatively cooperative and ones that more directly and immediately favor their own partisan interests. For example, consider two parties bargaining over legislation, say, the COVID-19 relief bill considered in the fall of 2020. Both parties likely had strong short-run incentives to bargain in bad faith and resist compromise (without admitting this publicly)—and to exaggerate the other party's bad faith.

But the partisan politics game differs from the standard theoretical repeated prisoner's dilemma in many ways. In politics, there are a lot more than two players. They don't repeatedly simultaneously choose between the exact same two actions, with the same payoffs in each stage of interaction. Actually, politicians are not only not playing a repeated prisoner's dilemma—they aren't technically playing a repeated game of any type. That's because they never repeat the exact same stage game. The players repeatedly interact, but the stage game always changes.

Still, why haven't incentives that generally arise in even "quasi-repeated games" like this—the ability to reward cooperation and punish defection—led the parties to maintain strategic cooperation? And why haven't incentives leading to cooperation in one-shot prisoner's dilemmas had any teeth? Again, people do often cooperate in these contexts. Half the players on *Golden Balls* "cooperated," and they weren't even trying to win votes from the audience. Why would a politician "defect" if that makes them look like a jerk?

Well, perhaps a stronger desire to cooperate—due to less cold feelings toward the out-party, different reputational factors, or just different types of people in politics—did contribute more to bipartisan cooperation in the past. There are several reasons, though, involving additional rational and behavioral factors, which have plausibly led to a decline in strategic incentives to cooperate over time, as I'll discuss in the remainder of this chapter. I'll first talk about how strategic incentives to cooperate have declined, independent of the quasi-repeated nature of the game between the parties. After that, I'll discuss how repeated game dynamics, and tit-for-tat attitudes in particular, have likely contributed to growth in conflict and affective polarization bias.

Strategic Intransigence

If [Obama] was for it, we had to be against it.
—Republican Senator George Voinovich, quoted in *The New New Deal*, by Michael Grunwald

In *Golden Balls*, and other publicly observable prisoner's dilemma-esque games, players cooperate partly to publicly signal their own positive character traits. There are two major reasons, however, why signaling motives specific to politics, and US politics in recent years in particular, have likely had the opposite effect, leading to strategic intransigence, so to speak. The first is that intransigence has plausibly become a *net positive* signal to many swing voters. That's because in politics, cooperation isn't just a signal about your own character but also about the opposition's. If the two parties make a joint decision, like agreeing on some bipartisan legislation, it's hard to disentangle how much credit each side deserves, much harder than it is when we can see directly whether each player simply chose either "split" or "steal." This can cause our side's "defection" to actually hurt the other side's reputation.

If the two sides split the credit for joint cooperation 50/50, then there might not be much of a problem. But when Congress passes a piece of legislation supported by the president, it's typically considered an accomplishment for the president and their party. It's a positive signal for them, signaling their leadership, competence, and productivity. So, it's clear why the "minority party" might want to avoid this.

For strategic obstruction to yield electoral benefits for the minority party—to hurt the majority's reputation more than it hurts their own—some voters have to not realize the obstruction was strategic. The minority must (at least somewhat credibly) claim they're blocking the new bill because it would be bad for the country. If the proposed legislation would be socially beneficial, the minority needs some swing voters to not realize this.

Unfortunately, this is often likely the case, perhaps even more so in recent years than in the past. Changes in the media environment are the subject of the next chapter, so I'll just touch on this topic here. But one especially relevant factor is that trust in the mainstream media, as an institution, has declined substantially over recent decades (Ladd, 2011). As a result, many voters, especially those without strong partisan loyalties, may be more likely to focus on verifiable outcomes, such as whether or not major legislation was passed, rather than media assessments of which party deserves credit for the legislation or blame for failure to legislate (Stone, 2013). This has plausibly enhanced the minority party's strategic incentive to obstruct, independent of the merits of the bill under consideration.

Separate from changes in the media, it's also possible the parties simply didn't realize in the past how strategically effective intransigence could be. Slow learning about optimal strategies is common in various contexts (Fudenberg and Levine, 2016)—it can take decades for players to learn strategically optimal actions. For instance, NBA teams started fully exploiting the three-point shot only in the last decade, over thirty years after the shot was introduced (Cohen, 2021). Another explanation for growth in strategic intransigence is that being somewhat more intransigent without straying too far from the norms of the moment has always been a smart move. A consistent incentive to be "marginally uncooperative" would lead to gradual growth in "defection" (broadly construed) over time.

The second reason that signaling motives to defect have likely grown is that intransigence has become a more *direct positive* signal for the in-party's character in the eyes of the in-party's base. As partisans have grown to increasingly view the opposition party as the "enemy," they've become more likely to view cooperation with the out-party as "bad" and refusal to cooperate as "good." Members of Congress increasingly have to pander to voters with these preferences due to the growing threat of "getting primaried"—losing the nomination for a seat to a more extreme copartisan (Anderson et al., 2020). This threat has grown due to geographic sorting, gerrymandering, and growth in affective polarization. When Representative Joe Wilson yelled out "You lie!" in the middle of a 2009 joint address to Congress by President Obama, it led to donations pouring in afterward *for Wilson*. Ezra Klein's *Why We're Polarized* discusses this example and more broadly how US politics has grown to increasingly incentivize related "hardball" discourse and actions.

Now you might be thinking "well yeah, politicians are often acting strategically, now more than ever—but that's *why* I dislike them." That's not an unreasonable thought since strategic behavior can indeed signal negative character traits. One might dislike a public servant who strategically puts partisan interests over the common good. But it's also possible for voters to *over*infer poor character from strategically noncooperative behavior. In fact, if incentives to be strategically noncooperative have grown through the years (as I argue above, and for direct evidence see Canen et al., 2020), then we'd see more of this hardball behavior even if politicians' actual character traits were held fixed. If voters understood changes in these incentives, their feelings toward politicians wouldn't have changed due to defection becoming more common. Voters would essentially say "don't hate the player, hate the game."

But the strategic incentives politicians face aren't obvious. (They haven't been obvious to me, anyway.) If they were, then there wouldn't be much point to me and Klein, among others, bothering to write about them in detail as we have. Almost nobody fully understands strategic motives intuitively—that's why we take college courses on game theory. And lack of intuitive understanding of strategic incentives has indeed been documented in the behavioral economics literature. A formal term for this phenomenon is *limited strategic thinking* (Camerer, 2003).

Limited strategic thinking is when someone underestimates the degree of strategic thinking by other players. This behavior is seen clearly in a now classic game often called the Keynesian beauty contest. It's an extremely elegant game—both simple and rich. There are two or more players, and each player simultaneously chooses a number between zero and one hundred. The player whose number is closest to two-thirds of the average number wins. If two or more players tie for the win, they split the payoff. It's called a Keynesian beauty contest because John Maynard Keynes famously compared the stock market to newspaper beauty contests from that era in which respondents became eligible for a prize not by picking the most beautiful person but by picking the person most often chosen by others. Players in this game needed to guess what others would guess, knowing that others needed to think this way as well.

In the "guess two-thirds of the average" game, players must also guess what others will guess, knowing that others will be trying to do the same thing. The only equilibrium in this game—the only situation in which no player has an incentive to unilaterally change her strategy—is when everyone chooses 0. All the players then tie for the win. In reality, however, most people don't choose 0, and a relatively common choice is 33 (Mauersberger and Nagel, 2018). That's because 33 is two-thirds of 50, the average of randomly drawn numbers between 0 and 100. But usually the other players aren't choosing randomly—they're choosing strategically. Thinking of their choices as random is a type of limited strategic thinking. It neglects others' strategic motives. It's even possible for all the players to underestimate each other's strategic thinking: suppose they all assume the others choose randomly, and so each player chooses 33 (two-thirds of 50). They'd then tie for the win, but they're not in equilibrium because each player would have been better off choosing a lower number and winning outright. If everyone else chooses 33, two-thirds of the average is 22 (two-thirds of 33), so you'd be closer to the average choosing 32 or other lower numbers.

Returning now to affective polarization bias: limited strategic thinking can cause voters to unduly attribute noncooperative behavior to bad character. If voters neglect politicians' strategic incentives, voters might overattribute the out-party's apparent refusal to compromise over legislation as purely due to undesirable traits like stubbornness, extreme ideology, or even spite. A simple model helps to clarify this point (the following is based on Stone, 2020a). Suppose two parties jointly choose a policy represented by a number between 0 and 100. (You could think of this as, say, the size of a tax cut.) The left-leaning party's optimal number is something between 0 and 50, and the right party's optimal number is between 50 and 100. Numbers further from 50 are considered more extreme and more disliked by the other side. Both parties simultaneously shout out a number, and the actual policy is determined by the average of the two. So, if the left shouts 25 and the right shouts 75, the actual policy will be 50.

If you're on the right, your ideal outcome is 75, and you expect the left to shout 25—then you better shout something bigger than 75. If 100 is the biggest number allowed, then that's what you'll go with (and you'll expect to get an outcome of $(100 + 25)/2 = 62.5$, less than your ideal point of 75 but better than the 50 you'd expect to get if you stated your policy preference truthfully). If the left thinks analogously, they'll shout out 0 and the actual outcome will be $(0 + 100)/2 = 50$. If both sides then interpret the other side's statement at face value (i.e., don't consider their strategic incentive to exaggerate), both sides will overestimate the other side's extremism, which could lead to biased dislike.

This just an illustrative example. The point is that, as discussed throughout this section, strategic incentives can in general make us act uncooperatively. If voters fail to consider strategic motives when interpreting these actions, they'll likely overinfer "bad" motives from those actions. And there's a large body of evidence showing that people do indeed underestimate how strategic thinking affects other people's behavior. In fact, improved media coverage of strategies underlying political behavior has been shown to reduce affective polarization (Zoizner et al., 2020).

Conflict Cycles and Spirals

But what about the repeated nature of political games and other relationships? Again, in general the incentive to cooperate tends to be greater in
repeated interactions. Even completely self-interested actors can sustain
cooperation "in the shadow of the future." Nevertheless, Democrats and
Republicans have obviously not figured out how to do this. Like most
of us, they do seem to often take a tit-for-tat approach to strategy, as I'll
discuss below. But this approach has likely contributed to the decline in
cooperation as opposed to being a simple formula for maintaining cooperation, as is the case in theory and in many lab experiments. Similarly,
tit for tat is known to lead to problems in a wide range of other contexts
and relationships, due to several important differences between repeated
prisoner's dilemmas in theory and the quasi-repeated versions that occur
in reality.

The first of these differences is that in reality, we of course don't know
who we're really dealing with. In game theoretic terms, we don't know the
other players' true payoffs as these can depend on their character traits
(how selfish they are, how patient they are, etc.). By contrast, in, for example, Axelrod's tournaments, each player knew that the others each had the
objective of maximizing their total intertemporal (explicit) payoff. Due to
this incomplete information about the character of others, every action
you take is a signal of your character to other players in real-world quasi-
repeated games. Naturally, we often interpret the other side's defection as a
signal of "bad" character; for example, it could signal selfishness or impa-
tience. This increases how much we dislike them and makes future cooperation less likely, as I'll explain in more detail below.

Another important difference between theory and reality is something I
alluded to earlier in the chapter: that quasi-repeated games in the real world
in general, and perhaps especially in partisan politics, are orders of magnitude more complex and ambiguous than textbook repeated games. In
politics, every time the parties interact is different, usually in unpredictable
ways. No one knows who will hold power in the future, for how long, what
decisions they'll be faced with, or the consequences of those decisions. We
have different memories and interpretations of what happened in the past.
We can thus be clueless about the true effects of different decisions for each
party in the future—and even the present.

Complexity and ambiguity in relationships can easily lead to confusion over whose defection is a justified "retaliation" to the other party's prior "cheating" as opposed to constituting cheating in its own right. As a result, tit-for-tat strategies can lead to disaster. See Rosenquist (2019) for a discussion of this dynamic occurring in US politics over recent decades. Ambiguity-driven misperceptions combined with retaliatory strategies are in fact well known to yield conflict "cycles" and "spirals" in a wide range of contexts. Robert Jervis's *Perception and Misperception in International Politics* is a seminal work on the central role of misperceptions in driving international conflict spirals. For instance, Cold War tensions flared up after a South Korean passenger plane mistakenly flew over the USSR and was shot down in 1983, and a radar error led to escalation of US involvement in the Vietnam War (Ball, 1991). Hoffman and Yoeli (2022) describe how the British and Germans refrained from bombing civilian targets at the start of World War II; however, after a small number of bombs were dropped on Central London likely by accident, retaliation and escalation by both sides quickly ensued.

Moreover, Andersson and Pearson (1999) discuss tit-for-tat-driven "incivility spirals" in the workplace often starting unintentionally due to ambiguous actions interpreted negatively; see also Wu and colleagues (2013). Porath and Gerbasi (2015, 284) write that "people [in the workplace] just do not realize how they affect others. They may have good intentions, but they fail to see how they are perceived." Relationship psychologist Garth Fletcher writes that "unhappy, short-lived marriages were characterized by individuals responding [to each other] in a fine-grained quid pro quo fashion" (Fletcher, 2008, 138). Online advice to avoid "tit-for-tat" behavior in relationships abounds (If curious, search for tit-for-tat relationships. Plenty of links that basically say "don't do this" pop up right away).

In reality, "noise" is everywhere.[4] Think about the game of telephone, where one person whispers a message to another, who then whispers what they heard to the next player, and so on. Usually, the last person hears something only loosely related to the original content. It's hard for a small group to communicate a simple message to one another, and it's even harder for larger groups to gain a shared understanding of more complex situations. In reality, accurate perceptions of complex situations are the exception and misperceptions the norm. Research has indeed shown that introducing noise and misperceptions into otherwise completely standard repeated prisoner's dilemmas makes tit for tat less effective.[5] One accidental misstep leads to reciprocation, and the players get stuck in a rut. In his later book, Axelrod (1997) writes that in repeated games with noise, strategies that exhibit more leniency and contrition than tit for tat are more successful; see Fudenberg and colleagues (2012) for research from economists with similar results.

A third important difference between standard repeated prisoner's dilemmas in the lab and the ambiguous quasi-repeated versions that occur in reality is that in the latter, the "magnitude" of defection can grow over time. The self-serving but socially harmful action is not fixed; it can escalate. When someone attacks us, we can attack back "100x more." While escalation can be a strategic attempt to force capitulation, it also tends to occur even when we consciously try to merely match the magnitude of the other side's transgression (Shergill et al., 2003). We tend to retaliate with stronger actions in response to negative actions by our counterparts while reciprocating more equally only in response to positive actions (Keysar et al., 2008).

Conflict cycles and *conflict spirals* are sometimes used as synonyms in these literatures (e.g., Kennedy and Pronin, 2008) but they're not quite the same. The term *cycle* implies repetition, and *spiral* implies escalation. Cycle thus seems to be a more appropriate term for situations in which the players go back and forth between taking equally "bad" actions: one side defects, the other defects in retaliation, the first side retaliates back, and so on, with the defections being roughly equal in scope. Spiral is the more appropriate term for when the level of retaliation is unconstrained and escalates over time.

Examples of escalation are easy to find. A minor one occurred when Nancy Pelosi ripped up Trump's 2020 State of the Union speech after he rejected her offer to shake hands before the speech (instead handing her a copy of the speech). Bench-clearing brawls in baseball typically begin with one player being hit by a pitch or even just being brushed back, perhaps unintentionally. Famed relationship psychologist John Gottman says that tit for tat isn't the problem as much as escalation, writing that "negative affect reciprocity [tit for tat] . . . because it is so [common in marriages] may be something that therapists can afford to ignore . . . the problem . . . is the escalation of negativity" (Gottman et al., 1998, 18).

The last—and not least—key difference between real-world and theoretical repeated prisoner's dilemmas is, of course, cognitive bias. In Axelrod's tournaments, game theorists submitted algorithms, which weren't subject to, say, motivated reasoning and overprecision. In reality, bias can wreak havoc in conjunction with the other factors mentioned here, as I'll discuss in detail soon. Actually, even in the absence of cognitive bias, one could have done better than tit for tat in the original Axelrod repeated the prisoner's dilemma tournament—by being more forgiving. It's a little-known fact that "tit for two tats" (wait for the opponent to defect *twice* before retaliating) would have performed even better than tit for tat and won the tournament. Apparently, there were some competing strategies that defected intentionally, but then if the other player was cooperative, they became cooperative in return. Tit for tat would thus retaliate too quickly in response to these strategies and fail to achieve the full benefits of mutual cooperation. As Axelrod (1984, 39) writes, "The implication is striking . . . even expert strategists do not give sufficient weight to the importance of forgiveness." This implication is even more clear in the presence of uncertainty about character traits, noise, potential escalation, and cognitive bias.

Tit for tat is sometimes a useful heuristic, especially in particularly straightforward contexts, and as a result is ingrained in our nature. But most of us (even game theorists) have grown wise enough to realize that the tit-for-tat strategy should be used judiciously, even sparingly. Most of us understand—at least in principle—that "an eye for an eye will make the whole world blind."

Systematic Evidence?

Formal evidence of tit for tat and behaviorally strategic escalation in American politics over the era of rising affective polarization is perhaps surprisingly lacking, however. Maybe this is due to the same factors that also partly *cause* these phenomena—the complexity and changing nature of the game in partisan politics. These factors also make research on this topic messier; it's hard to empirically identify when strategic retaliation and escalation have truly occurred.

Bipartisanship has certainly declined over time in Congress, as figure 5.2 illustrates. And there's suggestive evidence that this decline resulted from each side responding to perceived excessive obstruction in the recent past by the other side. George W. Bush campaigned as a "uniter, not a divider" but was perceived by Democrats as abandoning bipartisanship. Democrats

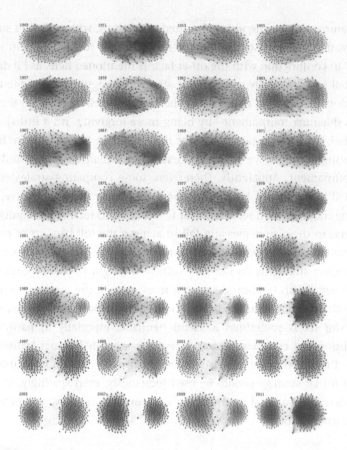

Figure 5.2
US House of Representatives voting network graphs. The nodes in the right clusters are Republicans, the left clusters are Democrats, and the lines connecting the nodes and the positions of the nodes indicate voting similarity. Source: Andris et al. (2015).

were then perceived by Republicans to obstruct social security reform in 2005, and Republicans were then seen as obstructing stimulus and health-care reform in 2009 and 2010 (Straka and Straka, 2020). But since each of these issues was quite distinct, and corresponding actions were complex, it's hard to make a clean comparison.

One issue that is relatively stable over time and is thus relatively well suited for this type of analysis is confirmations, and lack thereof, of presidential appointments. And this is indeed an area where tit-for-tat thinking has been said to have led to escalating disagreement and hostility (Adler, 2016; Rosenquist, 2019). In her book *Battle Over the Bench*, Amy Steigerwalt (2010, 13) writes that "between 1968 and 2000, only thirteen judicial nominees had cloture motions even filed in relation to their nominations; all were eventually confirmed, with the exception of Abe Fortas in 1968." (Cloture motions are filed to attempt to end filibusters. Since filibuster attempts are not directly recorded—and yes, it sure seems that they should be—and cloture motions indicate that there was a filibuster attempt, cloture motions are typically considered the best available measure of filibuster activity. We'll get back to Fortas later.) She goes on to say that "during the Bush (43) administration, this contentiousness reached new heights as ten circuit court nominees were successfully filibustered."

Steigerwalt's book was published in 2010. To say that contentiousness reached new heights in the early 2000s now seems quaint. While there were twenty-four cloture motions filed for judicial nominations between 2003 and 2010, there were twenty-six in the next Congress (2011–2012) alone (Beth et al., 2018). In response, in the first year of Obama's second term, in 2013, Democrat Senate Majority Leader Harry Reid exercised the so-called nuclear option for non-Supreme Court nominations, eliminating the filibuster for them. Republican Mitch McConnell did not even conduct hearings (much less allow a vote) for Merrick Garland, nominated by Obama for the Supreme Court in March 2016, ostensibly because it was an election year. McConnell then dropped the filibuster for Supreme Court nominations in 2017 and led the confirmation of Amy Coney Barrett to the court in the fall of (election year) 2020. After this, Democrats actively discussed court-packing as a countermeasure.

In addition to filibusters, there's also been more openly hostile questioning of nominees and more opposition in voting. The average number of votes against Supreme Court nominations increased from six during the Clinton years to forty-seven during the Trump administration. Figure 5.3 shows the increase in cloture votes (indicating filibusters) of all presidential nominees that have occurred since the Lyndon B. Johnson administration. As of May 31, 2021, Biden had made more nominations (244) than any of his last four predecessors at the same date but had fewer confirmations (53) than any except Trump (42), who had made fewer than half as many nominations (Thomas, 2021).

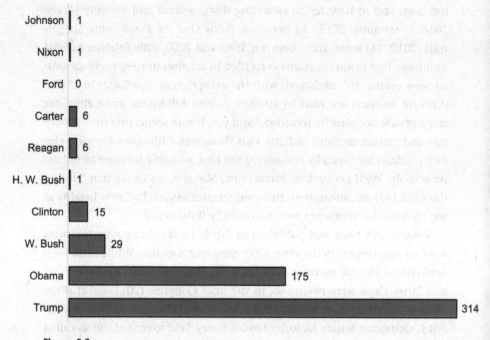

Figure 5.3
Cloture votes for presidential nominees. Source: adapted from Everett and Levine (2020).

Behavioral Conflict Cycles and Spirals: Overarching Biases and Limited Strategic Thinking

> When you go out for revenge, you have to dig two graves.
> —Yiddish saying

Summing up the two sections above, conflict cycles and spirals are common, destructive, often driven by ambiguity and misunderstanding, and often lead to intensely negative character judgments and feelings—and seem to have occurred in US politics over recent decades. These points are fairly well known, maybe even common sense—and yet the mechanisms driving our misunderstandings are certainly not always well understood, especially by the parties involved. What's even less clear is when, and why, spirals lead to *undue* dislike (especially for the parties involved but even for outside observers too). In the next two sections I'll talk through the perhaps surprisingly wide variety of such biases that arise in ambiguous quasi-repeated prisoner's dilemmas, contributing to conflict spirals—and spiraling undue dislike.

To clarify ideas, let me first quickly sketch a model of conflict cycles with "rational" growing dislike. This will also roughly show how a conflict cycle between even "good" players can occur. It will also show how a rational cycle has a hallmark characteristic at odds with real-world cycles and spirals: the players are aware the cycle may have started by mistake, which perpetually limits the growth in dislike. Consider a repeated *sequential* prisoner's dilemma: in each stage game, player 1 first chooses to cooperate or defect, and player 2 observes this choice and then also chooses one of these two actions. Also suppose there are two types of players, "good" and "bad," and players don't know each other's types. Only good players can sustain cooperation (bad players always defect.) That is, if the two players were each good and both knew this, they'd both always cooperate. If at least one player is bad and known to be bad, both always defect.

Let's assume each player knows only their own type and has some belief (probability) that the other player is good. And suppose actions and payoffs are observed with noise: good actions sometimes look bad and perhaps also vice versa. Consider an instance of the game in which both players by chance are good types, so both should cooperate forever and player 1 indeed initially cooperates. But player 2 misperceives this as defection or the action randomly turns out to be defection without player 1's knowledge. For example, a driver could accidentally cut off another without realizing this (aggressive driving would be defection, and courteous driving would be cooperation for this context).

Suppose this perception of player 1's action as defection then leads player 2 to Bayesian update to a sufficiently high probability that player 1 is "bad" to justify playing defect in response, which player 1 observes correctly. Player 1 knows she might have mistakenly observed player 2's cooperation as defection or that player 2 might have defected due to mistakenly thinking player 1 initially defected. But defection is always a signal of bad character (defection is always more likely to come from a "bad" type of player 2 than "good"), causing player 1 to Bayesian update that player 2 is more likely "bad," and thus causing player 1 to also optimally defect. Both players continue to defect and update toward the other being bad, and pretty soon even if defection is mistakenly interpreted as cooperation, it won't turn things around because the players will realize this must have been a misinterpretation.

In this case, the players will both dislike each other more than they truly should since they're both truly good. However, they won't experience biased dislike—they'll dislike each other the appropriate (Bayesian) amount given available information. Moreover, there's a limit to how much they'll dislike one another: being rational, they'll know there's a chance the conflict stemmed from a mistake, and they'll maintain uncertainty about the other side's type accordingly. Even after countless defections, they'll never update to the belief that "the other side is definitely bad."

Needless to say, this isn't very realistic. When we get into extended conflicts with one another, negative feelings tend to grow and psychological factors can play a large role in affecting how most of us actually think and behave. When these games go awry and tempers flare, rational beliefs are probably the exception, not the rule. We don't think the conflict might be a big mistake—we just think the other side is terrible.

Furthermore, our undue dislike toward the other side reduces our propensity to cooperate and makes us more likely to escalate conflict, for at least two main reasons. First, worse beliefs about the other side's character traits imply less trust in the other player(s) (Ho, 2021). We lose confidence that our cooperation will be rewarded by the other side in the future, giving us less incentive to cooperate. Second, when we dislike the other players more, we are simply less interested in helping them out, especially at our own expense, now and in the future, and can even desire to actively harm them (Webster et al., 2021). So it's very clear that biased dislike makes us more likely to take actions that will escalate conflict. If the other side fails to understand the biased dislike driving our actions, then biased dislike on both sides is likely to grow.

Let's call conflict cycles and spirals driven by biased beliefs "behavioral conflict cycles and spirals" to distinguish them from the potentially fully rational ones and discuss which biases are likely to occur and why. The ambiguity and complexity of real-world quasi-repeated prisoner's dilemmas don't just set the stage for random misperceptions—these are also the conditions that "activate" many of our cognitive biases. The blurrier the lines, the easier it is for our unconscious minds to control the image we see. These biases further exacerbate problems caused by tit for tat, beyond those shown by the literature on repeated prisoner's dilemmas with random noise.

Two key general biases are *under*estimation of our own past "defections" and *over*estimation of the other side's. The major overarching biases discussed in chapter 3 contribute to these self-serving views. First, and I suspect foremost, are motivated reasoning and myside bias: we're motivated to believe the other side deserves more blame for our conflicts (political or otherwise) for multiple reasons. It makes us feel better about ourselves, allows us to better advocate for our reputations, and allows us to better advocate for our own (self-serving) defection in the present and future (Zell et al., 2021). As a result, we interpret our own ambiguous actions that could be perceived as defection or escalation generously (as nondefection) or just ignore how these actions could offend. And we interpret the other side's ambiguous actions as defection when it behooves us to do so.[6]

For example, when Merrick Garland was denied a hearing by McConnell in 2016, he justified this decision in a few ways: that it was a presidential election year ("The American people should have a voice in the selection of their next Supreme Court Justice"), Republicans had taken control of the Senate in 2014 and thus there was a divided government, and Obama was a second-term lame duck president. In the fall of 2020 when McConnell and Republicans confirmed Amy Coney Barrett, Democrats focused on the apparent hypocrisy of McConnell and other Senate Republicans confirming a nominee even later in an election year. McConnell instead talked about reasons that the situation in 2020 was different from that of 2016: Republicans held unified control of government (as opposed to the Democrats in 2016) and Trump was not in his second term (in contrast to Obama).

As usual, both sides restricted their arguments to those supporting their interests. (Also, as usual, that doesn't mean both sides were equally wrong but does imply that, to the extent that arguments were made sincerely, at least one side was subject to motivated reasoning and myside bias.) Even if you don't think one or both leaders fully believed the arguments they made, the fact that they made them suggests they thought those arguments would be plausible, at least to copartisans.

Motivated reasoning can also make us forget our own intentional or unintentional defections relatively quickly. We'll then underestimate the other player's motivation for their defection (or what we perceive as defection), which leads us to judge their defection too negatively. And we don't neglect or forget the other player's aggressions so easily. We can even be motivated to (too) negatively interpret the other player's actions—to overestimate the degree of escalation represented by those actions—to justify our own self-serving retaliation and possible escalation in the present and future. If escalation yields immediate benefits to us (as is often the case, e.g., court-packing directly benefits the party currently in power), then we could be motivated to interpret others' actions in a way to justify our escalation.

Returning to some numbers may help clarify. Consider the example of payoffs from one player's choice in a sequential prisoner's dilemma shown in table 5.6. Suppose just one player, the in-party, is faced with the choice of A or B ("cooperate" or "defect"). Cooperation is socially efficient in the sense of yielding the higher combined payoff $(1 + 1 > 10 - 10)$. But, clearly, defection is best for the in-party in the short-run, yielding a payoff of 10 versus 1. The in-party could then be motivated to believe defection is socially optimal too and that this doesn't even make the out-party worse off. An example of such a motivated perception of payoffs is shown in the third column of the table. Consequently, the in-party would not believe the out-party has a right to retaliate to action B (defect) in the future. The fourth column shows an example of motivated out-party perceptions if the in-party actually cooperated. In this case, the out-party could still be motivated to perceive this cooperation as defection to justify their own (self-serving) defection in the next stage when it's their turn to act. Remember, accurate perceptions are the exception, and misperceptions are the norm. And the model I discuss here is just a model—reality is not so simple.

Table 5.6
Illustrative example of how motivated reasoning can affect perceived payoffs in a sequential prisoner's dilemma

Strategy chosen by the in-party	True payoffs	In-party's perceived payoffs (justifying B as socially optimal)	Out-party's perceived payoffs if the in-party chooses A
A = Cooperate	In-party payoff = 1	In-party payoff = 1	In-party payoff = 5
	Out-party payoff = 1	Out-party payoff = 1	Out-party payoff = 1
B = Defect	In-party payoff = 10	In-party payoff = 10	In-party payoff = 8
	Out-party payoff = −10	Out-party payoff = 5	Out-party payoff = 8

Confirmation bias, WYSIATI, naive realism, and overprecision are likely to contribute to behavioral conflict spirals as well. Confirmation bias (both motivated and unmotivated) leads our negative impressions to be self-perpetuating. WYSIATI makes us neglect noise and uncertainty, yielding overprecision and making us think that we understand the other player's character better than we do. Naive realism can make us overestimate the extent to which the other side knows what we know and consequently over-estimate the extent to which the other side understands our grievances.[7]

A minor example of naive realism and WYSIATI contributing to conflict happened to my spouse in a parking lot recently. She opened her car door and bumped the side mirror of a car in the next spot over. There happened to be a guy sitting in that car's driver's seat. After she started to walk away, he opened his door and yelled out, "Hey! You could have at least apologized!" He assumed she'd seen him and just ignored him, but she hadn't seen him and understandably assumed there was no one in the car given that it was parked in the spot before she got there. His WYSIATI and naive realism caused him to be subject to false consensus about the knowledge that he was in the car, leading to undue hostility toward her (hostility based on false beliefs).

Limited strategic thinking is again relevant too. If we fail to under-stand the other side's strategic reasons for defecting, we'll be more likely to attribute their defection directly to bad character—that they're simply taking the self-serving action that harms us purely due to short-sighted self-interest. If we're "sure" we saw the other player defect for no good reason, but we might be misinterpreting their action, then we'll be more likely to retaliate than if we properly understand the role of noise or their own stra-tegic motivation to defect.

An Example from "the Discourse"

Much of the discourse on the court nomination battles seems to exem-plify these biases. It's an understatement to say that commentary often appears biased toward supporting the in-party's interests. Here's a closer look at just one of practically countless examples. On October 26, 2020, Ezra Klein (who describes himself as liberal) tweeted a reference to McCo-nnell's "defections" on Garland and Barrett and potential retaliation by Democrats (Klein, 2020b): "I cannot emphasize enough how much McCon-nell's actions on Garland and Barrett have radicalized Democratic senators.

As I've argued before, McConnell's single most consequential legacy may be what he convinces Senate Democrats to do."

Numerous tweets responded by claiming Democrats' treatment of Republican Supreme Court nominees, Robert Bork in particular, justified McConnell's actions. Bork was nominated by President Reagan in 1987 and voted down by a Democrat-controlled Senate 58–42. Pundit Joe Nocera, often sympathetic to Democratic viewpoints, wrote in a 2011 *New York Times* column that "Bork was . . . deeply conservative. . . . It is, to be sure, completely understandable that the Democrats wanted to keep Bork off the court. . . . But liberals couldn't just come out and say that . . . So, instead, the Democrats sought to portray Bork as 'a right-wing loony' . . . [and engaged in] character assassination." Nocera even argued the Bork fight played a key role in driving subsequent growth in affective polarization: "The Bork fight, in some ways, was the beginning of the end of civil discourse in politics. . . . The anger between Democrats and Republicans, the unwillingness to work together, the profound mistrust—the line from Bork to today's ugly politics is a straight one." Thompson (2021) says the Bork fight had a profound impact on McConnell in particular.

At the risk of stating the obvious, Nocera's view was not the consensus then among those left of center. And it certainly didn't become the consensus view for the left in subsequent years.[8] Let's return to Ezra Klein's 2020 tweet about McConnell radicalizing Democrats and the responses essentially arguing "Democrats started it." In response to these responses, political scientist Scott Lemieux tweeted that "the bad faith of these ridiculous attempts to pretend Dems started a cycle which in fact started with the filibuster/removal of Abe Fortas is blindingly transparent."[9] Recall that Fortas was noted earlier in the chapter as the one judicial nominee not confirmed between 1968 and 2000. His nomination for chief justice by Lyndon Johnson was successfully blocked by conservative senators, ostensibly due to ethics issues but perhaps also due to ideological ones.[10] Of course, those who blocked him might have perceived this to be justified retaliation for the other side's prior defection.

I'll restate the main point that I am trying to illustrate here: the major general biases make us play the "who started it" game at the highest levels of discourse and politics. Our biases make us lean toward interpreting the other player's actions as uncooperative *and* toward underestimating our own past uncooperativeness, which our counterpart player(s) might in turn be responding to when they act uncooperatively. Both of these biases naturally contribute to affective polarization bias, in turn further exacerbating conflict and bias.

Behavioral Conflict Spirals: Other Factors

There are even more psychological factors that can exacerbate behavioral conflict spirals, worth discussing here at least briefly. First, as I discussed earlier, tit for two tats (ignoring an initial transgression before playing tit for tat) is often a more effective strategy in repeated prisoner's dilemmas than tit for tat. But we struggle to turn the other cheek because it seems unfair, allowing the other player to "get away with" bad behavior, or at least what looked like bad behavior to us. People of course care deeply about fairness in general (see, e.g., Fehr and Gächter, 2000), and we especially care about not being "played for a 'sucker'" (Hibbing and Alford, 2004). As a result, we'll feel a strong desire to retaliate to another player's defection even when we might know, at least in the back of our minds, that refraining from doing so is the smart thing to do to diffuse or prevent a conflict spiral.

Another factor contributing to spirals is our failure to foresee how other players will interpret our retaliation and how they'll respond in turn. Motivated reasoning and WYSIATI are part of the story here, causing us to be overconfident that the other side will share our understanding of the justification for our actions. Another reason is simple lack of strategic foresight (Stone, 2020a). We have a vague awareness of the shadow of the future but don't think it through precisely.

In early 2021, when Senate Democrats considered whether to eliminate or weaken the Senate filibuster, Mitch McConnell threatened multiple times that this would result in a "scorched-earth Senate" as retaliation. Perhaps he was making this threat explicit because he's aware of Democratic politicians' or voters' lack of strategic foresight. (And perhaps Democrats should have been more explicit about retaliation that would result from some of McConnell's past actions they perceived as escalatory to deter those actions.) Scholars of interpersonal conflict have found that explicit threats can indeed be useful for deterring escalation in conflict.

Yet another simple behavioral phenomenon that can exacerbate spirals is our tendency to focus on the most salient (noticeable) information (see, e.g., Bordalo et al., 2020). In relationships, political and otherwise, the most salient information is often what happened most recently. If the other side defected in the last period, I might neglect the history that led up to this (on both sides) and feel compelled to retaliate. This type of short memory, *recency bias*, driven conflict spiral happens with my kids all the time. One will either accidentally or thoughtlessly instigate a conflict with a minor transgression, say, a shove. The other escalates in retaliation. The first one then immediately reciprocates, seemingly completely forgetting his initial transgression. Before long, nearby household items start getting used as weapons and there is a risk of someone getting seriously hurt. (I call them the two stooges, but the real stooges had a much higher tolerance for pain.)

Yes, politicians *should* know better about this type of thing than kids, but it's not so clear that this is the case, and it's especially unclear if this is true for the loudest political commentators. In their defense, the complexity of partisan politics makes it natural to focus on salient information. Tit for tat might seem silly because of its exclusive focus on the most recent past. But given the overwhelming amount of potentially relevant historical information in most political situations, and even social relationships, a heuristic focus on the most recent event is not completely unreasonable. Negative emotions also heighten the desire to respond to the recent past—and the severity of many of our biases in general (Blanchette and Richards, 2009; Kramer et al., 2007; Fernback and Van Boven, 2021).

Some of you might now be thinking, hey, wait a second—there must be some reasonably sophisticated players in the world of politics, and shouldn't they at least be somewhat aware of the ambiguity inherent in these complex games and relevant biases? Shouldn't these relatively sophisticated players know that other players are subject to these biases? And shouldn't that make these players more sympathetic and less judgmental toward others when they take aggressive actions?

Well, yes, and as discussed in chapter 3 and elsewhere in the book, we are often aware of some of other people's cognitive biases. But when we see others act in a way that seems biased toward self-serving actions, this often makes us like them *less*, not more. Biased judgment is not a positive character trait. A fundamental problem, again, is the bias blind spot: we "see" their bias but not our own. We should grade them on a curve ("nobody's perfect"), but instead, we too harshly judge them for mistakes—or what we perceive are mistakes—due to underestimating our own mistakes. We're often biased toward overestimating their bias since we tend to underestimate the justification they perceive for their defection or escalation (including both our own sins provoking their retaliation and their lack of awareness of our own justification for our prior defection(s); see Kennedy and Pronin, 2008).[11]

Philosopher Kevin Dorst discusses "why the other side is more reasonable than you'd think" extensively on his *Stranger Apologies* blog and in ongoing research (e.g., Dorst, 2021). He argues that belief polarization is often more rational than it seems, as Bayesians predictably polarize when they face ambiguous information. This is an intriguing claim, and the jury is still out on its empirical relevance. Regardless, I agree with the conclusion—that partisans tend to underestimate the other side's reasonableness—in part because our side is *less* reasonable than we think. The *underestimation* of our own biases causes us to *overestimate* their biases, thereby disliking them more than we should.[12]

A Toy Model of Snowballing Misunderstanding

Before wrapping up the chapter, I'd like to quickly formalize a key general point: how the combination of tit-for-tat strategy, biased character inference, lack of strategic foresight, and escalation naturally cause misperceptions, and animosity, to snowball over time.[13] Suppose two players, A and B, take turns choosing a number, X, which must be greater than or equal to zero. For each player, when choosing X, a higher X is good for yourself and bad for the other player, and the harm to the other player from choosing a higher value of X is greater than the benefit to yourself, so higher values of X are "selfish" in that they are privately good but socially inefficient. Thus, both players consider a choice of high X by the other player to signal poor character. (One could interpret $X = 0$ as "cooperation" and higher values of X as higher degrees of "defection" to map this back to the prisoner's dilemma.) Each player has beliefs about the quality of the other's character, which is some number ranging from 0 to infinity (a higher number implies less selfishness and better character). Suppose these beliefs can be represented with a single value, the expected quality of their character, and each player dislikes the other more when this number is smaller.

Specifically, in round t, for odd values of t, suppose player A chooses the number:

$$X_t^A = \frac{1}{q_A} + 1 / E_{A,t}(q_B),$$

where q_A is A's character and $E_{A,t}(q_B)$ is A's expectation of (perceived average value of) B's character at the start of round t. So, player A chooses a higher X when her own character is lower and when her expectation of the other player's character is lower due to, for example, retaliation, dislike, mistrust—the exact reason is not important here. Each action is thus a signal of the player's own character to the other player (suppose there's a small amount of noise, so it's not a perfect signal, but let's ignore this here for simplicity too). Player B acts analogously in each round $t + 1$.

Now let's assume both players have character values of 1, and both have unbiased expectations of each other at the start of the game. So, player A chooses $X_{A,t} = 1 = 1/1+1/1 = 2$ in round 1. But suppose both players have a bias toward perceiving the other player's action as 10 percent higher than it is (for one of the reasons discussed above), so B perceives $X_{A,t} = 1$ as 2.1. Suppose also that A doesn't realize B perceives A's action this way—and B doesn't realize that A doesn't realize this—again, consistent with the discussion above. For simplicity, I'll assume each player's updated expectation of the other's character can be directly solved for using their observed action. (I won't model a more subtle and complex belief updating process.) Player B will then, assuming that $E_{A,t}(q_B) = 1$ and subtracting this off from 2.1, solve for q_A to be approximately $1/1.1 = 0.91$, and so B now likes A less and will choose $X_{B,t} = 2.1$ in round 2. Player A will perceive this as $2.1*(1.1) = 2.31$. However, A thinks $E_{B,t}(q_A) = 1$, and so A will infer that $1/q_B = 2.31 - 1$, implying $q_B = 1/1.31 = 0.76$. Player A thus now likes B even less than B likes A.

Note that there are two forces driving A's biased dislike of B: direct misinterpretation of B's action and unawareness of B's misinterpretation of A's action. Player A will thus next choose $X_{A,t} = 1/1+1/0.76 = 2.31$ in round 3. B perceives this as $2.31(1.1) = 2.54$, and B will update beliefs about q_A to $1/1.54 = 0.65$ (since B still thinks A thinks $q_B = 1$, so A's high action must have been due to A having lower character than B realized), implying that B's dislike of A grows further still. The pattern will continue. Each side attributes the other's escalation to worse and worse character, due to the other side's past misperception and retaliation, despite their actual character values being exactly the same.

Concluding Remarks

The main points from this chapter are as follows:

- Game theory 101 predicts that players "defect" in a one-shot prisoner's dilemma. In reality, people instead often "cooperate" because we're socially minded or want to appear that way.
- In repeated prisoner's dilemmas, we're more likely to cooperate, even if we're completely selfish, because defection can be punished, and cooperation rewarded, in the future by the other player.
- A simple strategy effectively yielding cooperation in repeated prisoner's dilemma tournaments and lab settings is tit for tat, which is consistent with direct reciprocity being evolutionarily adaptive.
- Short-run incentives to cooperate are lower in political games in reality because cooperation both makes the other side "look good" to swing voters and makes your side "look bad" to your partisan base. Limited strategic thinking can cause this strategic defection to be misinterpreted as an overly negative signal of character.
- Tit for tat often causes trouble in the quasi-repeated prisoner's dilemma games we often play in our bilateral relationships in reality. We fail to agree on justification for retaliatory defection due to ambiguity, noise, and a variety of cognitive biases (motivated reasoning, WYSIATI, naive realism, among other factors), leading to excessive defection and even escalation (behavioral conflict spirals).
- Misunderstanding excessive defection leads to unduly negative inferences about the other side's character traits, causing additional defection/escalation due to decreased trust that our side's cooperation will be reciprocated by the other side in future play, and decreased desire to behave prosocially. Affective polarization bias–driven defection can in turn be misinterpreted as overly negative signals of character, causing additional bias.
- Spiraling affective polarization bias is exacerbated by other factors including confirmation bias, overprecision, fairness/revenge motives, limited strategic foresight, limited memory/attention, emotions exacerbating bias, and the bias blind spot.

Political scientist Brendan Nyhan coined the phrase "negative partisanship rules everything around me" to describe the wide range of phenomena explained by out-party dislike. Negative partisanship even rules negative partisanship. We dislike them, so we act like jerks to them; they then dislike us and act like jerks back, causing us to dislike them further.

For a variety of reasons, polarization tends to snowball. And cognitive biases are often—perhaps almost always—fundamental causes of snowballs that grow large. Even if spirals can start by "mistake" due to ambiguity and miscommunication, if we're unbiased, we'll keep in mind the possibility of such mistakes, limiting growth in our dislike. Perhaps we'll have the foresight to turn the other cheek, maybe even a few times, to forestall escalation. By contrast, biased dislike naturally exacerbates, and is exacerbated, by tit-for-tat retaliation and escalation. The less aware we are of bias contributing to their "bad actions," the more we attribute them to bad character and the stronger we'll retaliate, leading to (biased) retaliation by them, ad nauseam.

So, it's actually not quite right to say "An eye for an eye will make the whole world blind." Taken literally, after one misstep, "an eye for an eye" might only cause a second person to become half-blind. That's bad news but not tragic. It's ambiguity and cognitive bias that cause actions to escalate, leading outcomes for everyone to become much worse.

Before proceeding to the next chapter, I want to briefly discuss an issue specific to conflict spirals in politics: the distinction between feelings of voters and politicians. I've been vague about this, largely because there are close connections between these players within the same party. When voters become more hostile toward the out-party, politicians are incentivized to behave accordingly—to act in a hostile way toward the out-party and blame them for the breakdown in cooperation. Similarly, voters influence each other: less affectively polarized voters may strategically conform and refrain from pushing back against more polarized, and more outspoken, copartisan voters for various reasons, such as the desire to not appear disloyal.

Perhaps even more significantly, politicians both unintentionally and strategically stir the pot and exacerbate affective polarization bias among voters themselves. Charles Barkley once commented that "our politicians, whether they're Republicans or Democrats, are designed to make us not like each other. They divide and conquer" (Salvador, 2021). Political consultant Roger Stone confirms this claim, saying that "politics is not about uniting people. It's about dividing people. And getting your fifty-one per cent" (Toobin, 2008). Political scientist Steven Webster's book *American*

Rage documents strategic provocation of anger and hostility toward the out-party by politicians. Amanda Ripley calls politicians and others who act this way due to benefiting from conflict "conflict entrepreneurs." Many members of the media, political consultants, marketers, and various party operatives might belong in this category. Limited strategic thinking (lack of awareness of politicians and others having incentives to exacerbate conflict) and sheer credulity would cause this behavior to increase voter affective polarization bias. I discuss the influence of divisive information further in the next chapter.

6 Information

The greatest enemy of knowledge is not ignorance, it is the illusion of knowledge.
—popularly attributed to Stephen Hawking

Maybe the most salient change in the political environment that's occurred over the era of rising affective polarization has been the transformation of the media. We've experienced the advent of several major new media technologies—cable news, the web, and social media—and the decline of various forms of legacy media. It's natural to suspect that these changes have contributed to growth in various types of polarization, including affective polarization bias. Empirical studies on this topic have been perhaps surprisingly unclear, however.[1] In this chapter, I'll argue that changes in our information ecosystem, more broadly defined, and interpreted in the context of a wide range of research on the psychology, and math, of information processing, have indeed contributed to growth in affective polarization—and to growth in affective polarization bias.

Technological Change, Echo Chambers, and Selective Exposure

I don't think it's necessary for me to describe in detail how technological changes have affected the media industry since 1980. The histories of how cable television took off in the 80s and 90s, followed by the proliferation of online media outlets, blogs, social media platforms, and smart phones—and the decline of print media, newspapers especially—are familiar to most of us and are well documented elsewhere.[2] But it's still useful to briefly talk through the economics and psychology of how these technological changes have affected media content.

Technological improvements often lower firms' costs of production, and it's indeed cheaper to produce news online than to publish and deliver in print. It's natural to think lower production costs would benefit firms, but that's not always the case since low costs can increase the intensity of competition in various ways. Lower firm costs are consequently more likely to benefit an industry's consumers than firms, for various reasons. When consumers have similar preferences, lower costs usually lead to lower prices or improved vertical product characteristics (higher quality). When consumer preferences are more heterogeneous, lower costs are likely to lead to greater horizontal differentiation and market segmentation, which allows firms to better cater to consumer preferences.

For example, when the cost of a permit to sell ice cream on a strip of beach declines, this can lead to market entry: more vendors on the strip. They might bunch up in the middle, or they might spread out (differentiate), depending on contextual factors (e.g., the distribution of consumers along the strip). But either way, consumers benefit. Bunched up vendors help consumers if they sell a wider variety of ice cream flavors, offer lower prices, or just reduce waiting times as compared to a single vendor in the same location. If the vendors spread out along the strip, then they cater better to consumers' varying tastes for location.

Technological growth has, of course, led to entry and increased horizontal differentiation in the news industry across various dimensions, including politics.[3] Many media outlets have moved away from the "objectivity norm" and come to differentiate themselves from each other politically. Researchers have shown that political differentiation across media outlets, often referred to as *slant* in the literature for short, can be defined and measured in various ways, such as looking at the similarity of language used by Democratic and Republican politicians (Gentzkow and Shapiro, 2010) or how news stories are framed in ways that favor one party (Garz et al., 2020a). While the most extreme slants tend to be used by outlets with relatively small audiences, major mainstream outlets can use substantially different slants as well (Garz et al., 2020a).

The proliferation of partisan outlets has led to prominent concerns about media *echo chambers*: that consumers will exclusively see one-sided news sources that "echo" both each other and the consumer's prior beliefs.

Echo chambers could result from consumer choices, algorithmic *filter bub-bles* (search engines or other algorithmic forces steering consumers toward prior belief-confirming sources), or a combination of both. There's actually a reasonably well-established view now in political science that hardcore echo chambers are fairly uncommon (Guess et al., 2018; Guess, 2021). Most media consumers frequently get news from mainstream outlets that are relatively nonpartisan. However, the citizens who are in real echo chambers are highly engaged and plausibly have inordinate influence and visibility (Guess, 2021), or may be relatively likely to take extreme actions. The litera-ture's understanding of the prevalence of echo chambers may also change as media consumption data becomes more granular or due to the media landscape continuing to develop. For example, the growth of Substack sub-scriptions and partisan social media platforms (e.g., Parler and QubeTV) may cause bona fide echo chambers to become more common.

Regardless, it's clear that the key force driving differentiation in news slant is that consumers generally prefer to get news from politically like-minded outlets and journalists. There might be a relatively small popula-tion of Republicans that only watch Fox News and get no other news. But it's undoubtedly true that Republicans are more likely than Democrats to watch Fox and the reverse is true for many other outlets; see figure 6.1. More broadly, as media choice has expanded, *selective exposure*—disproportionate attention to "congenial" or "attitude-congruent" information (information that we hope is true or already agree with)—has generally increased.[4] And selective exposure doesn't just mean inordinate exposure to information confirming our views on policy or ideology. It also means inordinate expo-sure to information that's critical of the opposition (which I'll call "anti-out-party information") since we also find this information congenial, for reasons discussed in chapter 3.

Selective exposure is intuitive and documented in a wide range of research. For example, Hart and colleagues (2009) present a metastudy of dozens of psychology studies and conclude that, in general, people tend to choose congenial information when given the option and this effect is somewhat stronger for political information. Selective exposure has also been shown to occur in more subtle ways. Kim and Kim (2021) show that people spend more time reading and watching news when current events are more favorable for their political views. Ho and colleagues (2020) show that people often prefer to receive no information at all than being exposed

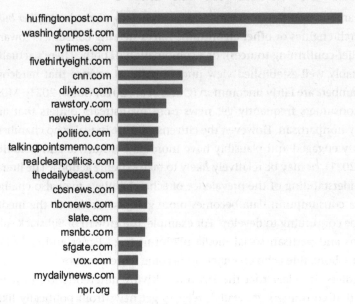

Traffic share for Democrats

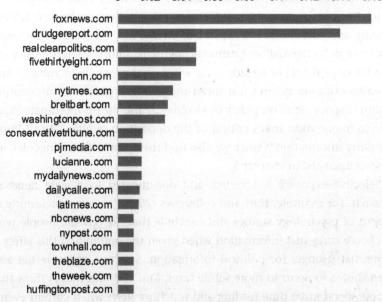

Traffic share for Republicans

Figure 6.1
Top twenty news websites visited by Republicans and Democrats, August to November 2016. Source: adapted from Peterson et al. (2021).

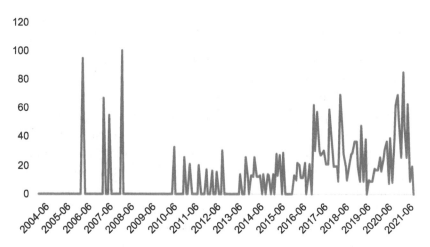

Figure 6.2
Google Trends for "echo chambers" in the US since 2004.

to potentially uncongenial information. And even research concluding that echo chambers are rare finds substantial evidence that partisans choose generally like-minded media diets (Guess, 2018).

Furthermore, despite the academic finding that echo chambers appear rare, the term *echo chambers* is still regularly used informally and by the media (see figure 6.2). It's part of the vernacular now. When we refer to echo chambers informally, we usually do so with the understanding that (of course) they're a real phenomenon.

I don't think this belief is misguided—the term is just being used more loosely outside of academia. When researchers say someone is in an echo chamber, they mean that person is getting all or nearly all of their political information from ideologically aligned sources. When nonacademics say someone's in an echo chamber, they're talking about a less extreme, but indeed much more common, version of the same idea: selective exposure. "Echo chambers" is a much catchier and more descriptive phrase than "selective exposure," after all.

So, technology has advanced, costs of publishing have declined, and as a result, selective exposure has increased. Economics 101 says this should make consumers better off; however, it's far from clear that this has been the case. Even if we assumed the quality of news was held fixed as horizontal differentiation increased, and that consumers were fully rational information processors, providing them with more "like-minded news" would raise concerns. Getting the information that maximizes one's own private interests does not necessarily make you optimally informed as a voter, from society's perspective.

Moreover, there are serious concerns, to say the least, about various ways that news quality has declined as new media has emerged (see, e.g., Cagé, 2016; Hasen, 2022). The reasons are complex, but one I'll note here is a potential *relationship* between horizontal and vertical characteristics of news that we often perceive precisely backward: we think more ideologically like-minded news is higher quality when the reverse is true (Stone, 2011). Consequently, growth in selective exposure can directly imply a decline in the quality of news that voters receive. I'll talk more about the causes and effects of selective exposure for political news soon, but first I want to talk about other ways our political "information sets"—the information relevant to politics we actually observe—have changed over the era of rising affective polarization.

Social Networks: Online and Off

In addition to major changes in the news industry, another enormous change in our information environment has been the emergence of online social networks. Most US adults now use at least one of these platforms, and by the time you're reading this, social media users will likely constitute a majority of the world's population as well (Chen, 2021). Since the pundits and news sources we "follow" on social media tend to be like-minded, we're also subject to selective exposure on these platforms. The evidence for whether these platforms increase selective exposure as compared to the web or other forms of news consumption is mixed (Barberá, 2020). But even if cross-cutting exposure on social media is substantial, selective exposure is substantial on social media as well (see also, e.g., Cinelli et al., 2020). Moreover, some direct comparisons imply selective exposure on social media is much higher than elsewhere on the web (Halberstam and Knight, 2016) and that the social media users who are exposed to a variety of sources only engage with the content they find congenial from ideologically misaligned sources (Green et al., 2021).

The peers that we connect with on social media tend to be like-minded too. Bakshy and colleagues (2015) report that for both self-identified lib-

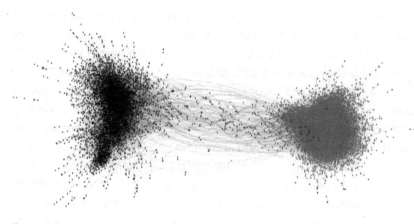

Figure 6.3
Visualization of a Twitter network. Nodes in the left cluster are almost entirely coded as liberal; nodes on the right are predominantly coded as conservative. Links between nodes are accounts that retweet one another, and nodes are located closer to one another when they retweet each other more often. Source: Brady et al. (2017); reprinted with permission.

erals and conservatives on Facebook, well over 50 percent of friends are ideologically aligned, and less than 25 percent come from the other side of the spectrum (the remainders are "moderates"). See also figure 6.3. In addition to connecting with offline friends and family who are generally like-minded, we're more likely to reciprocate online ties with copartisan strangers (Mosleh et al., 2021). Twitter networks of politicians and other elites are also largely ideologically like-minded (van Vliet et al., 2021). @LeaderMcConnell (Mitch McConnell) only follows his copartisans in the Senate, and @SpeakerPelosi (Nancy Pelosi) does the same for the House.[5]

Again, this selective exposure isn't absolute and universal. In fact, most of us have witnessed contentious interactions on Facebook between friends who don't see eye to eye on some political issue. (Sometimes they don't stay friends after these interactions.) But this behavior just highlights another way that our exposure to information online is not representative of reality: those of us who are most active online are not typical members of our party. Active social media users tend to be relatively extreme, close-minded, overconfident—and more affectively polarized (Settle, 2018). Moreover, when more typical partisans are politically active online, we can act in a way that is not typical of *ourselves*. Sometimes we're more disrespectful, belligerent, and aggressive—and get more attention when we act this way.[6] And even when we aren't trying to be combative, we dehumanize our online interlocutors and are relatively likely to be interpreted uncharitably by others (Roghanizad and Bohns, 2017).[7]

As a result, our limited exposure to the other side's views online can be misleading. Instead of helping us to understand the other side's point of view, and their general humanity, our worst suspicions of them are confirmed. I'll follow Bail (2021) and Kim's team (2021) and call this tendency to observe out-partisans online behaving in a misleadingly unlikable way the *social media prism*. (When we see copartisans express extreme opinions and act belligerently online, we don't mind it so much and maybe even like them for it, a phenomenon called *political acrophily*; see Clark, 2021.)

Both selective exposure and the social media prism are exacerbated by virality, driven by our own behavior, media manipulators (Marwick and Lewis, 2021), and the networks' algorithms. We're more likely to see content from our network that's been "liked" and shared more often, which is disproportionately likely to flatter our side and pillory the opposition, especially when expressed with "moral-emotional" language, determined using standard lists of terms referring to moral and emotional concepts, such as "greed" or "disgust" (Brady et al., 2017).[8] Out-party hostility drives engagement on social media (Rathje et al., 2021) and is the primary motivation behind sharing fake news in particular (Osmundsen et al., 2021)—and fake news has been shown to spread much more rapidly and further than truth (Vosoughi et al., 2018). The fact that posts and tweets loudly expressing anger toward the out-party are more likely to go viral can incentivize strategic outrage and distortion for users trying (perhaps unconsciously) to maximize engagement, making (false) outrage-infused content even more common.

We also see content that the platforms feed us that hasn't even been shared by people in our network. The algorithms that networks use to determine how to suggest such content are far from transparent and are a subject of debate in scholarly literature. But given our preferences for congenial and emotionally engaging content, and the platforms' goals of giving us engaging content, we'd expect that the platforms would in fact feed us such content. There's substantial evidence that this in fact has often occurred.

You can immediately see the effects of algorithms enhancing selective exposure when you click on someone's Twitter profile or follow them.

You'll get recommendations for other people "Suggested" by Twitter to also follow—who are nearly always ideologically similar. For example, Twitter immediately suggested I follow Jeanine Pirro and Sean Hannity after I followed (and unfollowed) Tucker Carlson and suggested I follow Elizabeth Warren and Jake Tapper after I followed (and unfollowed) Rachel Maddow. A Facebook internal presentation from 2018 provides explicit confirmation of social media engaging in this type of practice, saying that "our algorithms exploit the human brain's attraction to divisiveness. If left unchecked [Facebook would feed users] more and more divisive content in an effort to gain user attention & increase time on the platform" (Horwitz and Seetharaman, 2020). And while some academic studies have found limited evidence of algorithm effects on selective exposure (Bakshy et al., 2015), others do report evidence of substantial effects (Kitchens et al., 2020; Levy, 2021).

Selective exposure has also increased offline due to growth in partisan residential sorting and other social sorting (Bishop, 2009). We all know about "red states" and "blue states": most states now have clear majorities that consistently support one party. The same type of residential sorting has increasingly occurred at smaller scales within states as well. In 1992, less than 40 percent of counties had landslide presidential election results with one candidate winning by more than 20 percentage points; in 2016, over 60 percent of counties had such outcomes (Wasserman, 2017). Brown and Enos (2021) found that even within *neighborhoods*, people are now more likely to live near copartisans. See also McCartney and colleagues (2021), who found that people have become more likely to sell their homes when their next-door neighbors are out-partisans.

In addition to our nearby and less-nearby neighbors being more likely to share our political views, we're also much more likely now to date and marry copartisans and have copartisan children than in decades past. The correlation between spouses' party-feeling thermometer scores increased from 0.39 in 1965 to 0.77 in 2015. For parents' and their children's scores, this correlation increased from 0.20 to 0.64 over the same period (Iyengar et al., 2018). There's even evidence that friendships now regularly end over political disagreements: in a 2021 survey, 22 percent of "extreme conservatives" had ended a friendship over politics, and 45 percent of "extreme liberals" had done the same (Abrams, 2021).

Leading media economists Matthew Gentzkow and Jesse Shapiro conducted a study, published in 2011, that was one of the first to rigorously

Table 6.1
Estimates of ideological homogeneity for different sources of information

Setting	Ideological segregation
Offline media	4.1
Internet	7.5
Work, neighborhood, family	15–25
Trusted friends and political discussants	> 30

Source: Gentzkow and Shapiro (2011).

assess the echo chambers hypothesis. Estimates for their measure of selective exposure, which they call ideological segregation, for various contexts are shown in table 6.1. Ideological segregation is a measure of the fraction of copartisans using the same information sources for a given "setting." If members of both parties were equally likely to get news from all sources in a setting, then the ideological segregation would equal zero for that setting; if Republicans got news from just one source, and Democrats from another source, the measure would take its maximum value, 100.

The paper's main results were that ideological segregation was higher for online media than for traditional media, but not by much, and ideological segregation for both was quite low as compared to for offline interactions. These results were interpreted to imply that concerns about echo chambers online were unfounded and overblown. An alternative interpretation, however, is that selective exposure *offline* was already quite severe over ten years ago. And it's become even more so since then. Moreover, analogous estimates of online isolation have increased in more recent years as well (Peterson et al., 2021).

What Drives Homophily and Demand for Congenial News?

> No one loves the messenger who brings bad news.
> —Sophocles, *Antigone*

Before discussing the effects of selective exposure, let's briefly discuss causes of selective exposure in some more depth. There's an obvious explanation for why our friends, dating partners, and neighbors tend to be increasingly like-minded: that, as you know all too well by now, we increasingly dislike people with whom we disagree politically. Yes, it's more complicated than this; there are other factors that have caused partisans to inadvertently be more likely to end up living in the same places over time. For example, if conservatives prefer big yards more than liberals, and conservatives increasingly identify as Republican (due to partisan sorting), we'll see more and more Republicans in suburbs and less in cities. But there's also a wealth of evidence that we choose whom to associate with in a variety of settings specifically based on their political views (Huber and Malhotra, 2017; Shafranek, 2021), so as out-party hostility has grown, this has likely contributed to growth in ideological segregation offline.

It's somewhat less obvious why we prefer like-minded news—news from sources that we tend to agree with. Yes, disliking people who support the out-party will naturally make us want to avoid getting news from those people, for reasons similar to why we tend to avoid socializing with out-partisans offline. Yet the situation is different for sources of political information since we might have more to learn from those we disagree with. If we read and watch news to become well informed, it could even be optimal to seek neutral or even counterattitudinal information sources. There are several reasons, however, that help explain why we don't actually do this.[9]

The first is trust. Even if we truly wished to be as informed as possible, we may prefer to get news from like-minded sources due to trusting them to be more accurate. We might have valid reasons for placing more trust in like-minded media. And we might also excessively trust like-minded sources due to overconfidence in the validity of our own views. If I overestimate the accuracy my opinions on issues in general, and these opinions all happen to be left leaning, I'll then also overestimate the accuracy of left-leaning media propagating similar opinions (Stone, 2011).

A second explanation is that, of course, we don't just get news to become well informed. We also do so to attain what some economists call belief-based utility (Molnar and Loewenstein, 2021) but is really just basic emotional psychology: it's unpleasant to be told we're wrong, and it feels good to be told we're right or that something we wish to be true is true. Pro-in-party and anti-out-party news is fun to read and watch and is more likely to grab our attention when the news is more sensational. Truth is occasionally stranger than fiction but not often; usually fake news is more interesting than the real stuff, especially when we're motivated to believe it's true. Encountering belief-challenging information, ambiguity, and complexity can be annoying and frustrating.

It's also often useful for our social interactions to be armed with the latest news on the out-party's sins and the in-party's virtues given that this is the information our social network tends to value most. The desire to find anti-out-party news for social purposes grows stronger as our social networks become more like-minded—and finding and sharing this type of news in turn causes our networks to become more polarized. So once again, effects can snowball.

A final explanation for why news consumers prefer like-minded news is one that economists have focused on more than scholars from other disciplines: that such news can actually be optimal for making decisions. If news consumers have heterogeneous political preferences and simply don't have time to get all the news that's decision relevant, consumers can make better decisions when they get news that's curated to be most relevant for their personal preferences. Ideologically aligned media might thus provide the most usefully curated information. This would make demand for like-minded news completely rational from a standard economic perspective as opposed to being driven by beliefs about news accuracy or the desire to get news that makes us feel good. Gentzkow and colleagues (2015) call this the "delegation" mechanism for demand for like-minded news since it implies consumers essentially delegate decisions to like-minded advisors.

Here's an example to clarify this point, based on the model of Chan and Suen (2008). Suppose you lean right and would vote Republican 80 percent of the time if you were fully informed, knowing everything there was to know that's relevant to your vote. Perhaps the 20 percent of the time you optimally vote Democrat occurs if the Democratic candidate's character is particularly "good." Specifically, suppose their character can be measured on a scale of 0–100. Your prior is that each character value is equally likely, and you only vote for the Democrat if you expect their character to have a value of 80 or higher, so if you knew the exact value of their character you would vote Democrat 20 percent of the time. But you don't have time to read all the news, just a headline endorsement.

Suppose your local newspaper endorses the Democrat if and only if their character is greater than 50. This paper's partisan slant is neutral in the sense that the paper endorses each party with probability 0.5. A Democratic endorsement from this paper then isn't strong enough to flip your vote. Your Bayesian posterior beliefs about the Democrat's character even after this endorsement are that it's equally likely to be between 50 and 100, so equal to 75 on average. This is below your threshold of 80, so you optimally still vote Republican. This newspaper doesn't help you to make a more informed decision given your preferences.

By contrast, a right-leaning outlet that only endorses the Democrat in extreme circumstances, say, when the Democrat's character is greater than 80, can flip your vote. When they endorse the Democrat, you know their character value is high enough for you to want to vote Democrat. Only a right-leaning outlet—one that usually endorses the Republican—can provide you with useful information for your decision—and endorsement that is actually capable of changing your vote.

In summary, there are several theories of demand for congenial news, and it's at least conceivable that this demand is largely rational. Empirical work distinguishing between these theories using real news consumption data is difficult and therefore has been limited. Prima facie evidence against truth-seeking or instrumental information-seeking theories of congenial news demand is that more slanted media tends to be lower quality. Figure 6.4 provides an illustration (based on data from a private consulting firm and not peer-reviewed research; however, see figure 2 of Pennycook and Rand [2019a] for similar results). Figure 6.4 shows a trade-off between ideological slant and accuracy of reporting, suggesting consumers of slanted news either misguidedly trust ideologically aligned sources or simply enjoy news from these sources more. Kelly (2019) reports evidence that media consumers indeed overestimate the objectivity of like-minded news sources.[10]

A few papers providing more formal evidence against the rational delegation theory of selective exposure are as follows. Charness and colleagues (2019) found that people have a bias toward getting information from belief-confirming sources in an incentivized experiment that completely eliminates social identity motives and belief-based utility. Participants were given a choice of sources of information for a guess they had to make about a random variable and received a larger payment when their guess was correct. In some situations, the source most likely to reject the participant's prior maximized their probability of making a correct guess. But the

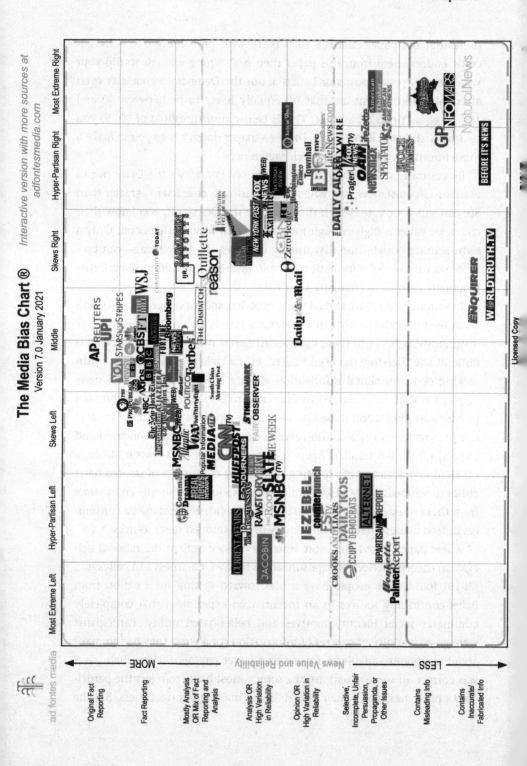

The Media Bias Chart ®
Version 7.0 January 2021

Interactive version with more sources at adfontesmedia.com

ad fontes media

News Value and Reliability

MORE — LESS

Original Fact Reporting
Fact Reporting
Mostly Analysis OR Mix of Fact Reporting and Analysis
Analysis OR High Variation in Reliability
Opinion OR High Variation in Reliability
Selective, Incomplete, Unfair Persuasion, Propaganda, or Other Issues
Contains Misleading Info
Contains Inaccurate/ Fabricated Info

Most Extreme Left · Hyper-Partisan Left · Skews Left · Middle · Skews Right · Hyper-Partisan Right · Most Extreme Right authors found participants were consistently most likely to choose sources slanted toward confirming priors even though there was no psychological or social motive for this. It seems people simply overestimated the value of information from a source likely to confirm their prior.

Another study shedding light on this topic is Cookson and colleagues (2021). They used data from the investor social network StockTwits and found that self-described bulls engage in selective exposure as they are five times more likely to follow other bullish investors than self-described bears. Users share investment advice, so if selective exposure were useful for making better investment decisions, we'd expect selective exposure to be associated with obtaining high returns. The paper shows that, on the contrary, investors subject to a greater degree of selective exposure had worse-performing investments, implying belief-confirming slanted news in fact worsened decisions made based on this news.

I've done some work on this topic too. Three coauthors and I (Garz et al., 2020a) conducted incentivized surveys of MTurk workers the mornings after the 2016 presidential debates to see how their interest in debate news, and source for debate news, depended on who "won" the debate according to Fox News and the *New York Times*. We found that Democrats were only interested in reading a Fox News story on the previous night's debate when its headline said the Democrat won the debate and otherwise chose either the *New York Times* debate story or a nonpolitical story. Trump supporters switched from a Fox story to a nonpolitical story when the Fox headline indicated Trump lost last night's debate and were consistently uninterested in the *New York Times* story. Subjects were paid to correctly answer a question on the content of the article of their choice, so they had an incentive to choose the article they were most interested in actually reading. Given that we held fixed both the story topic (the most recent debate winner) and outlet, these results suggest demand for real news was at least partly driven by the desire for belief-based utility (psychological forces), that is, whether the story was "good news" or "bad news."

Figure 6.4
Ad Fontes Media's "Media bias chart." See adfontesmedia.com for a description of the methodology. Copyright © 2021 Ad Fontes Media, Inc.; reprinted with permission.

We also looked at the demand and supply of slant for presidential poll stories by several outlets. We found that Fox generally slanted headlines toward favoring Trump's chances in comparison to Google News headlines and, compared to this same benchmark, the *New York Times* slanted headlines toward favoring Clinton's chances. A natural explanation for this slant is that the readers tended to enjoy it because it told them what they wanted to hear and therefore garnered more attention from those readers. It's hard, though possible, to come up with stories that justify this slant based on the outlet's desire to provide optimal information or gain trust.

However, we also found that headlines favoring Clinton's chances were more likely to make the lists of "trending" (most clicked) stories on Fox—and headlines favoring Trump's chances were most likely to be trending on the *New York Times*. We didn't have individual click data and thus didn't know who exactly clicked to make these stories so popular. Still, given Fox's strongly right-leaning readership and the *Times*'s left-leaning one, these results suggest many readers on both sides were willing to read uncongenial stories from trusted outlets (supporting the "trust" theory over the "psychology" one). Finally, we also found suggestive evidence that the *Wall Street Journal* was more likely to run stories on the polls when they favored the Democrats' chances. We interpreted this as potential evidence of the "delegation" mechanism: perhaps relatively affluent and conservative readers of the *Wall Street Journal* found these stories more useful for deciding when to make political donations (when the news was less favorable to Republicans).

Overall, our analysis was messier than we would have liked, but the messiness was an important result unto itself. Demand for like-minded news is complex and has many causes. The inconsistency of our results made us further appreciate this complexity and that the various theoretical reasons for demand for like-minded news all have real-world relevance at different times. These factors can even interact with, and reinforce, one another. "Psychological" components of demand have (some) rational underpinnings: it doesn't feel good to hear what we wish to be true unless we trust that it might actually be true. The influence of rational factors likely contributes to the persistence, and insidiousness, of less rational factors also driving news demand. If researchers struggle to cleanly identify the psychological component of news demand, it's unsurprising that media consumers struggle to see this in ourselves. However, the preponderance of evidence implies this component exists and has substantial effects.

Does Slanted News Imply Slanted Beliefs?

To summarize the above, for numerous reasons and through numerous interfaces, we've become increasingly exposed to anti-out-party information over the last few decades. The reasons are complex and unclear, even to us. It's possible, in theory, that we get news from sources slanted toward confirming our priors because it's optimal for our decisions. But several types of evidence suggest this isn't the case—that for various reasons we tend to get too much belief-confirming and otherwise congenial information, with respect to the goal of being best informed about issues and making optimal decisions. And to be clear, when I say "anti-out-party information," I'm using the term *information* loosely. I'm referring to a variety of types of content that, if taken at face value, could cause affective polarization bias to increase: nonrepresentative (cherry-picked) facts, slanted interpretations of events, misinformation, disinformation, and sheer insults and defamation.

Still, if we were fully aware of the way our political information sets were skewed (due to our choices and circumstances), we could, in theory, filter them appropriately. Our slanted information sets might not even bias our beliefs, on average. We'd say, more or less, "Well, I know that the media content that I see is skewed toward criticism of the other team, so I won't take it all that seriously. I'll also infer that they're doing pretty well if the strongest criticisms of them that I see are weak."

More precisely, an important theoretical property of Bayesian updating is that it causes one's beliefs to be a *martingale*, a statistical term for a variable whose changes are completely unpredictable. To see why Bayesian beliefs should have this property, suppose they didn't. That would mean that you could predict before an event occurred, say, watching cable news at 8:00 p.m., that this was likely to shift your beliefs in one particular direction (say, toward disliking the out-party even more than you did before). But if you knew this, then you'd use that information to go ahead and update your beliefs in that direction now. As a result, the show would then have either no effect or an unpredictable effect on your beliefs.

This means that for a Bayesian, exposure to news should be expected to have no effect on beliefs on average (ex ante)—even slanted news. Here's a quantitative example to illustrate. Suppose you're uncertain about whether politician Smith is "good" or "bad" and your prior is that there's a 40 percent chance he's good. Suppose an outlet either reports "He's bad!" or "He's good!" and is slanted toward the latter: anytime Smith is good, the outlet reports this, and even if he's bad, they report "He's good!" 90 percent of the time. This outlet reports "He's good!" the vast majority of the time, so the fact that the news is slanted toward this statement means this report doesn't affect your beliefs much.

And indeed, the Bayesian posterior probability that Smith is good given a "He's good!" report is then only 42.6 percent.[11] Your belief that Smith is good moves up just 2.6 percentage points. And the Bayesian posterior Smith is good given a "He's bad!" report is precisely 0 percent.[12] This outlet reports "He's good!" nearly all the time: 94 percent to be precise since they report this the 40 percent of the time Smith is good and also report this 90 percent of the 60 percent of the time he's bad (0.4 + 0.9*0.6 = 0.94). As a result, your average posterior belief that Smith is good is the probability of a good report times the posterior Smith is good in this case plus the probability of a bad report times the posterior Smith is good in that case: 0.94*42.6% + 0.06*0% = 40%. This average posterior is exactly the same as your prior.

The outlet's slant (its 94 percent chance of reporting "he's good!") has no effect on your beliefs, on average, because the slant causes your beliefs to not budge much when you get the "expected" news. Yes, most of the time your beliefs move toward "good" due to the slant, but your beliefs just move a little bit in that direction (due to the slant). A small fraction of the time your beliefs move the other way and move much further in this case. On average, these changes exactly cancel: your belief that Smith is good can increase or decrease but does neither, on average. A Bayesian expects to believe in the future what she believes now.

Undue Influence: Nonmotivated Factors

Trust me, Wilbur. People are very gullible. They'll believe anything they see in print.

—E. B. White, *Charlotte's Web*

If the Bayesian theory that getting slanted news has no predictable effect on our beliefs strikes you as implausible, you'd not be wrong. For a variety of reasons, we are indeed often predictably influenced by slanted information.[13] Again, this can be true for information about both political and nonpolitical relationships. If your best friend has a grudge against your spouse, and this friend is the main person you talk to about grievances with your spouse—you are engaging in selective exposure (and your spouse might be in trouble as a result). You're getting information from a source with a skewed, confirmatory, and congenial viewpoint ("It's not your fault . . . I can't believe they did that"). If you fail to take account of your friend's bias against your spouse, you'll be predictably influenced by your friend's input, and your posterior beliefs will be non-Bayesian.

In this section, I'll discuss "unmotivated" reasons for why we are indeed often unduly credulous of slanted information beyond excessive trust in the quality of ideologically like-minded media, as noted above. I'll talk about the role of motivated reasoning in the next section of the chapter. I highly recommend Pantazi and colleagues (2021) for an extensive review of the literature outside of behavioral economics on excessive credulity, that is, *truth bias*, with a focus on responses to political misinformation. I'll talk briefly about some of the topics they cover, but I'll focus here on complementary behavioral economic concepts and literature.

One fundamental explanation for truth bias is that belief is simply cognitively easier than disbelief, especially when new information is consistent with, or at least not in conflict with, our priors. Our instinct is, typically, to believe. Disbelief requires criticism, criticism requires "critical thinking," and critical thinking requires cognitive effort. We may or may not deploy this effort optimally to serve our own interests in general. But since forming accurate beliefs about news doesn't usually provide much in the way of direct benefits, we tend to use these cognitive resources especially sparingly when evaluating the accuracy of news (Kahneman, 2011; Pennycook and Rand, 2019b). For example, Breakstone and colleagues (2021) report that 52 percent of US high school students took a Russian propaganda video showing evidence of voter fraud in the US at face value, accepting it as true, and less than 0.1 percent bothered to track down the source. In related incentivized experiments, Serra-Garcia and Gneezy (2021) found that people are overconfident in their ability to detect fake news, even in the absence of motivated reasoning. Experiment participants believed they correctly assessed the accuracy of approximately 65 percent of videos while actually getting approximately 50 percent correct.

Second, limited strategic thinking makes us unduly credulous of information from a message sender with strategic incentives to skew or exaggerate information in one direction. The media has always had incentives to exaggerate conflict and extreme voices from both sides, contributing to the general prevalence of false polarization discussed in chapter 2. And partisan media outlets, and copartisan members of our social network, have incentives to exaggerate congenial news from their side (which again includes anti-out-party news) to gain the attention of like-minded consumers and followers (Levendusky, 2013). Limited strategic thinking likely makes us neglect both these factors and be too influenced by partisan news.

There's a wide variety of evidence demonstrating undue credulity in the presence of strategic incentives. A particularly clear recent example comes from Jin and colleagues (2021). They present results from an experiment in which communicators can't distort information but can strategically withhold information. Each experiment involved two subjects, a sender and a receiver. The sender privately observed an integer between 1 and 5 and could then report this number to the receiver or withhold it ("no report"). The receiver then guessed the private number, choosing from the set of possible integers and midpoints {1, 1.5, 2, . . . , 4.5, 5}, and receiving a higher payoff for a more accurate guess. The sender's payoff, however, was always higher whenever the receiver's guess was higher. So if the sender observed "3," she could either report "3" or say "no report." If she reported "3," then the receiver should guess "3" since the truth must be 3. But to maximize one's own payment, the sender wants the receiver to guess as high a number as possible. When should the sender withhold the report, and what should the receiver infer when information was withheld?

Standard economic theory provides a clear answer to both questions: in equilibrium, the sender should withhold the report only if the true number is 1, and the receiver should guess 1 when information is withheld. Here's why: suppose the sender only reported 5 and withheld everything else. Then the receiver should interpret "no report" to mean the number is equal to the average of the numbers withheld—1, 2, 3, and 4—and guess this average (2.5). However, the sender would then want to report numbers greater than 2.5 (3 and 4) since this would lead to higher guesses (and thus higher payoffs for the sender) than the guess for no report. The receiver, in equilibrium, must figure this out too. So, suppose the sender reports 3, 4, and 5, and the receiver knows this. Then, upon hearing "no report," the receiver should guess the average of the numbers withheld, 1 and 2, so 1.5. But then the sender would want to report 2. The receiver, realizing this, would then infer from no report that the number must be 1. And the sender then indeed prefers to report any number of 2 or greater given that the receiver guesses 1 if there is no report.

You can deduce this outcome with a paragraph's worth of thought like this. But the actual behavior was, unsurprisingly, not consistent with this equilibrium. What's interesting is that there wasn't just a small amount of noise affecting senders and receivers equally. Instead, receivers were systematically fooled: the average number withheld was 1.7, but the average receiver guess when the report was withheld was 2.2. Receivers systematically underestimated the strategic withholding of low numbers by senders, to a large degree, given the minimum guess was 1. Similar results implying excessive credulity due to limited strategic thinking have also been found in communication games with different structures (Blume et al., 2020).

A related, but distinct, cause of undue credulity is shown in recent work by Ben Enke (whom I also cited in chapter 4 and will cite again momentarily—yes, I'm a big fan of his work). He presents results from an experiment providing strong support for WYSIATI causing us to be systematically influenced by slanted information (2020b). It's worth also talking through the experiment's structure quickly to clarify what Enke showed. In each experiment, there was a true "state" consisting of the average of six randomly drawn numbers between 50 and 150. Subjects observed just one of these draws and then guessed if the average of all six was above or below 100. They then observed *all* other signals consistent with their guess (over or under 100) but only a random sample of the inconsistent numbers. Subjects were told exactly how this selective exposure process worked, and so in theory they could have accounted for it precisely and guessed correctly, on average. But subjects still ended up guessing numbers significantly too high when the initial draw was high (and additional draws were transparently skewed toward being high) and guessed numbers too low when observed information was (transparently) skewed low. The results imply that when we see a biased report, and know the reporter's bias, our interpretation of the report accounts for the bias somewhat—but not enough.

Obviously, in reality, the structure of the game played between media consumers and producers is not nearly as simple and transparent as the structure of these experiments. Consumers aren't told the rules that partisan news outlets use to select and report facts. However, the simplicity of experiments should make it relatively easy for participants to form accurate beliefs in experiments. If we're still fooled in simple settings like these experiments—and we are—we're even more likely to be fooled in more realistic (and thus more complex) environments.

Another unmotivated factor potentially causing undue influence is *correlation neglect* and its close cousin *naive herding*.[14] Many of the political opinions we see and hear online and offline originate from the same or related sources. These opinions should therefore be treated as correlated, and consequently discounted, as compared to independent sources of information. For example, suppose politician X takes ambiguous action Y. Pundit Z interprets this as bad. Five of your friends read pundit Z's take and decide the action was bad and then separately tweet their own opinions about why action Y was bad. If you don't realize the five opinions were influenced by the same source, you'll be more swayed by them than you should be. Enke and his coauthor Florian Zimmerman (2019, 313) provide experimental evidence of this "double-counting problem" and show experimentally that "beliefs are too sensitive to the ubiquitous 'telling and re-telling of stories' and exhibit excessive swings."

Matters can be even worse if three of the five friends were unconvinced by pundit Z's take but still said they agreed because they saw the other two friends do so first. This is called *herding* in the economics theory literature; naive herding occurs when we don't fully consider the degree to which conformist behavior is influenced by herding (a form of correlation neglect and limited strategic thinking) and therefore are unduly influenced by herds.

The biases described above, starting with limited strategic thinking, are examples of what some psychologists call *metacognitive myopia*: "an inability of human processors to assess the quality and history of information and a tendency to take such information at face value" (Pantazi et al., 2021, 272). In *behavioral* economics, we'd call these biases examples of *selection neglect*: the tendency to fail to properly account for sample selection biases in the information we observe, causing it to be misleading if taken at face value. For example, after President Joe Biden's joint session address in April 2021, there were trending news stories with headlines referring to a poll finding 85 percent of viewers approved of the speech. This was a strikingly high figure—if one assumed the poll was a representative sample of voters. (If one realized that most people who bothered to watch the speech were already Biden supporters, the very high approval rate wasn't nearly as interesting and tempting to click on.)

Selection neglect isn't mentioned by Bail (2021) in his book, but it's *why* we're unduly influenced by the social media prism and indeed the similar prism created by the media more broadly. When the media presents exaggerated evidence of polarization and excessively negative representations of out-partisans, this leads to excessive perceived polarization (false polarization) and affective polarization bias because we fail to account for the way the "sample" is selected. It's indeed hard to understand this selection process—that's why Bail had to write a book about it![15] Even journalists appear subject to selection neglect; for example, they treat Twitter users as a more representative sample of public opinion than they really are (McGregor, 2019).

There are still more reasons that we're likely subject to undue influence from selective exposure and media prism effects. The classic Kahneman and Tversky *availability* and *representativeness heuristics* make us both overestimate the general prevalence of examples that easily come to mind and overextrapolate from these examples. As we encounter bad actors on the other side online and in conversation more often, we'll thus be more likely to overestimate their general prevalence. Limited strategic thinking can make us underestimate the incentives of like-minded friends and media outlets to engage in *nut-picking*—choosing particularly unflattering representatives of the other side to quote and critique—because this appeals to their like-minded networks. *Social pressure* can make people hesitant to speak up when they think out-partisans are being characterized unfairly. Limited strategic thinking and selection neglect can again make us fail to account for the absence of these dissenting voices and be overly influenced by superficial consensus.

Moreover, the *out-group homogeneity effect* makes us overestimate the similarity of people on the other side to the extreme and unflattering examples we observe (Settle, 2018). The *mere exposure effect* makes us prefer content and ideas that we are exposed to repeatedly, and the *illusory truth effect* makes us more likely to believe false content when we hear it repeatedly (Kim, 2021; Lacassagne et al., 2022). And, last but far from least, unmotivated confirmation bias makes us see what we expect to see. Anti-out-group information consistent with our priors is especially likely to be perceived as valid.

Prism effects can influence nonpolitical relationships too. If your spouse tends to be in a bad mood after getting home from work simply because they're worn out and stressed, and you tend to see them then and not when they're at their best and most energetic, which happens to occur during their work hours, you might misjudge their general character. Anytime we overreact to something another person says or does when they're in a bad mood can be viewed as an example of prism-driven biased dislike. Just as our interpersonal feelings are, in general, at the mercy of our attitudes—whether or not we focus on negative attributes of the other person—our feelings are also at the mercy of the accuracy of information about the other person we're exposed to.

Undue Influence: Motivated Reasoning

Thus, for a good number of reasons, even in the absence of a motive to hold a particular belief, if we're exposed to information slanted toward criticizing one side, we'll probably end up feeling too negatively toward that side. And if we're motivated to be credulous of the information we're exposed to, undue negativity is even more likely to occur and be more pronounced.

Motivated reasoning makes us too credulous for a few reasons. As noted above, motivated overconfidence in our own opinions makes us think that like-minded outlets are more objective and accurate than they really are. This will also make us overestimate the degree to which nonlike-minded media are lower quality or unfairly biased against our side. (The latter belief is so common that there's a special term for it: the *hostile media phenomenon*; see, e.g., Perloff, 2015.) We're also motivatedly overconfident in our ability to discern real from fake news (Lyons et al., 2021).

Gilovich's maxim is worth repeating here: motivated reasoning makes us think "can I believe it?" when we wish the news to be true and "must I believe it?" when we wish it to be false. Selective exposure leads us to inordinately see news in the first category, with the answer to the question almost being always "yes."

I think this point is pretty intuitive, and since motivated reasoning and motivated confirmation bias are discussed extensively in chapter 3, I'm going to keep this discussion relatively brief. But there is one recent study on this topic by behavioral economist Michael Thaler that is worth describing in some detail. It provides especially clear support for the relevance of motivation in the context of political news specifically, where the literature has been surprisingly mixed (Pantazi et al., 2021; Pennycook and Rand, 2021).

Thaler (2019) came up with a very clever way to precisely identify motivatedly non-Bayesian interpretations of real political information.[16] He first asked participants in his experiment for the *median* value of their belief distribution for several potentially politically charged facts, like the murder rate under the Obama administration. That is, participants were asked to state a murder rate such that they thought the true murder rate was equally likely to be above or below the stated value. Thaler then randomly gave subjects either false or true news reports on the true values and asked for their beliefs about the probability that each report was true, with incentives for accuracy.

Given the setup, under Bayesian updating, the report's value should have actually had *no effect* on the subject's beliefs about the report's accuracy. This is because the true value was, by construction, equally likely to fall above or below the stated median. Motivated reasoning, however, could affect respondent beliefs. For example, suppose you don't like Obama and therefore are "motivated" to believe a higher value of the murder rate during his administration is true. Then, if motivated reasoning affects your beliefs, you'll think the news is more likely to be accurate when it says the murder rate was higher. And that's exactly what Thaler found: when the news report was consistent with partisan preferences, subjects believed it was more accurate, for a wide variety of topics. These beliefs about accuracy are credible because they were incentivized: subjects weren't just saying what they wished to be true without really believing it—they were paid more when they were correct. Effects were similar for subjects in both parties and across demographic groups (race, age, education). Oprea and Yuksel (2022) provide complementary results, finding that social exchange of information amplifies errors in beliefs driven by motivated beliefs about the accuracy of information. Both papers' results are perhaps far from shocking, but still very useful for confirming the importance of motivated reasoning in how we interpret political information and how these effects likely compound on social media.[17]

Predictable (Non-Bayesian) Polarization

The evidence from the last two sections on undue credulity implies that, given how people tend to be disproportionately exposed to anti-out-party information, we'd expect this to cause affective polarization bias. Moreover, given growth in exposure to this type of information over the last few decades, we'd expect this bias to increase over this period. In this section, I'll argue there are two other distinct bodies of research providing important indirect evidence in support of these hypotheses.

The first is the literature on the *law of group polarization* (Sunstein, 1999), the empirical regularity that beliefs tend to become more extreme after like-minded people communicate with one another. Yes, "law" is likely an overstatement—but perhaps not by much. Hastie and Sunstein (2015) write that "group polarization has been found in hundreds of studies involving more than a dozen countries." They explain group polarization via a combination of several factors discussed in the previous two sections: correlation neglect (and its close cousin, naive herding), social pressure deterring contrarians, and selection effects causing those with the most confident and extreme opinions to speak loudest and most often, plus selection neglect by those listening to these voices, making them unduly influential.[18]

The law of group polarization means that group members change beliefs in a predictable way. While some research proposes Bayesian explanations for this behavior (Pallavicini et al., 2021), the martingale property of Bayesian beliefs (that Bayesian belief changes are unpredictable) and other factors discussed above imply that group polarization is therefore typically non-Bayesian. Since group polarization applies to all kinds of beliefs, we would expect it to also apply to beliefs affecting interpersonal feelings. Offline sorting and social media have caused us to communicate more with like-minded groups today than we did forty years ago. Thus, the law of group polarization, in conjunction with offline and online sorting, has likely contributed to growth in affective polarization bias.[19]

The second additional literature I want to discuss here is the large literature showing that people being exposed to richer and more representative sources of information about out-groups causes a *decline* in affective polarization. This literature indirectly implies that limited exposure to like-minded information causes growth in affective polarization bias, as I'll explain. One such study for the US political context that's especially compelling is the America in One Room project, which brought together a representative sample of over five hundred Americans for a weekend of mediated conversations on a host of major issues in 2019. The results were almost stunningly positive: affective polarization declined by over 20 percent for members of both parties, and other attitudes improved substantially as well (Fishkin et al., 2021). Political scientists Matt Levendusky and Dominik Stecula describe numerous related studies with similar results in their book *We Need to Talk: How Cross-Party Dialogue Reduces Affective Polarization*.

Multiple other studies from the last few years report similar results as well, and three with particularly large samples are as follows. Levy (2021) reports that randomizing exposure to counterattitudinal media on Facebook caused lower affective polarization in a sample of over seventeen thousand participants. Peterson and Kagalwala (2021) find, in a sample of over eight thousand, that hostility to out-party media outlets was reduced by exposure to nonpolitical content from those outlets. Amsalem and colleagues (2021) find, in a combined sample of over nine thousand, that discussing politics with counterpartisans predicts lower affective polarization, for both face-to-face and online discussions.[20]

There are also several recent studies with smaller samples—but often more in-depth experimental "treatments"—finding further support. Baron and colleagues (2021) report that mediated in-person communication (workshops run by the nonprofit "bridge-building" organization Braver Angels) yielded depolarizing effects. Broockman and Kalla (forthcoming) find affective polarization was reduced for Democratic activists who engaged in "deep canvassing" (extended conversations) with Trump supporters. Bail (2021) reports that Discussit, a platform designed to facilitate productive conversation between counterpartisans, resulted in a decline in polarization among 1,200 test users. Rossiter (2020) reports that cross-partisan political chats facilitated with novel software (that she designed) reduced affective polarization. In a smaller study I conducted with Bowdoin College students, reading cross-partisan cable television email newsletters for one month led to reduced affective polarization (Stone et al., 2017).

These results are increasingly being interpreted as part of the much larger and broader literature on the *contact hypothesis*—the theory that increasing intergroup contact, under appropriate conditions, reduces hostility toward out-groups. Evidence varies somewhat, but the hypothesis has received tremendous support overall. Pettigrew and Tropp (2006) report results from a massive metastudy of over five hundred studies across thirty-eight countries and show that intergroup contact had positive effects 94 percent of the time. Paluck and colleagues (2019) present a meta-analysis of twenty-seven more recent studies largely confirming Pettigrew and Tropp's results. Bruneau and colleagues (2021) report on a metastudy of sixteen samples in five countries with nearly eight thousand subjects and conclude that contact consistently reduced dehumanization and metadehumanization. Even the *extended contact hypothesis*—"knowing that in-group members have cross-group friends improves attitudes toward this out-group"—has been confirmed in a metastudy (Zhou et al., 2019). See anthropologist Rutger Bregman's 2019 book *Humankind* for discussion of additional research. Even more recent studies across multiple disciplines finding positive effects of contact include, for example, Bazzi and colleagues (2019) and Mousa (2020).

By contrast, Bail and colleagues (2018) is an important study showing a polarizing effect from out-group contact. The authors found that randomized exposure to out-party tweets on Twitter for one month led to an increase in ideological polarization, for conservatives especially (the study didn't collect data on affective polarization). The authors interpret their results as evidence of the *backfire effect*—the idea that being presented with belief-challenging information typically backfires, leading us to dig in our heels and become more extreme. Bail's book (2021) focuses in large part on this study, and it's received a lot of attention elsewhere too. For example, Ezra Klein discusses it extensively in *Why We're Polarized*, concluding that "reading the other side doesn't change our mind, it deepens our certainty" (158).

However, a body of research has now concluded that the backfire effect is rare, at least for beliefs about political facts, and its generality was overstated (Porter and Wood, 2019; Nyhan, 2021). Backfire effects—and closely related phenomena, the boomerang effect and psychological reactance—may be more prevalent in other contexts (Osman, 2020), especially when individuals feel that a persuasion effort is imposed upon them. However, remember that the contact hypothesis stipulates conditions for contact to have positive effects. I won't go into detail on these conditions here, but it's intuitive that for contact to have positive effects, we can't present the worst aspects of ourselves, which is what we often tend to do on Twitter and other social media. Just because random tweets don't depolarize us doesn't mean that richer, more accurate information won't do this.

The evidence on the contact hypothesis doesn't imply that we need to present a positively distorted image of ourselves to improve intergroup relations. We basically just have to be ourselves. "Be yourself" is clichéd advice—for good reason. When we present ourselves sincerely, we are more likable. Contact with others where we accurately represent our true selves improves relations between groups at odds with each other. So, while the contact hypothesis is not usually described this way, it ultimately boils down to the idea that when we better understand who the out-group really is—when we're *better informed* about them—we like them better. In other words, the contact hypothesis implies that our initial dislike of the out-group is due to lack of information and misperceptions. Our out-group dislike before contact is driven, at least in part, by incorrect beliefs about the out-group. Intergroup contact doesn't depolarize because it convinces us that the other side is right and we were wrong—just that the other side has better reasons justifying their beliefs and actions than we realized.

Concluding Remarks

Key points from this chapter are as follows:
- New media technology and the proliferation of partisan media led to concerns about media echo chambers starting in the early 2000s.
- Exclusively one-sided media diets have been found to be rare; this could change as data on media consumption improves and entire platforms become more partisan, and the impacts of even a small percentage of citizens in echo chambers could be inordinately large.
- Regardless, selective exposure (getting news from like-minded sources) is still higher for online news and social media than for legacy news sources. Moreover, the exposure we do have to out-partisans on social media is skewed toward aggressive, extreme, and distorted content (the social media prism).
- Selective exposure has also grown in our offline social networks via residential and social sorting. Selective exposure in these settings is generally significantly more extreme than in our media diets.
- We tend to overestimate the quality and informativeness of ideologically like-minded media outlets and people in our social networks, causing these sources to have undue influence on our beliefs. The literature on

credulity suggests that while people are far from completely gullible, we are generally unduly influenced by slanted and skewed information for a wide variety of other reasons.

- Selective exposure (offline and online) would also be expected to lead to more extreme, non-Bayesian beliefs due to the law of group polarization, which appears to contradict the martingale property of Bayesianism.

- The contact hypothesis—that social contact with out-groups, under reasonable conditions, improves feelings toward out-groups—is now well established in many contexts, including US partisan politics. Recent work also suggests that the prevalence of the backfire effect has been overstated. Hostility toward out-groups declines when we get to know them better, implying that initial hostility is due partly to misperceptions and bias.

"What you see is all there is" causes us to think we know everything when we actually just know something. And our information networks are increasingly skewed toward causing us to know *some things* about the out-party being "bad" (and those things are often untrue). Moreover, as our beliefs about the out-party's bad character have grown stronger, many of us have grown to further trust those who confirm this—and to find challenges to these beliefs increasingly unpleasant.[21] Selective exposure can thus, like tit for tat, lead to snowballing affective polarization bias. The preponderance of theory and evidence implies that changes in our information environment have led us to become increasingly overconfident in our beliefs about the out-party's vices. I'll discuss implications of this point, and those covered in the previous chapters, in the next and final chapter.

III Implications

7   Undoing Hate?

> Were half the power, that fills the world with terror,
> Were half the wealth, bestowed on camps and courts,
> Given to redeem the human mind from error,
> There were no need of arsenals or forts
> —Henry Wadsworth Longfellow, "The Arsenal at Springfield"

My primary goals for this book have been to 1) clarify the notion of disagreement-driven undue dislike (affective polarization bias), 2) present evidence of this bias in US politics, and 3) use a behavioral economic lens to analyze causes of the bias, noting how many of these extend beyond intergroup bias (the focus of the prior literature on affective polarization) and afflict relationships both within and across social groups. Recognizing parallels between hostility in political and nonpolitical contexts helps us to better understand undue hostility in general.

I hope that awareness of this bias will make some of us think twice (or at least once) about our hard feelings toward those we disagree with. A rule of thumb I'd suggest is the more contempt you feel toward the other "party," the more likely it is that you're making a mistake about them and judging them too negatively—by your own standards. Especially if you feel hate toward someone, remind yourself that "they're probably not as bad as they seem."

Again, I recognize that many of us might wonder why we should even *want* to reduce our own affective polarization bias in the realm of politics. A fundamental practical reason is to improve our own decisions. Maybe this goes without saying but maybe not: more accurate beliefs really do typically lead to better decisions. If you think it's going to rain and it doesn't, you'll miss out on the chance to enjoy being outside. If you think it's not going to rain and it does, you'll get wet. More accurate beliefs can of course improve at least some of our political decisions as well. On the other hand, one could argue that biased political beliefs are useful for maintaining ties with like-minded friends and family. But overcoming delusions doesn't have to harm our relationships. Our friends might even value our open-mindedness more than we think (Heltzel and Laurin, 2021), especially when we discuss issues respectfully and inquisitively, as I'll discuss further below.

What's more, perhaps the most important reason we'll benefit from reducing our own bias is that it can radicalize the other side. Many of us at times have had thoughts like, "Sure, I might have some biases, but the other side's biases are much worse, so mine are no big deal." Remember, though, that the other side's biases also make them overreact to your mistakes, and the more the other side overreacts, the more valuable it is to not give them ammunition. Even if they're wrong on the issues, or their opinions on issues are motivated by self-interest—if you want to actually make progress addressing the issues, you'll benefit from the other side seeing your side as reasonable. Yes, saying something like "the less biased side should be extra careful to be unbiased" implies a larger burden for the already better-behaved side and might seem unfair. But this doesn't mean ceding power to them. It just means minimizing fodder for these overreactions, which will make you and your side better off in the long run. And don't worry too much about the apparent unfairness of your (less biased) side making a greater effort to reduce your bias further: if the other side really does have more biased judgment, they'll pay a price for this—more biased judgment really does lead to worse decisions in most aspects of life.

Most of the rest of this chapter discusses more specific implications and ideas stemming from the prior chapters. These range from well-known and widely embraced policy recommendations to new and very much unproven possibilities. Topics include areas for future research not mentioned in the earlier text and ideas for individuals, the private sector, and policymakers to consider in pursuit of the goal of reducing undue hate.

Chapters 1 and 2: Affective Polarization Bias, Theory, and Evidence

It might be useful to mathematically extend the analysis and definitions offered in chapter 1, but I suspect more research is especially needed for the topic of chapter 2, evidence. Most of this evidence is for affective polarization felt by mass partisans toward other mass partisans in the US. It seems clear that the bias exists in this context, to a substantial degree, but more work is necessary to better understand the precise magnitude and prevalence of bias and how it may be changing over time.

One shortcoming of chapter 2 worth noting is that I don't estimate the fraction of current partisan affective polarization driven by bias. The difference between in- and out-party thermometer scores grew from around 25 to 50 points from 1980 to 2020. I'm certainly not claiming that all of this growth is due to bias. Partisans did truly grow over that time to become, on average, more different from one another (due to sorting and other factors). Accordingly, if partisans accurately understood out-partisans as being increasingly "worse" (for given criteria), affective polarization could have conceivably grown without a change in bias. In Stone (2019) I show that, adjusting for ideological sorting, the growth in thermometer score polarization is approximately cut in half. In other words, holding fixed ideological differences between partisans, they still grew to dislike one another by around 12.5 thermometer score points. This suggests an approximate upper bound for growth in affective polarization bias-driven thermometer score polarization of 12.5 points, which is similar to the measured decline in polarization resulting from the America in One Room project (discussed in chapter 6). So, if I had to speculate, I would guess that, on average, affective polarization bias in recent years accounts for around 10 points of thermometer score polarization—that we dislike each other by at least 10 points more than we should (by our own criteria for interpersonal dislike). But it would be ideal to have a more precise estimate.

The affective polarization bias evidence that I find most compelling is the evidence on misperceptions of actions. Future work could build on this evidence by going beyond the lab and using field experiments— experiments taking place in natural, real-life environments. A relatively efficient way to do this research would be to elicit beliefs about actions actually taken by members of both parties from past field experiments, such as dating and hiring decisions, and to assess the accuracy of these beliefs. It would also be useful to conduct new field experiments reflecting basic values and compare partisans' beliefs about out-partisan behavior in these situations to their actual behavior. For example, it might be pretty

neat to run a "lost wallet experiment" (dropping wallets with cash and
contact information and tracking how often they're returned as a measure
of altruism) at, say, Republican and Democratic conventions, and compare results. And it could be helpful if future studies could directly address
possible reverse causality (dislike driving beliefs about character rather
than beliefs about character driving dislike) and to test for biased dislike
more directly.

The evidence I present for affective polarization bias outside of politics
is also limited, and I don't have direct evidence of this bias directed toward
political elites specifically or affecting elites specifically. It would be especially interesting to conduct field experiments on the behavior of politicians and other elites and compare this to both mass partisans' and elites'
expectations for this behavior. Similar experiments could be conducted for
contentious relationships outside of politics.

Chapter 3: Overarching Biases

Lee Drutman's 2020 book, *Breaking the Two-Party Doom Loop*, makes a compelling argument that, in large part due to some of the biases discussed in
this chapter being immutably baked into human nature, a two-party system is bound to lead to increasingly hostile conflict and growing political
dysfunction.[1] He points out that the Constitution's framers warned of this
problem—without the language of modern behavioral science—but with a
deep, historically rooted understanding of human nature. Drutman argues
that we therefore need to enact reforms to enable multiparty representation
to break what he calls the "doom loop" of spiraling affective polarization,
gridlock, undermining norms, and threats of violence.

Drutman is practical: he recognizes that Constitutional amendments are
likely infeasible, especially any that would seem to disadvantage one party
or the other, and therefore he only advocates changes requiring regular
legislative approval. These include expanding House districts and changing
them from having a single representative determined by plurality voting
to having multiple members elected by proportional representation with
ranked choice voting. These changes would allow parties to gain representation even with support in a district as low as 17 percent, which Drutman says would lead to four to six parties being represented in Congress.

He points out the US's system is antiquated; we're "one of only a handful of advanced democracies that still use single-member plurality-winner districts." Proportional representation also inherently makes gerrymandering less effective, especially with larger, more ideologically diverse districts (Drutman, 2018). Eighty-five percent of Americans say our political system needs "major change" or "to be completely reformed" (Wike et al., 2021), so perhaps such a large change is politically feasible.

I suspect these reforms would be improvements over the status quo. Our motivation to believe the out-party is "bad" is likely especially strong when there's a single out-party. As discussed in chapter 3, many aspects of American politics are zero-sum: what's bad for them is good for us. And, as also discussed earlier in the text, affective polarization has grown particularly quickly in the US as compared to countries with multiparty systems. It's reasonable to think that the intensity of partisan conflict would decline here with a multiparty system and as a result affective polarization bias would decline as well.

But I'm also more optimistic that this bias, and others discussed in the chapter, can also be mitigated through education. Evidence on the effectiveness of education on cognitive biases is admittedly mixed (Kristal and Santos, 2021; Morewedge, 2019). Nevertheless, even if we have yet to figure out the best methods for this type of education, that doesn't mean it's an impossible task. Civics education has been found to reduce affective polarization in subsequent years (Clark, 2021) and could incorporate content on cognitive biases to make it even more effective. More focused education on cognitive biases could also help build awareness of key overarching biases and norms that we should strive to avoid them.[2] Let's teach kids and teens to follow Ted Lasso's advice to "be curious, not judgmental," and the underlying psychology of its wisdom.[3]

Education on biases could be provided for adults in the workforce as well. Many workplaces require employees to undergo training on unconscious biases. These trainings could also include material on intergroup bias, motivated reasoning, confirmation bias, overprecision, intellectual humility, and related factors discussed in chapter 3—or organizations could provide separate trainings on these topics. Books on how to adopt a truth-seeking mindset (as opposed to one that's primarily driven by motivated reasoning and aversion to cognitive effort) that I'd highly recommend include

Julia Galef's *The Scout Mindset* and Adam Grant's *Think Again*. Both provide many practical tips for how to overcome bias and explanations for why we indeed benefit from doing so. This education would both help make employees better citizens and help make them better decision makers in the workplace, yielding direct dividends for the firm. It would also make a lot of sense to require politicians in particular to complete this type of training. This education should emphasize the bias blind spot, to avoid the risk of leading to greater awareness of the other side's biases and not one's own.

Another approach to reducing our overarching biases in general, which admittedly would be even harder to operationalize, is to socially stigmatize partisan bias. In *Thinking, Fast and Slow*, Kahneman says he's not optimistic that learning about various biases will directly cause readers to reduce their biases but hopes the book will indirectly achieve this goal by leading to more intelligent gossip at the "water cooler." Kahneman talks about how he hopes knowing our biases would be identified by our peers might be the most effective way to get us to be careful to avoid those biases in the first place. Let's call people out, so to speak, for saying or implying "I know" when they should say "I think" because the situation they're referring to is complex or ambiguous—especially when the speaker's overly certain prediction is aligned with their interests. Similarly, political actors of all types—mass voters, pundits, and politicians—should be called out, and not rewarded, for public displays of partisan bias. Politicians especially should be held to a high epistemic standard and held accountable for not meeting this standard. Perhaps a public "bias tracker," recording examples of various biases in statements by all major public officials, would be useful.

Chapter 4: Tastes and Truth

A basic recommendation for individuals that follows from this chapter's material is the simple and unoriginal point that we should try to be more accepting of our differences. Just because you say tomato and I say tomahto doesn't mean we should call the whole thing off. But this simple recommendation can, of course, be surprisingly tough to follow. How many spouses repeatedly hammer away at each other trying to make them change and end up frustrated, driving each other away?[4]

The analogy to partisan politics implies that citizens should also keep this point in mind when thinking about partisan differences. Conservative commentator David French makes a related argument in his excellent book *Divided We Fall*: that the broad solution to America's polarization is to embrace pluralism and federalism (to let "California be California and Tennessee be Tennessee"). If our "tastes" simply differ incorrigibly across regions of the country, we may need to accept regional differences in policy more than we'd naturally be inclined (while basic rights must continue to be universally protected).

There are two more specific policy options related to chapter 4 that I think are also worth noting here. The chapter provides an argument for why larger perceived ideological differences between the parties causes greater affective polarization bias. Thus, policies that would reduce such perceived differences would reduce bias. One such option is Gehl and Porter's (2020) "final-five voting" proposal to reduce extremism in Congress. Final-five voting consists of using nonpartisan primaries to nominate candidates for House seats, with the top five candidates advancing to the general election and the winner then being determined by ranked choice voting. The five candidates in the general election could all come from the same party or from two or more parties.

The logic for why this would help is as follows. Partisan primaries currently tend to engage a small fraction of voters with relatively extreme preferences. Nominees selected by these voters can still win in the general election against a moderate from the other party if the district is solidly "red" or "blue" due to geographic sorting and gerrymandering. With final-five voting, the five candidates advancing to the general election will likely span the ideological spectrum reasonably well. So, even in a mostly politically homogeneous district with, say, 70 percent of voters being Democrats, a relatively moderate Democrat candidate could easily win the general election. For example, suppose half of the 70 percent Democrat voters were "extreme" and half were "moderate" (so, each group comprised 35 percent of the district's electorate). With ranked choice voting, the moderate candidate would win the general election by getting support from the moderate Democrat voters (35 percent) and from the non-Democrat voters (30 percent) as they would rank the moderate Democrat above the more extreme Democrat.

A second, and more general, policy idea is to use *issue linkage* in legislative bargaining—making deals that combine multiple issues. Issue linkage is a term from the academic literature on international agreements (Maggi,

2016), but the term hasn't been used in the congressional bargaining literature to my knowledge. Logrolling (reciprocal voting among legislators) is a related concept, but I think it is distinct. The reason the issue linkage approach might make truly mutually beneficial deals more common is as follows. Issue linkage facilitates exploitation of what some trade economists have called *comparative interest* (Horstmann et al., 2005), a term that parallels *comparative advantage*, the classic economic theory of mutually beneficial trade. The theory of comparative advantage says that while two economic agents don't benefit from trading the same good to one another, they can both almost always gain from exchanging different goods—even if one of the two agents can produce more of both goods—as long as they produce the goods in "different" ways.

Similarly, Democrats and Republicans may struggle to make a mutually beneficial deal on a single issue, for example, immigration reform. A more relaxed policy, or a stricter one, will probably appeal to just one party and not the other. However, mutual benefits are more likely when a deal involves multiple issues that the two parties have different "tastes" for and thus different comparative interests in. If Democrats have a strong preference for policy X and Republicans only have a weak preference against it, and Republicans strongly prefer policy Y while Democrats only weakly oppose it, both parties would be better off enacting policies X and Y (as compared to having neither policy enacted). Senators Tom Cotton and Mitt Romney proposed a deal of this nature involving both immigration and minimum wage policy changes (Verbruggen, 2021). Admittedly, this proposal doesn't seem to have made any headway, and this general approach might be infeasible in the current political environment, but I think it warrants consideration.

Chapter 5: Strategy and Repeated Interactions

The most straightforward recommendation for behavior from this chapter is to be careful about playing tit for tat in our ongoing relationships, especially in situations that are relatively complex and ambiguous. As Linus Pauling is credited with having said, "Do unto others 20 percent better than you would expect them to do unto you, to correct for subjective error." I love the spirit of this advice but would revise the last part to say "to correct for motivated reasoning and other cognitive biases" (but yes, I know that wouldn't be nearly as snappy). In our ongoing relationships, turning the other cheek at least once after a perceived transgression, and probably two or three times, before drawing judgment or consciously retaliating, is usually wise. I understand the situation is much more complicated in US politics today—and in general, turning the other cheek is foolish when it's very clear the other side is playing "hardball." Still, overestimating the other side's "defection" and escalation, and the temptation to escalate ourselves, is a risk even in highly contentious relationships. In general, we'll benefit from being aware of this instinct and making a conscious effort to resist it. Moreover, since even seemingly superficial issues like perceived slights and insults can lead to conflict spirals, it's especially important to start on the right foot in many contexts.

Evidence of misperceptions driving escalation of conflict abounds. My main new claim in this chapter—that participants in protracted conflicts tend to negatively misjudge the other side's character traits, to a greater degree as conflict escalates—is intuitive and supported by a wide variety of evidence from multiple disciplines. But this claim has not been directly demonstrated to my knowledge.[5] I hope to pursue work on this topic myself, and I certainly welcome research by others too. Similarly, I'm not aware of work that precisely identifies tit-for-tat behavior in US politics. As I discuss, this might be due to the ambiguity and ever-changing nature of the real-world game. Still, I think there is potential for clarifying research on this topic. For example, it could be useful to measure how elites and voters in both parties perceive the histories of both parties playing political hardball. These perceptions could then be compared to the level of support for future aggressive actions to assess the theory that motivated perceptions and memories contribute to continued conflict and escalation.

This chapter also supports the need for policies to constrain, deter, or just prohibit various types of hardball escalation in politics. Ideas that have been discussed include creating term limits for Supreme Court justices (Ornstein, 2014) and dropping the debt limit and adding automatic economic stabilizers in recessions to prevent unnecessary congressional showdowns (Klein, 2019). More ambitious proposals include selecting Supreme Court justices randomly from a pool of eligible judges or rebalancing the Supreme Court with five justices appointed by each party, and five more chosen by those justices (Sitaraman and Epps, 2019). The stark growth in use of the filibuster over recent decades also suggests need for reform. One idea for "democratizing the filibuster" is to change it so that it can be broken by senators representing most of the country's population instead of the 60 percent of all senators currently required (Gould et al., 2021). Final-five voting would also help promote compromise in Congress as it would reduce Congress members' incentives to pander to extreme primary voters.

Another implication of this chapter—on the deep-rooted tangle of misunderstandings and skewed perceptions leading to escalating aggression—is the need for third-party mediation. Bilateral conflict is often fundamentally intractable due to strategic tension and conflict of interests but also because cognitive biases prevent the two "players" from figuring out who's at fault even when they'd truly like to do so. For example, suppose Joe accuses Jack of doing something wrong. Cognitive bias on either side, of course, could impinge on the two hashing out the issue with a productive dialogue. Moreover, even if both Joe and Jack were truly unbiased, they might each be unpersuaded by the other side's arguments due to mere suspicion of those arguments being biased. There are good reasons that "he said/he said" disputes are often intractable.

Historically, the closest thing to a third-party mediator and referee of US politics has been the press, but clearly it no longer effectively fills this role. Formal mediation of disputes in Congress seems like a reasonable option to consider. Senator Tim Kaine actually suggested this a few years ago (American Bar Association, 2018). There was no follow-up to my knowledge—why not give it a try?

I'll mention a few more informal recommendations for relationships of all types that are also based on the issues discussed in this chapter. First, we should try to be more forward-looking in choosing our actions in ongoing relationships—to consider how the other side will interpret and respond to these actions. We should even consider sometimes explicitly stating how we'll respond to potential defections by the other side (i.e., announce retaliatory threats) to deter conflict-escalating actions by the other side. This would risk increasing hostility in the short run but could be helpful in avoiding even larger increases in the future.

Another recommendation is to turn tit for tat from a bug into a feature in our relationships by exploiting the power of *positive* reciprocity. This might be impossible in-group conflicts or other conflicts with deep-rooted animosity, where "good" acts are unlikely to be reciprocated. However, even in politics it would be wise for players to take actions that entail short-term costs for the in-party if the long-term social benefits are higher. For example, the party that controls the White House should reform the presidential pardon power (Whittington, 2020) even though this would reduce their immediate power. In addition to benefits from improved policy, it would also signal to at least some members of the general public a willingness to engage in cooperative behavior.

But especially in less damaged relationships with minor signs of tension, momentum can sometimes be turned around easily via unsolicited generous or just unselfish actions. When you feel snubbed by a friend, snubbing them back might start a cold war; act warmly, and things will probably get back to normal quickly. Even in discussions of issues with those you disagree with, you can exploit positive reciprocity. Instead of just emailing articles to your "wacky uncle" to prove you're right on the issue you've been debating, try sometimes sending him high-quality pieces you know he'll agree with. He'll then be more likely to agree with other points you make that he'd otherwise be resistant to.

In conversations with those who disagree with you on a political topic, ask questions and indicate that you agree with your discussion partner's goals and specific points as much as possible. They'll become more likely to "reciprocate" by being open-minded to your points. Adam Grant's *Think Again* describes the well-documented effectiveness of *motivational interviewing*, an approach to persuasion in conversation that helps others find their own motivation to change their minds on an issue. Motivational interviewing avoids negative reciprocity in conversation and implicitly "exploits" positive reciprocity. If you're aggressive in conversation, your counterpart will probably reciprocate—and their beliefs won't budge. But when you engage in motivational interviewing, you signal that you respect the person you're speaking with, inducing their respect for you and making them more open-minded to your input.

Grant (2020, 150) describes an example of talking to a friend about possibly getting back together with an ex: "I was a fan of the idea, but instead of offering my opinion I asked her to walk me through the pros and cons and tell me how they stacked up against what she wanted in a partner. She ended up talking herself into rekindling the relationship. The conversation felt like magic, because I hadn't tried to persuade her or even given any advice." See figure 7.1 for a more general illustration of motivational interviewing. Mónica Guzmán's *I Never Thought of It That Way* and Ian Leslie's *Conflicted* are also excellent books on managing disagreement in conversation productively.

Grant also suggests asking "What would convince you?" when you're struggling to get the person you're speaking with to recognize a point. If the other person says, "Nothing," that makes it clear that the conversation won't be productive. But the question itself could also prompt them to think more carefully about the possibility of changing their minds and to recognize that this is something they should, at least in theory, be willing to do. I also suggest making a comment like, "I'm not trying to win a point in a debate—I'm just trying to work with you to understand the situation as well as we can." This might make them realize they unconsciously had been trying to prevent you from "winning" and nudge them to be more collaborative.

Whatever approach you take to conversations, remember that belief change can take time—sometimes a very long time, like years or decades. Try not to get frustrated if you don't see whomever you're talking to change their mind on the spot, even if you're pretty sure you've basically made a flawless argument. Your partner might seem like they're just not listening, but you never know when you're planting seeds.

Chapter 6: Information

This chapter presents various arguments and evidence that changes in the information we observe via the media and our social networks have led to growth in affective polarization bias. However, I'm not aware of any research *directly* showing this.[6] Doing so would be difficult since one would have to show changes in information both increase negative misperceptions of out-party character traits and affective polarization. But I hope future work tackles this challenge.

The main overall implication of this chapter is that it would be valuable to reduce the anti-out-party slant in most partisans' political information sets. Many nonprofit organizations and websites are working on pursuing this goal, encouraging people to both have conversations and read news

WILL YOU CHANGE MY MIND?

Figure 7.1

An illustration of motivational interviewing and lack thereof. Source: "Will You Change My Mind?" by Matt Shirley; from *Think Again: The Power of Knowing What You Don't Know* by Adam Grant, copyright © 2021 by Adam Grant. Used by permission of Viking Books, an imprint of Penguin Publishing Group, a division of Penguin Random House LLC. All rights reserved.

"across the divide."[7] Of course, changing this type of behavior is easy to talk about and hard to do. Nudges to get news from diverse sources and foster relationships with people with different viewpoints are easily ignored. The "good news" is that reading the other side's news is not as unpleasant to see as we expect (Dorison et al., 2019). It might even be habit-forming (Stone et al., 2017).

But why resist social sorting? Why should we politically diversify our own interpersonal interactions? For one thing, maintaining good relationships with friends and family members with different political viewpoints from our own might help eventually win them over. You never know. Even if this is a longshot, we can at least be good ambassadors for our side of the aisle. Actually, we can do this with all the people in our lives with different political views from ourselves. Remember, our words and actions often, perhaps nearly always, are interpreted as representing our side. If you want to fight affective polarization and the out-party's hostility toward your side, be friendliest to your neighbors and plumbers with whom you disagree politically—not least friendly to them as you might instinctively be inclined.

Moreover, if you've got a Trump sticker on your car, and you don't like the idea of Trump supporters being thought of as "deplorable," you might want to be an extra considerate driver. If you're wearing an N95 mask in a store with mostly maskless people, you might try to be extra friendly to show that mask wearers aren't "elitist" or otherwise unlikable. There's always a possibility something you do or say will have lasting impact. Every time you interact with the other side, there's a chance it will resonate—either pushing them further away or pulling them closer. We all have opportunities to build bridges this way almost every day.

Another principle to consider when encouraging people to diversify their political information sets is to "make it easy" (Richard Thaler's favorite policy advice). For example, antipolarization organizations could suggest that every voter employs a rule of thumb of finding a single voice from the other side that they (relatively) enjoy and trust and then try to read, watch, or listen to that person regularly. You might even create a weekly event on your calendar reminding yourself to do this. Pundits and politicians themselves might actively support this endeavor. Let's ask Tucker Carlson: who's someone on the left you'd suggest your viewers turn to for their perspective on the issues of the day? Rachel Maddow, who would you suggest your viewers for a thoughtful right-leaning viewpoint? Emphasizing the importance of getting news from different points of view in civics education at various ages, middle school through college, might be helpful too, but this is a longer-term solution.

These ideas may be worth exploring. Still, at least in the short- and medium-term future, more structural changes are likely necessary for meaningful, large-scale impacts. Perhaps the most feasible way to make such impacts is through changes to social media platform policies. Facebook and Twitter have both made several such changes to combat misinformation and improve the quality of discourse on their platforms since 2016 (see, e.g., Conklin, 2020), but both could still do much more. Moreover, even if both platforms are hesitant to do so, they might be compelled to via public pressure or threat of regulation, like the European Union's new Digital Services Act. Robert Wright's recommendations of transparent disclosure of algorithms and requiring platforms to offer an API (application programming interface) so third parties can develop add-ons to reduce polarizing content seem very sensible (Wright, 2021).[8]

And while, yes, Facebook and Twitter have taken positive steps, as far as I know, neither platform currently does anything to *encourage* constructive engagement with diverse viewpoints. Rather, on the contrary, both still push users toward selective exposure. Countering these tendencies might take some creativity and even courage, but there are many potential options. For instance, instead of simply showing on a user's profile page that she has one hundred thousand followers (as Twitter currently does), the profile page could also show a measure of the ideological distribution of followers or at least provide users with the option of seeing this information.

There are many ways to measure the partisanship of social media users; for example, the distribution of parties of politicians followed (or those followed by people we follow)—how many more conservatives does one follow than liberals or vice versa. Similarly, Twitter could report metrics for the ideological diversity of users who like and retweet tweets. These would highlight whether the user (and whether particular tweets) is simply preaching to the choir or has broader appeal—which could help to incentivize the latter. I think most of us would find a tweet liked by one hundred thousand people on the left less impressive than one liked by the same number of people spanning the ideological spectrum. Maybe social media companies could even intervene to warn or even educate users who appear to be subject to affective polarization bias. Or the platforms could at least steer users toward depolarizing content rather than material likely to get them even more worked up. Yes, this could lead to a decline in short-term user engagement and revenues, but perhaps shareholders could be assuaged by an argument that this cost is outweighed by a better long-term reputation for the company and even improved political stability. See Aral (2021) for a discussion of other options platforms could adopt, such as better labeling of news credibility and prompts for readers to consider accuracy of stories and sources, which have been shown to be effective in reducing the influence of false information.

I've worked on a project with the goal of creating a scalable way to incentivize diverse news consumption, a website called Media Trades, with David Francis, who works in academic IT at my institution, Bowdoin College. On the site, users choose a political "side" that they generally lean toward, left or right, and then can submit links to news articles or videos they'd like someone on the *other* side to see. In exchange for each link submitted, the user agrees to read an article from someone on the other side they're matched up with. A user's incentive to participate is that they get to provide news to someone on the other side—that is, to infiltrate the other side's news bubble. To show you did your part of the trade, you write a brief summary of the piece you received, with the option for a separate editorial response. Both partners rate each other's review, thumbs up or down, and users with more thumbs ups get prioritized for future trades and have the option to share their ratings publicly.

With collaborators Shilpi Mukherjee, a Clemson economics PhD student at the time, and Mike Franz, a colleague in the government department here at Bowdoin, I ran a project with classes at Bowdoin (whose students lean left) and students at Clemson (who lean right) in February 2021. Over one hundred students made over two hundred trades in total, and we surveyed students before and after the trades. Most students from both schools said they enjoyed the trades (and Clemson students enjoyed the trades much more than they expected to). Moreover, Bowdoin students' thermometer polarization declined by 2.4 points and Clemson students' declined by 7.5 points. For both schools, around 70 percent of students said that their interest in getting more diverse news going forward had "maybe" or "probably" increased because of the trading experience.

Figure 7.2
Source: mediatrades.org; illustration by Sarah Caplan.

For Media Trades to have a chance of making a significant impact, we'd need to find a way to scale up the number of users and trades. Perhaps the best way to do this would be a social media platform building in a trading feature. Categorizing trades by issue and having users pick a different side for each issue, for example, "generally in favor of stronger or weaker gun restrictions," would be preferable to forcing people to join one of two sides in general. Alternatively, online outlets with readers who tend to be on different sides, for example, foxnews.com and nytimes.com, could set up a trading agreement with one another. Readers could have the option to trade a story with readers from the partner outlet with just one click, in the same way that we can now email or post to social media this easily. Alternative methods of incentivizing substantial exposure to counterpartisan media could also be useful. I suspect that, for many liberals and conservatives, watching a solid month of Fox News and MSNBC could be painful at first but would eventually help them understand the other side's views better and soften hostility toward them.

Still, even if we found ways to enhance citizens' exposure to diverse news, it would also be ideal to have at least one major watchdog media outlet trusted by voters across the aisle. Market forces have not successfully led this to happen. Public media is thus a natural alternative to consider, but in the US it currently has a less-than-stellar reputation in the eyes of many citizens. One idea to improve public media's reputation for nonpartisanship that's admittedly far-fetched but parallels the proposal of Sitaraman and Epps discussed above for rebalancing the Supreme Court is to create a new public outlet, with an equal number of journalists chosen by members of both parties. Perhaps this outlet or a private one could carefully monitor pundit predictions—tracking those made with confidence that turned out to be incorrect—to help media consumers better understand which pundits are more accurate and to reduce the incentives of pundits to make overconfident proclamations.

Finally, given the strong evidence in support of the contact hypothesis, especially for in-person contact, policymakers and nonprofits should consider ways to promote this type of contact between members of the parties at all levels. How to do this is unclear, but there are many possibilities.[9] For example, the American Exchange Project is a new organization working on bringing together recent high school graduates from red- and blue-leaning parts of the country to spend two weeks together. Perhaps this type of program could be expanded to allow high school students to spend entire semesters in Democratic and Republican homes or college students to spend semesters in politically different campuses. Politicians themselves could certainly make a more structured effort to regularly engage in contact in various ways. (How about participating in small bipartisan book club groups discussing, say, *Divided We Fall*, *Scout Mindset*, *Think Again*, or *I Never Thought of It That Way*?)

Last Words

> Kindness is the only nondelusional response to the human condition.
> —George Saunders, "What It Means to Be Kind in a Cruel World," *The Ezra Klein Show* podcast

Again, many of the ideas I discuss above are speculative, and I'm sure there are many ideas worth consideration that I'm unaware of. Who knows, maybe affective polarization will ebb naturally or due to the emergence of unforeseen forces or events. A major external threat to the nation (that's less ambiguous than COVID-19) could unify the US, though obviously this isn't something to hope for.

But I don't think we should just cross our fingers and wish for good luck. We need to act. Individual actions can help, perhaps more than we realize due to social contagion (Frank, 2020). Still, I suspect we need a large-scale, top-down endeavor to have a chance at making significant progress on reducing affective polarization bias in the near-term future. Structural political changes like final-five voting and others discussed above may be necessary to remove the conditions that have led to the stark growth in affective polarization the US has experienced over recent decades. But to make these structural changes, we may need to learn to get along better first, especially if we want the changes to have bipartisan support and avoid the appearance of partisan motives.

I'm imagining something like a Depolarization Manhattan Project—a major endeavor with buy-in from top leadership in both parties, supported by significant resources and a commitment to implement recommendations and charged with coming up with short- and long-term solutions like those discussed above. Or perhaps the project could simply focus on eradicating misperceptions. Right, I know—asking our political leaders to agree on anything of substance now seems like a pipe dream. However, the one thing that most (maybe even all) members of both parties do agree on today is that our politics is broken. Representative Derek Kilmer (D-WA), chair of the Select Committee on the Modernization of Congress, summarizes this broad sentiment, saying that "a lot of what happens in Congress . . . feels frustrating at best and maddening at worst. And that feeling, by the way, is bipartisan. I haven't met anyone who actually enjoys working in a dysfunctional environment" (Ripley, 2021b). So, the need for such a project seems like something that we might be able to agree on as well. There is a real urgency.[10]

Just as problems in relationships between friends and partners can heal with improved interpersonal understanding, continued growth in animosity between the parties is not a foregone conclusion. "Humans . . . are not fated to be fanatics" (Worthen, 2021). Even misanthropes think "deep inside, every person is motivated to behave in morally good ways" (De Freitas et al., 2018, 134). How many more people could undergo a change like George Wallace's if they were visited by a Shirley Chisholm?

We are living in an animosity bubble. Bubbles eventually burst. But they can do a lot of damage if they grow too large first. Let's all do what we can to let the hot air out of this one gently.

Acknowledgments

I am very grateful to my editor, Emily Taber, for extensive helpful comments on style and content and expert guidance throughout this project. I also offer special thanks to Bowdoin College for supporting this work, and to the anonymous reviewers, Elizabeth Schroeder, David J. Stone (my father), Laura McCandlish (my spouse), Tom McCandlish (my father-in-law), Matt Gentzkow, Yphtach Lelkes, Matt Levendusky, and Ro'ee Levy for especially helpful feedback. I also greatly appreciate useful input from Michael Kozuch, Ben Williams, Nate Torda, Dan Wood, Jessica Feldman, Andrew Hamilton, Alan Sillars, Andy Rudalevige, Jeff Lees, Patrick Warren, Keith Stanovich, Eugen Dimant, Ben Tappin, Egon Tripodi, Ben Enke, Jesse Shapiro, Matt Brown, Chris Bail, Andrea Robbett, Scott Sehon, Jeff Selinger, Rob Sobak, Kana Takematsu, Nimra Siddiqui, John Hood, Ben Ho, Matt Nagler, Brendan Nyhan, Peter Dahlgren, Eli Finkel, Aditya Pall-Pareek, and Victoria Parker, and thank Ginny Crossman and Antonn Park for helpful assistance with copyediting. Finally, I thank you, the reader, for your time and attention. I believe that this material will be relevant beyond the current political moment, but please bear in mind the book was primarily written in 2021. And if you disagree with anything I've said, please don't hold it *too much* against me.

Notes

Introduction

1. See Perlez (1982), Capehart (2019), and Sommers (2020).

2. See, for example, Hocker and Wilmot (2014, 2), who write that "perception is at the core of all conflict analysis. In interpersonal conflicts, people react as though there are genuinely different goals . . . but sorting out what is perceived and what is interpersonally accurate forms the basis of conflict analysis."

3. See also Tuchman (1962).

4. See, for example, Menchaca (2021) for recent evidence and cites.

5. Affective polarization is also called *social polarization* in some literature, for example, Mason (2018).

6. More informal examples of elite affective polarization abound. See, for example, Calicchio (2021) on House members nearly coming to blows.

7. For additional evidence of affective polarization contributing to democratic backsliding, see also, for example, Graham and Svolik (2020) and Orhan (forthcoming), and for counterevidence, Broockman et al. (2020).

8. See, for example, Mason (2018), Chua (2018), Iyengar et al. (2019), Klein (2020a), and Harris et al. (2022).

9. See, for example, Orr and Huber (2020) for other work arguing that group identity factors are unlikely to be the complete explanation for partisan affective polarization.

10. See Whiting (2020), Bates (2016), and Lewis (2016).

11. Prominent examples include Claude and Shelby Steele (Kronen, 2020) and the Viljoen twins, whose reconciliation helped prevent civil war in South Africa after the end of apartheid (Bregman, 2020). And yes, academics are notorious for squabbling

both across and within departments. (So, relatively low stakes don't guarantee peaceful coexistence.)

12. See Bursztyn and Yang (2021) for a behavioral economic meta-analysis that's particularly relevant to this book, on interpersonal misperceptions across a wide range of settings.

Chapter 1

1. Goodwin et al. (2014, 166) write that "moral character plays a key role in impression formation, and in person perception more generally." Brambilla and Leach (2014, 398) write that "morality has a primary role over sociability (and competence/agency) in the impressions that we form and the evaluations that we make of people."

2. See, for example, Jones (1990) and Kenny (1994) for psychology research on interpersonal perceptions and White et al. (2020) for work showing perceived stability of character traits.

3. See, for example, Siegel et al. (2018) for research on updating beliefs about other people's character traits.

4. Bayes' rule is that the probability of Y being true given that X is observed, $\Pr(Y|X)$, is equal to $\Pr(X|Y)\Pr(Y)/[\Pr(X|Y)\Pr(\sim Y) + \Pr(X|Y)\Pr(\sim Y)]$, with $\sim Y$ denoting "not Y." For our example, X is the action of giving, and Y is being a "generous" type, so $\Pr(X|Y) = 0.75$ and $\Pr(X|\sim Y) = 0.1$, while $\Pr(Y) = 0.5$ and $\Pr(\sim Y) = 0.5$. So this Bayesian posterior is equal to $0.75*0.5/(0.75*0.5 + 0.1*0.5) = 0.88$. See, for example, Tetlock and Gardner (2015) and Jervis (2017) for nonmathematical discussions of the validity of Bayesianism as the ideal way to revise beliefs and https://arbital.com/p/bayes_rule/?l=1zq for a guide to theoretical and practical use of Bayes' rule.

5. Another of these ways is noted at the start of chapter 4.

6. See, for example, Acemoglu et al. (2016) for a discussion of long-run convergence of Bayesian beliefs to true values and the potential nonrobustness of this result.

7. In a previous draft of this book, I also defined a distinct type of mistaken dislike that's independent of a person's priors and private information, "excessive dislike," which is an overestimation of probabilities of "bad" actions as compared to the actual, or true, probabilities of those actions. This is a useful distinction at times; however, since this book is mainly about biased information processing, it seemed to best to drop this additional term and avoid the potential distraction. See Stone (2021) for further discussion.

8. See Tesler (2016), Klein (2020a), and Stout (2020) for books that discuss the role of race in the era of rising affective polarization.

9. See Nasby et al. (1980). Another related term is the "sinister attribution error" (Kramer, 1994).

10. See Webster (2020) and Phoenix (2019) on anger in US politics over recent decades.

11. For a good discussion of both perspectives on US partisan conflict, I recommend French (2020).

Chapter 2

1. See also, for example, Martherus et al. (2019).

2. See, for example, Chambers and Melnyk (2006), Moore-Berg et al. (2020b), and Levendusky and Malhotra (2016). Yang (2016) reports evidence of false polarization outside the US.

3. See Lenz et al. (2021) and Mernyk et al. (2021) for additional evidence of negatively biased metaperceptions in US politics.

4. Parts of this section are adapted, with permission, from Stone (2020b).

5. All original data analysis for this book is publicly available at https://osf.io /crb2u/.

6. These results are not reported in the paper but were shared with me by Dimant and are available at https://osf.io/crb2u/.

7. Another study providing similar evidence indicating that partisans have too pessimistic beliefs about out-partisan behavior in incentivized games is Hernández-Lagos and Minor (2020); however, they did not collect data on the degree of polarization. Two other papers that came out around the time of this book's writing are Zhang and Rand (2021), who found that partisans underestimate the quality of each other's judgment in rating the accuracy of nonpolitical news headlines, and Puryear et al. (2022), who found that partisans overestimate the fraction of out-partisans endorsing basic moral wrongs like child pornography even when incentivized for accuracy.

8. See, for example, Gulzar (2021).

9. Bradbury and Bodenmann (2020) report that marriage counseling is beneficial for 60 to 80 percent of couples, also implying marital problems are often due to partners misunderstanding each other.

10. Fletcher and Kerr (2010) show results from a meta-analysis of research on romantic relationships and report no overall association between relational adjustment and partners' understanding of one another.

Chapter 3

1. See Hetherington and Weiler (2018), whose book's title poses the "Prius or pickup?" question.

2. For an explanation of the history of the sorting phenomenon, see, for example, Levendusky (2009) and Klein (2020a).

3. See Greene (2013) and Clark et al. (2019) for more discussion of adaptive inter-group bias and Cikara and Van Bavel (2014) for a review of relevant neuroscience.

4. See also Julia Galef's book *The Scout Mindset* for an in-depth general discussion of the power and prevalence of motivated reasoning.

5. See, for example, Chew et al. (2020) and Derreumaux et al. (2021) for recent evidence. See Guay and Johnston (2021) and Ditto et al. (2018) for evidence that motivated political reasoning is similar for Democrats and Republicans.

6. More broadly, "identity-protective cognition" is a somewhat common term for motivated reasoning used for the purpose of protecting beliefs shared by a group central to one's identity (Kahan et al., 2007).

7. See Mercier and Sperber (2017), Solda et al. (2019), and Schwardmann et al. (2022).

8. Haidt and Klein both discuss motivated reasoning's effects on voters in their books. See Christensen and Moynihan (2020) for evidence of politicians engaging in motivated reasoning.

9. See Yon (2019) for a good discussion and references.

10. Stanovich notes in the book that he restricts attention to motivated processing.

11. A related term from psychology is "omission neglect" (see, e.g., Kardes et al., 2006).

12. See López-Pérez et al. (2021) for a discussion of WYSIATI as a cause of overprecision.

13. Note that the term naive realism has a distinct meaning in philosophy.

14. Fernbach and Van Boven (2021) discuss how categorical thinking contributes to false polarization.

Chapter 4

1. See Orr and Huber (2020) and Kingzette (2021) on policy and ideological differences as causes of affective polarization, respectively, and for work on moral convictions, see Garrett and Bankert (2020) and Enders and Lupton (2021).

2. See, for example, Thompson (2017).

3. Reeder et al. (2005) discuss a similar point.

4. Settle (2018, 183) writes that "the false consensus effect is especially pernicious in the realm of politics."

5. See Lizzeri and Siniscalchi (2008) for an economic analysis of this topic.

Chapter 5

1. Is it a "prisoner's" or "prisoners'" dilemma? Actually, the name of the game is often written both ways, and there are reasonable interpretations for both versions. The latter has the benefit of referring to both prisoners. But I still prefer the former since the players do not make a choice jointly; each individually faces a dilemma (as explained further in this section). However, there are, of course, two prisoners. So I think it's ideally written as "a prisoner's dilemma game" but can still be called just "prisoner's dilemma" for short.

2. See the literature on psychological games for an analysis of related issues. Carpenter and Robbett (2022) provide a good discussion.

3. See Axelrod (1984) for a detailed discussion.

4. See Kahneman et al. (2021) for a discussion of our general tendency to underestimate the prevalence of noise.

5. See, for example, Molander (1985) and Kollock (1993).

6. The literature on conflict analysis discusses (asymmetric) attribution bias—giving ourselves too much credit for good outcomes and the other side too much blame for bad (Jeong, 2008). The psychology literature on relationships has obtained related findings (see, e.g., Acitelli et al., 1993; Hinnekens et al., 2020).

7. Sammut et al. (2015) discuss naive realism contributing to conflict spirals via overestimation of the other side's bias, a topic I discuss again at the end of the chapter.

8. In a recent conversation with politically minded left-leaning friends and colleagues, they indicated thinking that Democrats' treatment of Bork was one hundred percent fair and failed to recognize even the perception that Bork was the victim of inappropriate "character assassination" (as described by Nocera and others).

9. See Lemieux (2020). These tweets are used with his permission.

10. Senate Judiciary Committee chair James Eastland told Johnson he "had never seen so much feeling against a man as against Fortas" (Kalman, 1992).

11. See also the evidence discussed in chapter 2 on perceptions of closed-mindedness (the character trait most closely related to cognitive bias that the Pew Research Center study asked about).

12. Dorst has told me he agrees that we are subject to excessive dislike (defined in chapter 1's note 7), but he's less sure about biased dislike. In a nutshell, Dorst thinks most of us are "doing the best we can" given our information—that we form nearly Bayesian beliefs. As I think this book makes clear, I disagree. But Dorst and I do agree that both sides overestimate the other side's biases—he'd say this overestimation is typically "rational," whereas I'd say we should usually know better. Still, the distinction between our views is perhaps mostly semantic. We both agree many partisans should tone down their dislike as it is driven by misperceptions and that in general the other side is more reasonable than we tend to think.

13. This model is also based on Stone (2020a).

Chapter 6

1. For example, see Settle (2018).

2. See, for example, Herndon (2012), Cagé (2016), and Napoli (2019).

3. See Levendusky (2013) for a discussion of the expansion of "partisan media" in recent decades and Hirano and Snyder (2020) for evidence that newspapers were relatively nonpartisan after 1950.

4. See, for example, Gentzkow and Shapiro (2011), Rodriguez et al. (2017), and Peterson et al. (2021).

5. See also the website https://ground.news/blindspotter/twitter/, which estimates the ideological distribution of news interactions for any Twitter account.

6. The degree to which behavior becomes more hostile online is a subject of debate, but see Bail (2021) for examples of this occurring.

7. See Elwood (2021) for a good discussion of related issues.

8. Bakshy et al. (2015) assume Facebook users are more likely to share politically aligned content. Garz et al. (2020b) provide evidence of such "selective engagement."

9. The discussion here is based on Gentzkow et al. (2015).

10. See Benkler et al. (2018) for a discussion of asymmetry in news quality across the ideological spectrum.

11. Using the Bayes' rule formula, this posterior probability is $1*0.4/(1*0.4 + 0.9*0.6)$ = 0.426.

12. The full formula for the Bayesian posterior of Smith being "good" given a "bad report" is $0*0.4/(0*0.4 + 0.1*0.6)$.

13. Predictable belief changes can be due to non-Bayesian information processing or biased priors or signal probabilities. But since these beliefs (priors and beliefs about signal probabilities) are based on past information processing, if they are systematically biased, this also suggests non-Bayesian information processing in the past.

14. A related term sometimes used in the literature is "redundancy neglect" (Angrisani et al., 2021).

15. See also Bowen et al. (2021).

16. See also Molleman et al. (2021).

17. See also Roozenbeek et al. (2022) for additional evidence of motivated reasoning and myside bias contributing to susceptibility to misinformation. See Hugo Mercier's very good book *Not Born Yesterday* for an argument that people are less gullible than commonly perceived. He acknowledges that we are more influenced by information consistent with our priors and does not discuss experiments like Jin et al.'s (2021) in which there is a normatively correct level of credulity that can be used as a benchmark. That is, Mercier shows that people show skepticism when interpreting new information, but most of the evidence he discusses doesn't assess whether people demonstrate the correct degree of skepticism. Mercier also acknowledges other factors that can cause undue credulity like correlation neglect (what he calls "hidden dependencies") (2020, 174).

18. Sunstein and Hastie don't use all of this terminology as some of it has emerged in more recent years.

19. See Fisk (2021) and Iandoli et al. (2021) for evidence of group polarization contributing to affective polarization.

20. In another recent large study, Casas et al. (2022) found that randomized exposure to relatively extreme counterpartisan sites have little effect on polarization.

21. Gentzkow et al. (2020) present a model in which trust in ideologically aligned outlets snowballs over time with arbitrarily small initial biases.

Chapter 7

1. Amanda Ripley also discusses binary competition as a key "fire starter" in *High Conflict* (2021a).

2. Organizations working on improving this type of education include the Alliance for Decision Education, a nonprofit working to promote education about cognitive bias for middle and high school students, and Narrative 4, a global organization

using story exchange to enhance empathy. Warner et al. (2020) find that polarization is reduced by taking others' perspectives in narrative writing.

3. See Lowney (2020).

4. Lusinski (2018) provides an excellent discussion of this issue.

5. Robbett and Matthews (2021) study the effects of partisanship in a repeated public goods experiment with relatively encouraging results, finding polarized and nonpolarized groups attain similar levels of cooperation when punishment is possible. However, their experiment doesn't include some factors discussed in this chapter that can lead to behavioral spirals (noise, ambiguity, potential escalation).

6. Schroeder and Stone (2015) present evidence that Fox News caused a decline in knowledge about information favorable to Democrats but do not examine affective polarization. Garrett et al. (2019) show that conservative media exposure was associated with higher levels of both misperceptions and affective polarization, but the causal relationship is unclear. Lelkes et al. (2017) show that quasi-random increased access to broadband internet due to variation in state right-of-way regulations caused greater partisan media consumption and out-party hostility, but the authors don't directly study misperceptions. Similarly, Levendusky (2013) presents experiments showing partisan cable news increases out-party hostility, but not that misperceptions are the mechanism. Bursztyn et al. (2022) show that media consumers mistakenly interpret opinions in media as facts, implying undue influence. Other papers show, without examining affective polarization or misperceptions, that partisan media and online media have causally increased ideological polarization (e.g., Martin and Yurukoglu, 2017).

Counterevidence worth noting is presented by Boxell et al. (2017, 2020). Their 2017 paper shows that affective polarization in the US grew fastest in demographic groups least likely to use online media. Their 2020 paper shows that affective polarization grew faster in the US than eight other OECD nations despite online and social media being used extensively by all of them. The authors write that their results imply US polarization growth has been due to "changes that are more distinctive to the US (e.g., changing party composition, growing racial divisions, the emergence of partisan cable news)" (3).

These studies do provide persuasive evidence that the internet has not been the dominant cause of growth in affective polarization in the US. On the other hand, their results don't imply that information and media in general aren't important causes of polarization. The authors highlight the potential key role of cable news, and their results don't rule out online media being a significant factor. Social media may have had an especially strong impact in the US due to factors unique to the US. Demographic groups that use the internet less often being more susceptible to false information (Guess et al., 2018) could have caused them to experience larger impacts.

7. A few examples include allsides.com, listenfirstproject.org, and braverangels.org.

8. Acemoglu et al. (2022) provide a thoughtful discussion of additional regulatory options.

9. Again, see Levendusky and Stecula (2021). I also recommend Hartman et al.'s (2022) excellent review of interventions to address partisan animosity.

10. Another admittedly far-fetched, top-down possibility would be some type of detente agreement among top media outlets or pundits.

References

Abrams, Samuel J. 2021. "My New Study Proves It: Cancel Culture Is Much Worse on the Left." *Newsweek*, June 8.

Acemoglu, Daron, Victor Chernozhukov, and Muhamet Yildiz. 2016. "Fragility of Asymptotic Agreement under Bayesian Learning." *Theoretical Economics* 11 (1): 187–225.

Acemoglu, Daron, Asuman Ozdaglar, and James Siderius. 2022. "A Model of Online Misinformation." Working Paper. National Bureau of Economic Research.

Acitelli, Linda K., Elizabeth Douvan, and Joseph Veroff. 1993. "Perceptions of Conflict in the First Year of Marriage: How Important Are Similarity and Understanding?" *Journal of Social and Personal Relationships* 10 (1): 5–19.

Adler, Jonathan H. 2016. "The Senate Has No Constitutional Obligation to Consider Nominees." *George Mason Law Review* 24 (1): 15–34.

Ahler, Douglas J., and Gaurav Sood. 2018. "The Parties in Our Heads: Misperceptions About Party Composition and Their Consequences." *Journal of Politics* 80 (3): 964–981.

Ahrens, Steffen, Ciril Bosch-Rosa, and Bernhard Kassner. 2021. "Overconfidence and the Political and Financial Behavior of a Representative Sample." Working paper. Ludwig Maximilian University of Munich and Humboldt University of Berlin.

American Bar Association. 2018. "Kaine Suggests Congress Should Consider Formal Mediation to Settle Some Disputes." https://www.americanbar.org/news/abanews/aba-news-archives/2018/04/kaine_suggests_congr/.

Amsalem, Eran, Eric Merkley, and Peter John Loewen. 2021. "Does Talking to the Other Side Reduce Inter-Party Hostility? Evidence from Three Studies." *Political Communication* 39 (1): 61–78.

Anderson, Sarah E., Daniel M. Butler, and Laurel Harbridge-Yong. 2020. *Rejecting Compromise: Legislators' Fear of Primary Voters*. Cambridge, UK: Cambridge University Press.

Andersson, Lynne M., and Christine M. Pearson. 1999. "Tit for Tat? The Spiraling Effect of Incivility in the Workplace." *Academy of Management Review* 24 (3): 452–471.

Andris, Clio, David Lee, Marcus J. Hamilton, Mauro Martino, Christian E. Gunning, and John Armistead Selden. 2015. "The Rise of Partisanship and Super-Cooperators in the US House of Representatives." *PlOS One* 10 (4).

Angrisani, Marco, Antonio Guarino, Philippe Jehiel, and Toru Kitagaw. 2021. "Information Redundancy Neglect versus Overconfidence: A Social Learning Experiment." *American Economic Journal: Microeconomics* 13 (3): 163–197.

Aral, Sinan. 2021. *The Hype Machine: How Social Media Disrupts Our Elections, Our Economy, and Our Health—and How We Must Adapt*. New York: Currency.

Axelrod, Robert. 1984. *The Evolution of Cooperation*. New York: Basic Books.

Axelrod, Robert. 1997. *The Complexity of Cooperation*. Princeton, NJ: Princeton University Press.

Bail, Chris. 2021. *Breaking the Social Media Prism: How to Make Our Platforms Less Polarizing*. Princeton, NJ: Princeton University Press.

Bail, Christopher A., Lisa P. Argyle, Taylor W. Brown, John P. Bumpus, Haohan Chen, M. B. Fallin Hunzaker, Jaemin Lee, Marcus Mann, Friedolin Merhout, and Alexander Volfovsky. 2018. "Exposure to Opposing Views on Social Media Can Increase Political Polarization." *Proceedings of the National Academy of Sciences* 115 (37): 9216–9221.

Bakshy, Eytan, Solomon Messing, and Lada A. Adamic. 2015. "Exposure to Ideologically Diverse News and Opinion on Facebook." *Science* 348 (6239): 1130–1132.

Ball, M. A. 1991. "Revisiting the Gulf of Tonkin Crisis: An Analysis of the Private Communication of President Johnson and His Advisers." *Discourse & Society* 2 (3): 281–296.

Barber, Michael, and Ryan Davis. 2019. "Partisanship and the Trolley Problem: Understanding Republicans' and Democrats' Willingness to Sacrifice Members of the Other Party." Working paper. Brigham Young University.

Barberá, Pablo. 2020. "Social Media, Echo Chambers, and Political Polarization." In *Social Media and Democracy: The State of the Field, Prospects for Reform*, edited by Nathaniel Persily and Joshua A. Tucker, 34. Cambridge, UK: Cambridge University Press.

Barker, David C., Ryan Detamble, and Morgan Marietta. 2021. "Intellectualism, Anti-Intellectualism, and Epistemic Hubris in Red and Blue America." *American Political Science Review* 111 (1): 1–16.

Baron, Hannah, Robert Blair, Donghyun Danny Choi, Laura Gamboa, Jessica Gottlieb, Amanda Lea Robinson, Steven Rosenzweig, Megan Turnbull, and Emily A. West. 2021. "Can Americans Depolarize? Assessing the Effects of Reciprocal Group Reflection on Partisan Polarization." OSF Preprints. May 10. doi:10.31219/osf.io /3x7z8.

Bates, Karen G. 2016. "Muhammad Ali and Malcolm X: A Broken Friendship, an Enduring Legacy." *NPR*, February 25.

Bazzi, Samuel, Arya Gaduh, Alexander D. Rothenberg, and Maisy Wong. 2019. "Unity in Diversity? How Intergroup Contact Can Foster Nation Building." *American Economic Review* 109 (11): 3978–4025.

Benkler, Yochai, Robert Faris, and Hal Roberts. 2018. *Network Propaganda: Manipulation, Disinformation, and Radicalization in American Politics.* Oxford: Oxford University Press.

Benson, Buster. 2019. *Why Are We Yelling? The Art of Productive Disagreement.* London: Penguin Books.

Beth, Richard S., Elizabeth Rybicki, and Michael Greene. 2013. *Cloture Attempts on Nominations: Data and Historical Development through November 20, 2013.* Washington, DC: Congressional Research Service.

Bishop, Bill. 2009. *The Big Sort: Why the Clustering of Like-Minded America Is Tearing Us Apart.* Boston: Mariner Books.

Blanchette, Isabelle, and Anne Richards. 2009. "The Influence of Affect on Higher Level Cognition: A Review of Research on Interpretation, Judgement, Decision Making and Reasoning." *Cognition and Emotion* 24 (4): 561–595.

Blume, Andreas, Ernest K. Lai, and Wooyoung Lim. 2020. "Strategic Information Transmission: A Survey of Experiments and Theoretical Foundations." In *Handbook of Experimental Game Theory*, edited by C. Mónica Capra, Rachel T. A. Croson, Mary L. Rigdon, and Tanya S. Rosenblat, 311–347. Cheltenham, UK: Edward Elgar Publishing.

Bordalo, Pedro, Marco Tabellini, and David Yang. 2020. "Issue Salience and Political Stereotypes." Working paper. National Bureau of Economic Research.

Bowen, Renee, Danil Dmitriev, and Simone Galperti. 2021. "Learning from Shared News: When Abundant Information Leads to Belief Polarization." Working paper. National Bureau of Economic Research.

Bowes, Shauna M., Madeline C. Blanchard, Thomas H. Costello, Alan I. Abramowitz, and Scott O. Lilienfeld. 2020. "Intellectual Humility and Between-Party Animus: Implications for Affective Polarization in Two Community Samples." *Journal of Research in Personality* 88: 103992.

Boxell, Levi, Matthew Gentzkow, and Jesse M. Shapiro. 2017. "Greater Internet Use Is Not Associated with Faster Growth in Political Polarization among US Demographic Groups." *Proceedings of the National Academy of Sciences* 114 (40): 10612–10617.

Boxell, Levi, Matthew Gentzkow, and Jesse M. Shapiro. 2020. "Cross-Country Trends in Affective Polarization." Working paper 26669. National Bureau of Economic Research. Last revised 2021. https://www.nber.org/papers/w26669.

Bradbury, Thomas N., and Guy Bodenmann. 2020. "Interventions for Couples." *Annual Review of Clinical Psychology* 16: 99–123.

Brady, William J., Julian A. Wills, John T. Jost, Joshua A. Tucker, and Jay J. Van Bavel. 2017. "Emotion Shapes the Diffusion of Moralized Content in Social Networks." *Proceedings of the National Academy of Sciences* 114 (28): 7313–7318.

Brambilla, Marco, and Colin W. Leach. 2014. "On the Importance of Being Moral: The Distinctive Role of Morality in Social Judgment." *Social Cognition* 32 (4): 397–408.

Breakstone, Joel, Mark Smith, Sam Wineburg, Amie Rapaport, Jill Carle, Marshall Garland, and Anna Saavedra. 2021. "Students' Civic Online Reasoning: A National Portrait." *Educational Researcher* 50 (8): 505–515.

Bregman, Rutger. 2020. *Humankind: A Hopeful History*. London: Bloomsbury Publishing.

Broockman, David, Joshua Kalla, and Sean Westwood. "Does Affective Polarization Undermine Democratic Norms or Accountability? Maybe Not." *American Journal of Political Science* (forthcoming).

Brown, Jacob R., and Ryan D. Enos. 2021. "The Measurement of Partisan Sorting for 180 Million Voters." *Nature Human Behaviour* 5: 998–1008.

Bruneau, Emile, Boaz Hameiri, Samantha L. Moore-Berg, and Nour Kteily. 2021. "Intergroup Contact Reduces Dehumanization and Meta-Dehumanization: Cross-Sectional, Longitudinal, and Quasi-Experimental Evidence from 16 Samples in Five Countries." *Personality and Social Psychology Bulletin* 47 (6): 906–920.

Bursztyn, Leonardo, Aakaash Rao, Christopher Roth, and David Yanagizawa-Drott. 2022. "Opinions as Facts." ECONtribute Discussion Papers Series 159. University of Bonn and University of Cologne, Germany.

Bursztyn, Leonardo, and David Y. Yang. 2021. "Misperceptions About Others." Working paper no. w29168. National Bureau of Economic Research.

Cagé, Julia. 2016. *Saving the Media*. Cambridge, MA: Harvard University Press.

Calicchio, Dom. 2021. "House Members Harris, Allred Nearly Come to Blows during Pennsylvania Certification Debate: Reports." FoxNews.com. January 7. https://www.foxnews.com/politics/house-members-harris-allred-nearly-come-to-blows-during-pennsylvania-certification-debate-reports.

Camerer, Colin F. 2003. "Behavioural Studies of Strategic Thinking in Games." *Trends in Cognitive Sciences* 7, no. 5 (May): 225–231.

Canen, Nathan J., Chad Kendall, and Francesco Trebbi. 2021. "Political Parties as Drivers of US Polarization: 1927–2018." Working paper no. w28296. National Bureau of Economic Research.

Capehart, Jonathan. 2019. "Opinion: How Segregationist George Wallace Became a Model for Racial Reconciliation: 'Voices of the Movement' Episode 6." *Washington Post*, May 16.

Carpenter, Jeffrey, and Andrea Robbett. 2022. *Game Theory and Behavior*. Cambridge, MA: MIT Press.

Casas, Andreu, Ericka Menchen-Trevino, and Magdalena Wojcieszak. 2022. "Exposure to Extremely Partisan News from the Other Political Side Shows Scarce Boomerang Effects." *Political Behavior*.

Cassese, Erin, Nathan P. Kalmoe, Lilliana Mason, and Alexander Theodoridis. 2021. "Pro-Trump Capitol Riot Violence Underscores Bipartisan Danger of Dehumanizing Language." NBC News: Think. January 17. https://www.nbcnews.com/think/opinion/pro-trump-capitol-riot-violence-underscores-bipartisan-danger-dehumanizing-language-ncna1254530.

Chambers, John R., and Darya Melnyk. 2006. "Why Do I Hate Thee? Conflict Misperceptions and Intergroup Mistrust." *Personality and Social Psychology Bulletin* 32 (10): 1295–1311.

Chan, Jimmy, and Wing Suen. 2008. "A Spatial Theory of News Consumption and Electoral Competition." *Review of Economic Studies* 75 (3): 699–728.

Charness, Gary, Ryan Oprea, and Sevgi Yuksel. 2021. "How Do People Choose between Biased Information Sources? Evidence from a Laboratory Experiment." *Journal of the European Economic Association* 19 (3): 1656–1691.

Chen, Jenn. 2021. "20 Facebook Stats to Guide Your 2021 Facebook Strategy." Sprout Social. February 17. https://sproutsocial.com/insights/facebook-stats-for-marketers/.

Chew, Soo Hong, Wei Huang, and Xiaojian Zhao. 2020. "Motivated False Memory." *Journal of Political Economy* 128 (10): 3913–3939.

Christakis, Nicholas A. 2019. *Blueprint: The Evolutionary Origins of a Good Society*. New York: Little, Brown Spark.

Christensen, Julian, and Donald P. Moynihan. 2020. "Motivated Reasoning and Policy Information: Politicians Are More Resistant to Debiasing Interventions than the General Public." *Behavioural Public Policy*: 1–22.

Chua, Amy. 2018. *Political Tribes: Group Instinct and the Fate of Nations*. London: Penguin Books.

Cikara, Mina, and Jay J. Van Bavel. 2014. "The Neuroscience of Intergroup Relations: An Integrative Review." *Perspectives on Psychological Science* 9 (3): 245–274.

Cinelli, Matteo, Gianmarco De Francisci Morales, Alessandro Galeazzi, Walter Quattrociocchi, and Michele Starnini. 2021. "The Echo Chamber Effect on Social Media." *Proceedings of the National Academy of Sciences* 118 (9).

Clark, Andy. 2015. *Surfing Uncertainty: Prediction, Action, and the Embodied Mind*. Oxford: Oxford University Press.

Clark, Christopher H. 2021. "Civic Education's Relationship to Affective Partisan Divides Later in Life." *Education, Citizenship and Social Justice*.

Clark, Cory. 2021. "How We Empower Political Extremists." *Psychology Today*, January 19.

Clark, Cory J., Brittany S. Liu, Bo M. Winegard, and Peter H. Ditto. 2019. "Tribalism Is Human Nature." *Current Directions in Psychological Science* 28 (6): 587–592.

Cohen, Ben. 2021. "The One Number That Explains the NBA's 3-Point Revolution." *Wall Street Journal*, January 21. https://www.wsj.com/articles/nba-3-point-revolution -11611190418.

Cohen, Taya R., R. Matthew Montoya, and Chester A. Insko. 2006. "Group Morality and Intergroup Relations: Cross-Cultural and Experimental Evidence." *Personality and Social Psychology Bulletin* 32 (11): 1559–1572.

Conklin, Audrey. 2020. "How Facebook, Twitter Policies Have Changed since 2016 in the Name of Voter Integrity." Foxbusiness.com. October 28. https://www.foxbusi ness.com/technology/facebook-twitter-changes-since-2016-election.

Connors, Elizabeth C. 2021. "Partisan Social Pressure and Affective Polarization." Working paper. University of South Carolina.

Cookson, J. Anthony, Joseph Engelberg, and William Mullins. 2021. "Echo Chambers." Working paper. University of California at San Diego and University of Colorado at Boulder.

Curry, Oliver S. 2019. "What's Wrong with Moral Foundations Theory, and How to Get Moral Psychology Right." *Behavioral Scientist*, March 26.

Daks, Jennifer S., and Ronald D. Rogge. 2020. "Examining the Correlates of Psychological Flexibility in Romantic Relationship and Family Dynamics: A Meta-Analysis." *Journal of Contextual Behavioral Science* 18 (October): 214–238.

De Freitas, Julian, Hagop Sarkissian, George E. Newman, Igor Grossmann, Felipe De Brigard, Andres Luco, and Joshua Knobe. 2018. "Consistent Belief in a Good True Self in Misanthropes and Three Interdependent Cultures." *Cognitive Science* 42: 134–160.

Derreumaux, Yrian, Robin Bergh, and Brent L. Hughes. 2021. "Partisan-Motivated Sampling: Re-Examining Politically Motivated Reasoning across the Information Processing Stream." Working paper. University of California, Riverside and Uppsala University.

Dimant, Eugen. 2021. "Hate Trumps Love: The Impact of Political Polarization on Social Preferences." Working paper. University of Pennsylvania.

Ditto, Peter H., Brittany S. Liu, Cory J. Clark, Sean P. Wojcik, Eric E. Chen, Rebecca H. Grady, Jared B. Celniker, and Joanne F. Zinger. 2018. "At Least Bias Is Bipartisan: A Meta-Analytic Comparison of Partisan Bias in Liberals and Conservatives." *Perspectives on Psychological Science* 14 (2): 273–291.

Dorison, Charles A., Julia A. Minson, and Todd Rogers. 2019. "Selective Exposure Partly Relies on Faulty Affective Forecasts." *Cognition* 188 (July): 98–107.

Dorst, Kevin. 2021. "Rational Polarization." Working paper. University of Pittsburgh.

Druckman, James N., Samara Klar, Yanna Krupnikov, Matthew Levendusky, and John Barry Ryan. 2022. "(Mis-)Estimating Affective Polarization." *Journal of Politics* 84 (2): 1106–1117.

Druckman, James N., and Matthew S. Levendusky. 2019. "What Do We Measure When We Measure Affective Polarization?" *Public Opinion Quarterly* 83 (1): 114–122.

Drutman, Lee. 2018. "The Best Way to Fix Gerrymandering Is to Make It Useless." *New York Times*, June 19. https://www.nytimes.com/2018/06/19/opinion/gerrymandering-districts-multimember.html.

Drutman, Lee. 2020. *Breaking the Two-Party Doom Loop: The Case for Multiparty Democracy in America*. Oxford: Oxford University Press.

Dunn, Will. 2021. "Harvard's Top Astronomer Says Our Solar System May Be Teeming with Alien Technology." *New Statesman*, January 22.

Elwood, Zachary. 2021. "Inherent Aspects of social Media That May Be Amplifying Polarization (Short Version)." Zachary Elwood Medium. February 27. https://apokerplayer.medium.com/how-social-media-divides-us-abridged-version-c8fc924ba2a4.

Enders, Adam M. 2021. "Issues vs. Affect: How Do Elite and Mass Polarization Compare?" *Journal of Politics* 83 (4).

Enders, Adam M., and Miles T. Armaly. 2019. "The Differential Effects of Actual and Perceived Polarization." *Political Behavior* 41 (3): 815–839.

Enders, Adam M., and Robert N. Lupton. 2021. "Value Extremity Contributes to Affective Polarization in the US." *Political Science Research and Methods* 9, no. 4 (October): 1–10.

Enke, Benjamin. 2020a. "Moral Values and Voting." *Journal of Political Economy* 128 (10): 3679–3729.

Enke, Benjamin. 2020b. "What You See Is All There Is (WYSIATI)." *Quarterly Journal of Economics* 135, no. 3 (August): 1363–1398.

Enke, Benjamin, and Florian Zimmermann. 2019. "Correlation Neglect in Belief Formation." *Review of Economic Studies* 86, no. 1 (January): 313–332.

Everett, Burgess, and Marianne Levine. 2020. "The Senate's Record-Breaking Gridlock under Trump." *Politico*, June 8.

Everett, Jim Albert Charlton, Cory J. Clark, Peter Meindl, Jamie B. Luguri, Brian D. Earp, Jesse Graham, Peter H. Ditto, and Azim F. Shariff. 2021. "Political Differences in Free Will Belief Are Associated with Differences in Moralization." *Journal of Personality and Social Psychology* 120 (2): 461–483.

Fehr, Ernst, and Simon Gächter. 2000. "Fairness and Retaliation: The Economics of Reciprocity." *Journal of Economic Perspectives* 14 (3): 159–181.

Fernbach, Philip M., and Leaf Van Boven. 2021. "False Polarization: Cognitive Mechanisms and Potential Solutions." *Current Opinion in Psychology* 43: 1–6.

Finkel, Eli J., Christopher A. Bail, Mina Cikara, Peter H. Ditto, Shanto Iyengar, Samara Klar, Lilliana Mason et al. 2020. "Political Sectarianism in America." *Science* 370 (6516): 533–536.

Fischer, Agneta, Eran Halperin, Daphna Canetti, and Alba Jasini. 2018. "Why We Hate." *Emotion Review* 10 (4): 309–320.

Fisher, Matthew, and Frank C. Keil. 2018. "The Binary Bias: A Systematic Distortion in the Integration of Information." *Psychological Science* 29 (1): 1846–1858.

Fishkin, James, Alice Siu, Larry Diamond, and Norman Bradburn. 2021. "Is Deliberation an Antidote to Extreme Partisan Polarization? Reflections on America in One Room." *Cambridge University Press* 115 (4).

Fisk, Colin A. 2021. "How Electoral Environments Shape Behavior: The Dynamics of Ideology and Party Identification." Dissertation. Indiana University, May.

Fletcher, Garth J. O. 2008. *The New Science of Intimate Relationships*. New York: Wiley-Blackwell.

Fletcher, Garth J. O., and Patrick S. G. Kerr. 2010. "Through the Eyes of Love: Reality and Illusion in Intimate Relationships." *Psychological Bulletin* 136 (4): 627.

Frank, Robert H. 2020. *Under the Influence*. Princeton, NJ: Princeton University Press.

French, David. 2020. *Divided We Fall: America's Secession Threat and How to Restore Our Nation*. New York: St. Martin's Press.

Fudenberg, Drew, and David K. Levine. 2016. "Whither Game Theory? Towards a Theory of Learning in Games." *Journal of Economic Perspectives* 30 (4): 151–170.

Fudenberg, Drew, David G. Rand, and Anna Dreber. 2012. "Slow to Anger and Fast to Forgive: Cooperation in an Uncertain World." *American Economic Review* 102 (2): 720–749.

Galef, Julia. 2021. *The Scout Mindset: Why Some People See Things Clearly and Others Don't*. London: Penguin Books.

Garrett, Kelly R., Jacob A. Long, and Min Seon Jeong. 2019. "From Partisan Media to Misperception: Affective Polarization as Mediator." *Journal of Communication* 69, no. 5 (October): 490–512.

Garrett, Kristin N., and Alexa Bankert. 2020. "The Moral Roots of Partisan Division: How Moral Conviction Heightens Affective Polarization." *British Journal of Political Science* 50 (2): 621–640.

Garz, Marcel, Gaurav Sood, Daniel F. Stone, and Justin Wallace. 2020a. "The Supply of Media Slant Across Outlets and Demand for Slant Within Outlets: Evidence from US Presidential Campaign News." *European Journal of Political Economy* 63: 101877.

Garz, Marcel, Jil Sörensen, and Daniel F. Stone. 2020b. "Partisan Selective Engagement: Evidence from Facebook." *Journal of Economic Behavior & Organization* 177: 91–108.

Gaukroger, Stephen. 2012. *Objectivity: A Very Short Introduction*, vol. 316. Oxford: Oxford University Press.

Gehl, Katherine M., and Michael E. Porter. 2020. *The Politics Industry: How Political Innovation Can Break Partisan Gridlock and Save Our Democracy*. Cambridge, MA: Harvard Business Review Press.

Gentzkow, Matthew, and Jesse M. Shapiro. 2010. "What Drives Media Slant? Evidence from US Daily Newspapers." *Econometrica* 78 (2010): 35–71.

Gentzkow, Matthew, and Jesse M. Shapiro. 2011. "Ideological Segregation Online and Offline." *Quarterly Journal of Economics* 126 (4): 1799–1839.

Gentzkow, Matthew, Jesse M. Shapiro, and Daniel F. Stone. 2015. "Media Bias in the Marketplace: Theory." In *Handbook of Media Economics*, vol. 1, edited by Simon P. Anderson, Joel Waldfogel, and David Stromberg, 623–645. Amsterdam: North-Holland.

Gentzkow, Matthew, Michael B. Wong, and Allen T. Zhang. 2020. "Ideological Bias and Trust in Information Sources." Working paper. Harvard University.

Gilovich, Thomas. 1991. *How We Know What Isn't So: The Fallibility of Human Reason in Everyday Life*. New York: Free Press.

Golman, Russell, George Loewenstein, Karl Ove Moene, and Luca Zarri. 2016. "The Preference for Belief Consonance." *Journal of Economic Perspectives* 30 (3): 165–188.

Goodwin, Geoffrey P., Jared Piazza, and Paul Rozin. 2014. "Moral Character Predominates in Person Perception and Evaluation." *Journal of Personality and Social Psychology* 106 (1): 148–168.

Gottman, John M., James Coan, Sybil Carrere, and Catherine Swanson. 1998. "Predicting Marital Happiness and Stability from Newlywed Interactions." *Journal of Marriage and the Family* 60, no. 1 (February): 5–22.

Gould, Jonathan, Kenneth Shepsle, and Matthew Stephenson. 2021. "Opinion: Don't Eliminate the Filibuster. Democratize It." *Washington Post*, April 6. https://www.washingtonpost.com/opinions/2021/04/06/dont-eliminate-filibuster-democratize-it/.

Graham, Matthew H., and Milan W. Svolik. 2020. "Democracy in America? Partisanship, Polarization, and the Robustness of Support for Democracy in the United States." *American Political Science Review* 114 (2): 392–409.

Grant, Adam. 2021. *Think Again: The Power of Knowing What You Don't Know*. New York: Viking.

Green, Jon, Stefan McCabe, Sarah Shugars, John Harrington, Hanyu Chwe, Luke Horgan, Shuyang Cao, and David Lazer. 2021. "Curation Bubbles: Domain versus URL Level Analysis of Partisan News Sharing on Social Media." Working paper. 2021 meeting of the American Political Science Association.

Greene, Joshua D. 2013. *Moral Tribes: Emotion, Reason, and the Gap between Us and Them*. London: Penguin Books.

Grubb, Michael D. 2015. "Overconfident Consumers in the Marketplace." *Journal of Economic Perspectives* 29 (4): 9–36.

Guay, Brian, and Christopher D. Johnston. 2021. "Ideological Asymmetries and the Determinants of Politically Motivated Reasoning." *American Journal of Political Science*.

Guess, Andrew M. 2021. "(Almost) Everything in Moderation: New Evidence on Americans' Online Media Diets." *American Journal of Political Science* 65, no. 4 (October): 1007–1022.

Guess, Andrew, Jonathan Nagler, and Joshua Tucker. 2019. "Less Than You Think: Prevalence and Predictors of Fake News Dissemination on Facebook." *Science Advances* 5, no. 1 (January): eaau4586.

Guess, Andrew, Brendan Nyhan, Benjamin Lyons, and Jason Reifler. 2018. "Avoiding the Echo Chamber About Echo Chambers: Why Selective Exposure to Like-Minded Political News Is Less Prevalent than You Think." Knight Foundation. https://kf-site-production.s3.amazonaws.com/media_elements/files/000/000/133/original/Topos_KF_White-Paper_Nyhan_V1.pdf.

Gulzar, Saad. 2021. "Who Enters Politics and Why?" *Annual Review of Political Science* 24: 253–275.

Guzmán, Mónica. 2022. *I Never Thought of It That Way: How to Have Fearlessly Curious Conversations in Dangerously Divided Times.* London: Penguin Books.

Haidt, Jonathan. 2007. "The New Synthesis in Moral Psychology." *Science* 316 (5827): 998–1002.

Haidt, Jonathan. 2012. *The Righteous Mind: Why Good People Are Divided by Politics and Religion.* New York: Vintage.

Halberstam, Yosh, and Brian Knight. 2016. "Homophily, Group Size, and the Diffusion of Political Information in Social Networks: Evidence from Twitter." *Journal of Public Economics* 143: 73–88.

Hall, Andrew B. 2019. *Who Wants to Run? How the Devaluing of Political Office Drives Polarization.* Chicago: University of Chicago Press.

Haran, Uriel, Don A. Moore, and Carey K. Morewedge. 2010. "A Simple Remedy for Overprecision in Judgment." *Judgment and Decision Making* 5, no. 7 (December): 467–476.

Harris, Elizabeth Ann, Philip Pärnamets, Anni Sternisko, Claire Robertson, and Jay J. Van Bavel. 2022. "The Psychology and Neuroscience of Partisanship." In *The Cambridge Handbook of Political Psychology*, edited by Danny Osborne and Chris G. Sibley, 50–67. Cambridge, UK: Cambridge University Press.

Hart, William, Dolores Albarracín, Alice H. Eagly, Inge Brechan, Matthew J. Lindberg, and Lisa Merrill. 2009. "Feeling Validated versus Being Correct: A Meta-Analysis of Selective Exposure to Information." *Psychological Bulletin* 135 (4): 555–588.

Hartman, Rachel, Jay William Blakey, Jake Womick, Christopher A. Bail, Eli Finkel, Juliana Schroeder, Paschal Sheeran, Jay J. Van Bavel, Robb Willer, and Kurt Gray.

2022. "Interventions to Reduce Partisan Animosity." Working paper. University of North Carolina at Chapel Hill.

Hasen, Richard. 2022. "How to Keep the Rising Tide of Fake News from Drowning Our Democracy." *New York Times*, March 7. https://www.nytimes.com/2022/03/07/opinion/cheap-speech-fake-news-democracy.html.

Hastie, Reid, and Cass R. Sunstein. 2015. "Polarization: One Reason Groups Fail." *Chicago Booth Review*, July 21. https://www.chicagobooth.edu/review/one-reason-groups-fail-polarization.

Hatemi, Peter K., Charles Crabtree, and Kevin B. Smith. 2019. "Ideology Justifies Morality: Political Beliefs Predict Moral Foundations." *American Journal of Political Science* 63 (4): 788–806.

Heltzel, Gordon, and Kristin Laurin. 2021. "Seek and Ye Shall Be Fine: Attitudes towards Political Perspective-Seekers." *Psychological Science* 32 (11): 1782–1800.

Hernández-Lagos, Pablo, and Dylan Minor. 2020. "Political Identity and Trust." *Quarterly Journal of Political Science* 15 (3): 337–367.

Herndon, Keith. 2012. *The Decline of the Daily Newspaper: How an American Institution Lost the Online Revolution*. New York: Peter Lang.

Hetherington, Marc, and Jonathan Weiler. 2018. *Prius or Pickup? How the Answers to Four Simple Questions Explain America's Great Divide*. Boston: Houghton Mifflin.

Hewstone, Miles. 1990. "The 'Ultimate Attribution Error'? A Review of the Literature on Intergroup Causal Attribution." *European Journal of Social Psychology* 20 (4): 311–335.

Hibbing, John R., and John R. Alford. 2004. "Accepting Authoritative Decisions: Humans as Wary Cooperators." *American Journal of Political Science* 48 (1): 62–76.

Hinnekens, Céline, Alan Sillars, Lesley L. Verhofstadt, and William Ickes. 2020. "Empathic Accuracy and Cognitions during Conflict: An In-Depth Analysis of Understanding Scores." *Personal Relationships* 27 (1): 102–131.

Hirano, Shigeo, and James M. Snyder Jr. 2020. "Measuring the Partisan Behavior of US Newspapers, 1880 to 1980." Working paper. Harvard University and National Bureau of Economic Research.

Ho, Benjamin. 2021. *Why Trust Matters: An Economist's Guide to the Ties That Bind Us*. New York: Columbia University Press.

Ho, Emily H., David Hagmann, and George Loewenstein. 2020. "Measuring Information Preferences." *Management Science* 67 (1): 126–145.

Hocker, Joyce L., and William W. Wilmot. 2014. *Interpersonal Conflict*. New York: McGraw-Hill.

Hoffman, Moshe, and Erez Yoeli. 2022. *Hidden Games: The Surprising Power of Game Theory to Explain Irrational Human Behavior.* New York: Basic Books.

Horstmann, Ignatius J., James R. Markusen, and Jack Robles. 2005. "Issue Linking in Trade Negotiations: Ricardo Revisited or No Pain No Gain." *Review of International Economics* 13, no. 2 (April): 185–204.

Horwitz, Jeff, and Deepa Seetharaman. 2020. "Facebook Executives Shut Down Efforts to Make the Site Less Divisive." *Wall Street Journal,* May 26. https://www.wsj.com/articles/facebook-knows-it-encourages-division-top-executives-nixed-solutions-11590507499.

Huber, Gregory A., and Neil Malhotra. 2017. "Political Homophily in Social Relationships: Evidence from Online Dating Behavior." *Journal of Politics* 79 (1): 269–283.

Iandoli, Luca, Simonetta Primario, and Giuseppe Zollo. 2021. "The Impact of Group Polarization on the Quality of Online Debate in Social Media: A Systematic Literature Review." *Technological Forecasting and Social Change* 170 (September): 120924.

Islam, Marco. 2021. "Motivated Risk Assessments." Working paper. Lund University.

Isler, Ozan, Onurcan Yilmaz, and Burak Doğruyol. 2021. "Are We at All Liberal at Heart? High-Powered Tests Find No Effect of Intuitive Thinking on Moral Foundations." *Journal of Experimental Social Psychology* 92 (January): 104050.

Iyengar, Shanto, Tobias Konitzer, and Kent Tedin. 2018. "The Home as a Political Fortress: Family Agreement in an Era of Polarization." *Journal of Politics* 80 (4): 1326–1338.

Iyengar, Shanto, Yphtach Lelkes, Matthew Levendusky, Neil Malhotra, and Sean J. Westwood. 2019. "The Origins and Consequences of Affective Polarization in the United States." *Annual Review of Political Science* 22: 129–146.

Jeong, Ho-Won. 2008. *Understanding Conflict and Conflict Analysis.* Los Angeles: Sage Publications.

Jervis, Robert. 2017. *Perception and Misperception in International Politics.* Princeton, NJ: Princeton University Press.

Jin, Ginger Zhe, Michael Luca, and Daniel Martin. 2021. "Is No News (Perceived as) Bad News? An Experimental Investigation of Information Disclosure." *American Economic Journal: Microeconomics* 13 (2): 141–173.

Jones, Edward E. 1990. *Interpersonal Perception.* New York: Freeman.

Kahan, Dan M., Donald Braman, John Gastil, Paul Slovic, and C. K. Mertz. 2007. "Culture and Identity-Protective Cognition: Explaining the White-Male Effect in Risk Perception." *Journal of Empirical Legal Studies* 4 (3): 465–505.

Kahneman, Daniel. 2011. *Thinking, Fast and Slow.* New York: Macmillan.

Kahneman, Daniel, Olivier Sibony, and Cass R. Sunstein. 2021. *Noise: A Flaw in Human Judgment*. New York: Little, Brown Spark.

Kalla, Joshua L., and David Broockman. 2021. "Voter Outreach Campaigns Can Reduce Affective Polarization among Implementing Political Activists." OSF Preprints. doi:10.31219/osf.io/5yahr.

Kalman, Laura. 1992. *Abe Fortas: A Biography*. New Haven: Yale University Press.

Kalmoe, Nathan P., and Lilliana Mason. 2019. "Lethal Mass Partisanship: Prevalence, Correlates, and Electoral Contingencies." Working paper. National Capital Area Political Science Association American Politics Meeting.

Kardes, Frank R., Steven S. Posavac, David Silvera, Maria L. Cronley, David M. Sanbonmatsu, Susan Schertzer, Felicia Miller, Paul M. Herr, and Murali Chandrashekaran. 2006. "Debiasing Omission Neglect." *Journal of Business Research* 59 (6): 786–792.

Kelly, Dimitri. 2019. "Evaluating the News: (Mis)Perceptions of Objectivity and Credibility." *Political Behavior* 41 (2): 445–471.

Kennedy, Kathleen A., and Emily Pronin. 2008. "When Disagreement Gets Ugly: Perceptions of Bias and the Escalation of Conflict." *Personality and Social Psychology Bulletin* 34 (6): 833–848.

Kenny, David A. 1994. *Interpersonal Perception: A Social Relations Analysis*. New York: Guilford Press.

Keysar, Boaz, Benjamin A. Converse, Jiunwen Wang, and Nicholas Epley. 2008. "Reciprocity Is Not Give and Take: Asymmetric Reciprocity to Positive and Negative Acts." *Psychological Science* 19 (12): 1280–1286.

Kim, Hyunjung. 2021. "The Mere Exposure Effect of Tweets on Vote Choice." *Journal of Information Technology & Politics* 18 (4): 455–465.

Kim, Jin W., Andrew Guess, Brendan Nyhan, and Jason Reifler. 2021. "The Distorting Prism of Social Media: How Self-Selection and Exposure to Incivility Fuel Online Comment Toxicity." *Journal of Communication* 71 (6): 922–946.

Kim, Jin Woo, and Eunji Kim. 2021. "Temporal Selective Exposure: How Partisans Choose When to Follow Politics." *Political Behavior* 43: 1663–1683.

Kingzette, Jon. 2021. "In-Party Love, Out-Party Hate, and the Ideological Roots of Partisan Animosity in the United States." Dissertation. The Ohio State University.

Kitchens, Brent, Steven L. Johnson, and Peter Gray. 2020. "Understanding Echo Chambers and Filter Bubbles: The Impact of Social Media on Diversification and Partisan Shifts in News Consumption." *MIS Quarterly* 44, no. 4 (December): 1619–1649.

Kivikangas, J. Matias, Belén Fernández-Castilla, Simo Järvelä, Niklas Ravaja, and Jan-Erik Lönnqvist. 2021. "Moral Foundations and Political Orientation: Systematic Review and Meta-Analysis." *Psychological Bulletin* 147 (1): 55–94.

Klein, Ezra. 2020a. *Why We're Polarized*. New York: Simon and Schuster.

Klein, Ezra (@ezraklein). 2020b. "I Cannot Emphasize Enough How Much McConnell's Actions on Garland and Barrett Have Radicalized Democratic Senators." Twitter, October 26. https://twitter.com/ezraklein/status/1320786555737239553.

Kollock, Peter. 1993. "'An Eye for an Eye Leaves Everyone Blind': Cooperation and Accounting Systems." *American Sociological Review* 58, no. 6 (December): 768–786.

Kramer, Roderick M. 1994. "The Sinister Attribution Error: Paranoid Cognition and Collective Distrust in Organizations." *Motivation and Emotion* 18 (2): 199–230.

Kristal, Ariella S., and Laurie R. Santos. 2021. "G.I. Joe Phenomena: Understanding the Limits of Metacognitive Awareness on Debiasing." Working paper no. 21-084. Harvard Business School.

Kronen, Samuel. 2020. "The Prescience of Shelby Steele." *Quillette*. October 8.

Krueger, Joachim, and Russell W. Clement. 1994. "The Truly False Consensus Effect: An Ineradicable and Egocentric Bias in Social Perception." *Journal of Personality and Social Psychology* 67 (4): 596–610.

Krumrei-Mancuso, Elizabeth J., and Brian Newman. 2020. "Intellectual Humility in the Sociopolitical Domain." *Self and Identity* 19 (8): 989–1016.

Lacassagne, Doris, Jérémy Béna, and Olivier Corneille. 2022. "Is Earth a Perfect Square? Repetition Increases the Perceived Truth of Highly Implausible Statements." *Cognition* 223.

Ladd, Jonathan M. 2011. *Why Americans Hate the Media and How It Matters*. Princeton, NJ: Princeton University Press.

Lees, Jeffrey, and Mina Cikara. 2020. "Inaccurate Group Meta-Perceptions Drive Negative Out-Group Attributions in Competitive Contexts." *Nature Human Behaviour* 4 (3): 279–286.

Lelkes, Yphtach, Gaurav Sood, and Shanto Iyengar. 2017. "The Hostile Audience: The Effect of Access to Broadband Internet on Partisan Affect." *American Journal of Political Science* 61 (1): 5–20.

Lemieux, Scott. 2020. "Five if (*sic*) Them Got Up-or-Down Votes, Four Were Confirmed, and One Was Rejected by an Overwhelming Bipartisan Majority—What 'Actions'?" Twitter, October 26. https://twitter.com/LemieuxLGM/status/1320831 784062316544.

Lenz, Gabriel, Alia Braley, Dhaval Adjodah, Hossein Rahnama, and Alex Pentland. 2021. "The Subversion Dilemma: Why Voters Who Cherish Democracy Vote It Away." Working paper. University of California, Berkeley, and MIT.

Leslie, Ian. 2021. *Conflicted: Why Arguments Are Tearing Us Apart and How They Can Bring Us Together*. London: Faber and Faber.

Levendusky, Matthew. 2009. *The Partisan Sort: How Liberals Became Democrats and Conservatives Became Republicans*. Chicago: University of Chicago Press.

Levendusky, Matthew. 2013. *How Partisan Media Polarize America*. Chicago: University of Chicago Press.

Levendusky, Matthew, and Dominik Stecula. 2021. *We Need to Talk: How Cross-Party Dialogue Reduces Affective Polarization*. Cambridge, UK: Cambridge University Press.

Levendusky, Matthew S., and Neil Malhotra. 2016. "(Mis)Perceptions of Partisan Polarization in the American Public." *Public Opinion Quarterly* 80 (S1): 378–391.

Levy, Ro'ee. 2021. "Social Media, News Consumption, and Polarization: Evidence from a Field Experiment." *American Economic Review* 111 (3): 831–870.

Lewis, Michael. 2016. *The Undoing Project: A Friendship That Changed the World*. London: Penguin Books.

Lieberman, Matthew D. 2022. "Seeing Minds, Matter, and Meaning: The CEEing Model of Pre-reflective Subjective Construal." *Psychological Review*.

Lizzeri, Alessandro, and Marciano Siniscalchi. 2008. "Parental Guidance and Supervised Learning." *Quarterly Journal of Economics* 123, no. 3 (August): 1161–1195.

Locker, Melissa. 2020. "'Green Needle' or 'Brainstorm'? A Puzzling Audio Clip Is Burning Up the Internet." *Time*, July 30.

López-Pérez, Raúl, Antonio Rodriguez-Moral, and Marc Vorsatz. 2021. "Simplified Mental Representations as a Cause of Overprecision." *Journal of Behavioral and Experimental Economics* 92 (June): 101681.

Lowney, Declan, dir. 2020. *Ted Lasso*. Season 1, episode 8, "The Diamond Dogs." Aired September 18, on Apple TV+. https://tv.apple.com/us/episode/the-diamond-dogs /umc.cmc.eaaizh8wdtnjuohaebw843ft?showId=umc.cmc.vtoh0mn0xn7t3c643 xqonfzy.

Lusinski, Natalia. 2018. "9 Differences Between Accepting Your Partner and Tolerating Them." *Bustle*, August 9.

Lyons, Benjamin A., Jacob M. Montgomery, Andrew M. Guess, Brendan Nyhan, and Jason Reifler. 2021. "Overconfidence in News Judgments Is Associated with False News Susceptibility." *Proceedings of the National Academy of Sciences* 118, no. 23 (April).

Maggi, Giovanni. 2016. "Issue Linkage." In *Handbook of Commercial Policy*, vol. 1, edited by Kyle Bagwell and Robert Staiger, 513–564. Amsterdam: Elsevier.

Martherus, James L., Andres G. Martinez, Paul K. Piff, and Alexander G. Theodoridis. 2019. "Party Animals? Extreme Partisan Polarization and Dehumanization." *Political Behavior* 43: 517–540.

Martin, Gregory, and Ali Yurukoglu. 2017. "Bias in Cable News: Persuasion and Polarization." *American Economic Review* 107 (9): 2565–2599.

Marwick, Alice, and Rebecca Lewis. 2017. *Media Manipulation and Disinformation Online*. New York: Data and Society Research Institute.

Mason, Lilliana. 2018. *Uncivil Agreement: How Politics Became Our Identity*. Chicago: University of Chicago Press.

Mauersberger, Felix, and Rosemarie Nagel. 2018. "Levels of Reasoning in Keynesian Beauty Contests: A Generative Framework." In *Handbook of Computational Economics*, vol. 4, edited by Cars Hommes and Blake LeBaron, 541–634. Amsterdam: Elsevier.

McCartney, W. Ben, John Orellana, and Calvin Zhang. 2021. "Sort Selling: Political Polarization and Residential Choice." Working paper. Federal Reserve Bank of Philadelphia.

McGregor, Shannon C. 2019. "Social Media as Public Opinion: How Journalists Use Social Media to Represent Public Opinion." *Journalism* 20 (8): 1070–1086.

McHugh, Cillian, Marek McGann, Eric R. Igou, and Elaine L. Kinsella. 2021. "Moral Judgment as Categorization (MJAC)." *Perspectives on Psychological Science* 17 (1).

Meier, Brian P., and Verlin B. Hinsz. 2004. "A Comparison of Human Aggression Committed by Groups and Individuals: An Interindividual–Intergroup Discontinuity." *Journal of Experimental Social Psychology* 40 (4): 551–559.

Menchaca, Marcos. 2021. "Are Americans Polarized on Issue Dimensions?" *Journal of Elections, Public Opinion and Parties* (April): 1–19.

Mercier, Hugo. 2020. *Not Born Yesterday: The Science of Who We Trust and What We Believe*. Princeton, NJ: Princeton University Press.

Mercier, Hugo, and Dan Sperber. 2017. *The Enigma of Reason*. Cambridge, MA: Harvard University Press.

Mernyk, Joseph S., Sophia L. Pink, James N. Druckman, and Robb Willer. 2021. "Correcting Inaccurate Metaperceptions Reduces Americans' Support for Partisan Violence." Working paper. Stanford University and Northwestern University.

Molander, Per. 1985. "The Optimal Level of Generosity in a Selfish, Uncertain Environment." *Journal of Conflict Resolution* 29, no. 4 (December): 611–618.

Molleman, Lucas, Andrea Gradassi, Mubashir Sultan, and Wouter van den Bos. 2021. "Partisan Biases in Social Information Use." Working paper. University of Amsterdam.

Molnar, Andras, and George Loewenstein. 2021. "Thoughts and Players: An Introduction to Old and New Economic Perspectives on Beliefs." Working paper. Carnegie Mellon University and University of Chicago.

Montoya, R. Matthew, Robert S. Horton, and Jeffrey Kirchner. 2008. "Is Actual Similarity Necessary for Attraction? A Meta-Analysis of Actual and Perceived Similarity." *Journal of Social and Personal Relationships* 25 (6): 889–922.

Moore, Don A. 2020. *Perfectly Confident: How to Calibrate Your Decisions Wisely.* New York: Harper Business.

Moore-Berg, Samantha L., Lee-Or Ankori-Karlinsky, Boaz Hameiri, and Emile Bruneau. 2020a. "Exaggerated Meta-Perceptions Predict Intergroup Hostility between American Political Partisans." *Proceedings of the National Academy of Sciences* 117 (26): 14864–14872.

Moore-Berg, Samantha L., Boaz Hameiri, and Emile Bruneau. 2020b. "The Prime Psychological Suspects of Toxic Political Polarization." *Current Opinion in Behavioral Sciences* 34: 199–204.

Morewedge, Carey K. 2019. "How to Stop Cognitive Bias from Affecting Our Decisions." *Hill*, October 29. https://thehill.com/opinion/finance/467892-how-to-stop -cognitive-bias-from-affecting-our-decisions/.

Mosleh, Mohsen, Cameron Martel, Dean Eckles, and David G. Rand. 2021. "Shared Partisanship Dramatically Increases Social Tie Formation in a Twitter Field Experiment." *Proceedings of the National Academy of Sciences* 118 (7).

Mousa, Salma. 2020. "Building Social Cohesion between Christians and Muslims through Soccer in Post-ISIS Iraq." *Science* 369 (6505): 866–870.

Mullen, Brian, Jennifer L. Atkins, Debbie S. Champion, Cecelia Edwards, Dana Hardy, John E. Story, and Mary Vanderklok. 1985. "The False Consensus Effect: A Meta-Analysis of 115 Hypothesis Tests." *Journal of Experimental Social Psychology* 21, no. 3 (May): 262–283.

Napoli, Philip M. 2019. *Social Media and the Public Interest.* New York: Columbia University Press.

Nasby, William, Brian Hayden, and Bella M. DePaulo. 1980. "Attributional Bias among Aggressive Boys to Interpret Unambiguous Social Stimuli as Displays of Hostility." *Journal of Abnormal Psychology* 89 (3): 459.

Nickerson, Raymond S. 1998. "Confirmation Bias: A Ubiquitous Phenomenon in Many Guises." *Review of General Psychology* 2 (2): 175–220.

Nocera, Joe. 2011. "The Ugliness Started with Bork." *New York Times*, October 21. https://www.nytimes.com/2011/10/22/opinion/nocera-the-ugliness-all-started -with-bork.html.

Nyhan, Brendan. 2021. "Why the Backfire Effect Does Not Explain the Durability of Political Misperceptions." *Proceedings of the National Academy of Sciences* 118 (15).

Oprea, Ryan, and Sevgi Yuksel. 2022. "Social Exchange of Motivated Beliefs." *Journal of the European Economic Association* 20 (2): 667–699.

Orhan, Yunus E. "The Relationship between Affective Polarization and Democratic Backsliding: Comparative Evidence." *Democratization* (forthcoming).

Ornstein, Norm. 2014. "Why the Supreme Court Needs Term Limits." *Atlantic*, May 22.

Orr, Lilla V., and Gregory A. Huber. 2020. "The Policy Basis of Measured Partisan Animosity in the United States." *American Journal of Political Science* 64 (3): 569–586.

Ortoleva, Pietro, and Erik Snowberg. 2015. "Overconfidence in Political Behavior." *American Economic Review* 105 (2): 504–535.

Osman, Magda. 2020. "Backfiring, Reactance, Boomerang, Spillovers, and Rebound Effects: Can We Learn Anything from Examples Where Nudges Do the Opposite of What They Intended?" Working paper. University of Cambridge.

Osmundsen, Mathias, Alexander Bor, Peter Bjerregaard Vahlstrup, Anja Bechmann, and Michael Bang Petersen. 2021. "Partisan Polarization Is the Primary Psychological Motivation behind Political Fake News Sharing on Twitter." *American Political Science Review* 115 (3): 999–1015.

Pallavicini, Josefine, Bjørn Hallsson, and Klemens Kappel. 2021. "Polarization in Groups of Bayesian Agents." *Synthese* 198 (1): 1–55.

Paluck, Elizabeth Levy, Seth A. Green, and Donald P. Green. 2019. "The Contact Hypothesis Re-evaluated." *Behavioural Public Policy* 3 (2): 129–158.

Pantazi, Myrto, Scott Hale, and Olivier Klein. 2021. "Social and Cognitive Aspects of the Vulnerability to Political Misinformation." *Political Psychology* 42, no. 51 (December): 267–304.

Parker, Victoria, Matthew Feinberg, Alexa Tullett, and Anne E. Wilson. 2021. "The Ties That Blind: Misperceptions of the Opponent Fringe and the Miscalibration of Political Contempt." Working paper. Wilfrid Laurier University, University of Toronto, and University of Alabama.

Parrish, Shane, and Daniel Kahneman. 2019. "#68 Daniel Kahneman: Putting Your Intuition on Ice." *The Knowledge Project*. Podcast, MP3 audio, 1:06:41. https://fs.blog /knowledge-project-podcast/daniel-kahneman/.

Pennycook, Gordon, and David G. Rand. 2019a. "Fighting Misinformation on Social Media Using Crowdsourced Judgments of News Source Quality." *Proceedings of the National Academy of Sciences* 116 (7): 2521–2526.

Pennycook, Gordon, and David G. Rand. 2019b. "Lazy, Not Biased: Susceptibility to Partisan Fake News Is Better Explained by Lack of Reasoning than by Motivated Reasoning." *Cognition* 188: 39–50.

Pennycook, Gordon, and David G. Rand. 2021. "The Psychology of Fake News." *Trends in Cognitive Sciences* 24, no. 5 (May): 388–402.

Perlez, Jane. 1982. "Rep. Chisholm's Angry Farewell." *New York Times*, October 12. https://www.nytimes.com/1982/10/12/us/rep-chisholm-s-angry-farewell.html.

Perloff, Richard M. 2015. "A Three-Decade Retrospective on the Hostile Media Effect." *Mass Communication and Society* 18 (6): 701–729.

Petersen, Michael Bang, Mathias Osmundsen, and John Tooby. 2020. "The Evolutionary Psychology of Conflict and the Functions of Falsehood." Working paper. Aarhus University and University of California, Santa Barbara.

Peterson, Erik, Sharad Goel, and Shanto Iyengar. 2021. "Partisan Selective Exposure in Online News Consumption: Evidence from the 2016 Presidential Campaign." *Political Science Research and Methods* 9 (2): 242–258.

Peterson, Erik, and Ali Kagalwala. 2021. "When Unfamiliarity Breeds Contempt: How Partisan Selective Exposure Sustains Oppositional Media Hostility." *American Political Science Review* 115 (2): 585–598.

Pettigrew, Thomas F., and Linda R. Tropp. 2006. "A Meta-Analytic Test of Intergroup Contact Theory." *Journal of Personality and Social Psychology* 90 (5): 751–783.

Pew Research Center. 2019. "How Partisans View Each Other." October 10. https://www.pewresearch.org/politics/2019/10/10/how-partisans-view-each-other/.

Pew Research Center. 2020. "Democratic Edge in Party Identification Narrows Slightly." June 2. https://www.pewresearch.org/politics/2020/06/02/democratic-edge-in-party-identification-narrows-slightly/.

Phoenix, Davin L. 2019. *The Anger Gap: How Race Shapes Emotion in Politics*. Cambridge, UK: Cambridge University Press.

Porath, Christine L., and Alexandra Gerbasi. 2015. "Does Civility Pay?" *Organizational Dynamics* 44 (4): 281–286.

Porter, Ethan, and Thomas J. Wood. 2019. *False Alarm: The Truth About Political Mistruths in the Trump Era*. Cambridge, UK: Cambridge University Press.

Puryear, Curtis, Emily Kubin, Chelsea Schein, Yochanan Bigman, and Kurt Gray. 2022. "Bridging Political Divides by Correcting the Basic Morality Bias." Working paper. University of North Carolina, Chapel Hill, University of Koblenz-Landauc, The Wharton School of Business, University of Pennsylvania, and Yale University. https://psyarxiv.com/fk8g6/.

Rathje, Steve, Jay J. Van Bavel, and Sander van der Linden. 2021. "Out-Group Animosity Drives Engagement on Social Media." *Proceedings of the National Academy of Sciences* 118 (26).

Reeder, Glenn D., John B. Pryor, Michael J. A. Wohl, and Michael L. Griswell. 2005. "On Attributing Negative Motives to Others Who Disagree with Our Opinions." *Personality and Social Psychology Bulletin* 31 (11): 1498–1510.

Resnick, Brian. 2019. "Intellectual Humility: The Importance of Knowing You Might Be Wrong." *Vox.* January 4. https://www.vox.com/science-and-health/2019/1/4/179 89224/intellectual-humility-explained-psychology-replication.

Ripley, Amanda. 2021a. *High Conflict.* New York: Simon and Schuster.

Ripley, Amanda. 2021b. "My Field Trip to Congress." *Unraveled* (blog). https://aman daripley.substack.com/p/my-field-trip-to-congress?s=r.

Robbett, Andrea, and Peter Hans Matthews. 2021. "Polarization and Group Cooperation." Working paper. Middlebury College.

Robinson, Robert J., Dacher Keltner, Andrew Ward, and Lee Ross. 1995. "Actual versus Assumed Differences in Construal: 'Naïve Realism' in Intergroup Perception and Conflict." *Journal of Personality and Social Psychology* 68 (3): 404.

Rodriguez, Cristian G., Jake P. Moskowitz, Rammy M. Salem, and Peter H. Ditto. 2017. "Partisan Selective Exposure: The Role of Party, Ideology and Ideological Extremity over Time." *Translational Issues in Psychological Science* 3 (3): 254–271.

Roghanizad, M. Mahdi, and Vanessa K. Bohns. 2017. "Ask in Person: You're Less Persuasive than You Think over Email." *Journal of Experimental Social Psychology* 69: 223–226.

Roozenbeek, Jon, Rakoen Maertens, Stefan M. Herzog, Michael Geers, Ralf H. J. M. Kurvers, Mubashir Sultan, and Sander van der Linden. 2022. "Susceptibility to Misinformation Is Consistent across Question Framings and Response Modes and Better Explained by Myside Bias and Partisanship than Analytical Thinking." *Judgment and Decision Making.*

Rosenquist, Niels. 2019. "How Tit-for-Tat Game Theory Hacked Politics." The Bulwark. June 10. https://www.thebulwark.com/how-tit-for-tat-game-theory-has-hacked -politics/.

Ross, Lee. 2018. "From the Fundamental Attribution Error to the Truly Fundamental Attribution Error and Beyond: My Research Journey." *Perspectives on Psychological Science* 13 (6): 750–769.

Ross, Lee, and Richard E. Nisbett. 1991. *The Person and the Situation: Perspectives of Social Psychology*. New York: McGraw-Hill.

Rossiter, Erin. 2020. "The Consequences of Interparty Conversation on Outparty Affect and Stereotypes." Working paper. Washington University in St. Louis.

Rowley, Chris, and Nagiah Ramasamy. 2016. "Horns Effect." In *Encyclopedia of Human Resource Management*, edited by Adrian Wilkinson and Stewart Johnstone, 182. Cheltenham, UK: Edward Elgar Publishing Limited.

Ruggeri, Kai, Bojana Većkalov, Lana Bojanić, Thomas L. Andersen, Sarah Ashcroft-Jones, Nélida Ayacaxli, Paula Barea-Arroyo et al. 2021. "The General Fault in Our Fault Lines." *Nature Human Behaviour* 5: 1369–1380.

Salvador, Joseph. 2021. "Charles Barkley on Politicians: 'They Divide and Conquer.'" *Sports Illustrated*, April 4. https://www.si.com/college/2021/04/04/charles-barkley-on-politicians-they-divide-and-conquer.

Sammut, Gordon, Frank Bezzina, and Mohammad Sartawi. 2015. "The Spiral of Conflict: Naïve Realism and the Black Sheep Effect in Attributions of Knowledge and Ignorance." *Peace and Conflict: Journal of Peace Psychology* 21, no. 2 (May): 289.

Schroeder, Elizabeth, and Daniel F. Stone. 2015. "Fox News and Political Knowledge." *Journal of Public Economics* 126: 52–63.

Schwardmann, Peter, Egon Tripodi, and Joël J. Van der Weele. 2022. "Self-Persuasion: Evidence from Field Experiments at Two International Debating Competitions." *American Economic Review* 112, no. 4 (April): 1118–1146.

Serra-Garcia, Marta, and Uri Gneezy. 2021. "Mistakes, Overconfidence, and the Effect of Sharing on Detecting Lies." *American Economic Review* 111, no. 10 (October): 3160–3183.

Settle, Jaime E. 2018. *Frenemies: How Social Media Polarizes America*. Cambridge, UK: Cambridge University Press.

Shafranek, Richard M. 2021. "Political Considerations in Nonpolitical Decisions: A Conjoint Analysis of Roommate Choice." *Political Behavior* 43: 271–300.

Shergill, Sukhwinder S., Paul M. Bays, Chris D. Frith, and Daniel M. Wolpert. 2003. "Two Eyes for an Eye: The Neuroscience of Force Escalation." *Science* 301 (5630): 187.

Shiller, Robert J. 2017. "Narrative Economics." *American Economic Review* 107 (4): 967–1004.

Siegel, Jenifer Z., Christoph Mathys, Robb B. Rutledge, and Molly J. Crockett. 2018. "Beliefs About Bad People Are Volatile." *Nature Human Behaviour* 2 (10): 750–756.

Sillars, Alan, and Doug Parry. 1982. "Stress, Cognition, and Communication in Interpersonal Conflicts." *Communication Research* 9 (2): 201–226.

Sillars, Alan L. 2002. "For Better or for Worse: Rethinking the Role of Communication and 'Misperception' in Family Conflict." Paper presented at the 16th annual B. Aubrey Fisher Memorial Lecture, University of Utah.

Sillars, Alan L. 2011. "Motivated Misunderstanding in Family Conflict Discussions." In *Managing Interpersonal Sensitivity: Knowing When and When Not to Understand Others*, edited by Jessi L. Smith, William Ickes, Judith A. Hall, and Sara D. Hodges, 193–213. Hauppauge, NY: Nova Science Publishers.

Sitaraman, Ganesh, and Daniel Epps. 2019. "How to Save the Supreme Court." *Yale Law Journal* 148.

Skitka, Linda J., Brittany E. Hanson, G. Scott Morgan, and Daniel C. Wisneski. 2021. "The Psychology of Moral Conviction." *Annual Review of Psychology* 72 (January): 347–366.

Solda, Alice, Changxia Ke, Lionel Page, and William Von Hippel. 2019. "Strategically Delusional." *Experimental Economics* 23: 604–631.

Sommers, Cristina H. 2020. "Lessons of a Black Pioneer." *Persuasion*, December 14.

Stanley, Matthew L., Alyssa H. Sinclair, and Paul Seli. 2020. "Intellectual Humility and Perceptions of Political Opponents." *Journal of Personality* 88 (6): 1196–1216.

Stanovich, Keith E. 2021. *The Bias That Divides Us: The Science and Politics of Myside Thinking*. Cambridge, MA: MIT Press.

Steigerwalt, Amy. 2010. *Battle over the Bench: Senators, Interest Groups, and Lower Court Confirmations*. Charlottesville: University of Virginia Press.

Stone, Daniel F. 2011. "Ideological Media Bias." *Journal of Economic Behavior & Organization* 78 (3): 256–271.

Stone, Daniel F. 2013. "Media and Gridlock." *Journal of Public Economics* 101: 94–104.

Stone, Daniel F. 2019. "'Unmotivated Bias' and Partisan Hostility: Empirical Evidence." *Journal of Behavioral and Experimental Economics* 79: 12–26.

Stone, Daniel F. 2020a. "Just a Big Misunderstanding? Bias and Bayesian Affective Polarization." *International Economic Review* 61 (1): 189–217.

Stone, Daniel F. 2020b. "Your Political Counterparts Are Not Moral Monsters." Arc -Digital.com. November 2. https://medium.com/arc-digital/your-political-counterparts -are-not-moral-monsters-7877c98ec773.

Stone, Daniel F. 2021. "Biased Dislike, Excessive Dislike, and the Affective Polarization Bias." Working paper. Bowdoin College.

Stone, Daniel F., Drew Van Kuiken, and Justin Wallace. 2017. "Extended Exposure to Diverse News: Evidence from a Campus Project." Working paper. https://ssrn.com/abstract=3049015.

Stout, Christopher T. 2020. *The Case for Identity Politics: Polarization, Demographic Change, and Racial Appeals.* Charlottesville: University of Virginia Press.

Straka, John W., and Brenda C. Straka. 2020. "Reframe Policymaking Dysfunction through Bipartisan-Inclusion Leadership." *Policy Sciences* 53 (4): 779–802.

Sunstein, Cass R. 1999. "The Law of Group Polarization." Working paper 91. University of Chicago Law School.

Tappin, Ben M., and Ryan T. McKay. 2019. "Moral Polarization and Out-Party Hostility in the US Political Context." *Journal of Social and Political Psychology* 7 (1): 213–245.

Tappin, Ben M., Leslie Van Der Leer, and Ryan T. McKay. 2017. "The Heart Trumps the Head: Desirability Bias in Political Belief Revision." *Journal of Experimental Psychology: General* 146 (8): 1143.

Tesler, Michael. 2016. *Post-Racial or Most-Racial? Race and Politics in the Obama Era.* Chicago: University of Chicago Press.

Tetlock, Philip E., and Dan Gardner. 2015. *Superforecasting: The Art and Science of Prediction.* Crown Publishing.

Thaler, Michael. 2019. "The 'Fake News' Effect: An Experiment on Motivated Reasoning and Trust in News." Working paper. Harvard University.

Thomas, Ken. 2021. "Biden Leads Predecessors in Nominations, Lags Behind in Confirmations." *Wall Street Journal*, May 30. https://www.wsj.com/articles/biden-leads-predecessors-in-nominations-lags-in-confirmations-11622367002.

Thompson, Alex. 2021. "Enemies, a Love Story: Inside the 36-Year Biden and McConnell Relationship." *Politico*, January 22.

Thompson, Derek. 2017. *Hit Makers: How to Succeed in an Age of Distraction.* London: Penguin Books.

Toobin, Jeffrey. 2008. "The Dirty Trickster: Campaign Tips from the Man Who Has Done It All." *New Yorker*, May 23.

Traister, Rebecca. 2019. *Good and Mad: The Revolutionary Power of Women's Anger.* New York: Simon and Schuster.

Tuchman, Barbara W. 1962. *The Guns of August.* New York: Macmillan.

Van den Assem, Martijn J., Dennie Van Dolder, and Richard H. Thaler. 2012. "Split or Steal? Cooperative Behavior When the Stakes Are Large." *Management Science* 58, no. 1 (January): 2–20.

Van Vliet, Livia, Petter Törnberg, and Justus Uitermark. 2021. "Political Systems and Political Networks: The Structure of Parliamentarians' Retweet Networks in 19 Countries." *International Journal of Communication* 15: 21.

Verbruggen, Robert. 2021. "The Cotton-Romney Deal: $10 Minimum Wage for Immigration Enforcement." *National Review*, February 23.

Vosoughi, Soroush, Deb Roy, and Sinan Aral. 2018. "The Spread of True and False News Online." *Science* 359 (6380): 1146–1151.

Waldman, Paul. 2020. "Opinion: Hatred of Liberals Is All That's Left of Conservatism." *Washington Post*, December 11. https://www.washingtonpost.com/opinions /2020/12/11/hatred-liberals-is-all-thats-left-conservatism/.

Warner, Benjamin R., Haley Kranstuber Horstman, and Cassandra C. Kearney. 2020. "Reducing Political Polarization through Narrative Writing." *Journal of Applied Communication Research* 48 (4): 459–477.

Wasserman, David. 2017. "Purple America Has All But Disappeared." FiveThirty-Eight. March 8. https://fivethirtyeight.com/features/purple-america-has-all-but-dis appeared/.

Webster, Steven W. 2020. *American Rage: How Anger Shapes Our Politics*. Cambridge, UK: Cambridge University Press.

Webster, Steven W., Adam N. Glynn, and Matthew P. Motta. 2021. "Partisan Schadenfreude and the Demand for Candidate Cruelty." Working paper. Indiana University-Bloomington, Emory University, and Oklahoma State University.

West, Richard F., Russell J. Meserve, and Keith E. Stanovich. 2012. "Cognitive Sophistication Does Not Attenuate the Bias Blind Spot." *Journal of Personality and Social Psychology* 103 (3): 506–519.

White, Cindel J. M., Ara Norenzayan, and Mark Schaller. 2020. "How Strongly Do Moral Character Inferences Predict Forecasts of the Future? Testing the Moderating Roles of Transgressor Age, Implicit Personality Theories, and Belief in Karma." *PLOS One* 15 (12).

Whiting, Amanda. 2020. "Gloria Steinem and Betty Friedan's Friendship Was as Messy as It Looks on Mrs. America." *Bustle*, April 21.

Whitt, Sam, Alixandra B. Yanus, Brian McDonald, John Graeber, Mark Setzler, Gordon Ballingrud, and Martin Kifer. 2021. "Tribalism in America: Behavioral Experiments on Affective Polarization in the Trump Era." *Journal of Experimental Political Science* 8 (3): 247–259.

Whittington, Keith E. 2020. "Time to Amend the Presidential Pardon Power." *Lawfare* (blog). July 14. https://www.lawfareblog.com/time-amend-presidential-pardon-power.

Wike, Richard, Janell Fetterolf, Shannon Schumacher, and J. J. Moncus. 2021. "Citizens in Advanced Economies Want Significant Changes to Their Political Systems." Pew Research Center. https://www.pewresearch.org/global/2021/10/21/citizens-in-advanced-economies-want-significant-changes-to-their-political-systems/.

Williams, Daniel. 2020. "Socially Adaptive Belief." *Mind & Language* 36, no. 3 (April): 333–354.

Worthen, Molly. 2021. "Is There a Way to Dial Down the Political Hatred?" *New York Times*, June 11. https://www.nytimes.com/2021/06/11/opinion/god-religion-politics-partisanship.html.

Wright, Robert. 2021. "Mark Zuckerberg Must Be Stopped: How to Turn Facebook and Other Social Media Platforms from Bugs into Features." *Nonzero Newsletter*, June 28.

Wu, Long-Zeng, Haina Zhang, Randy K. Chiu, Ho Kwong Kwan, and Xiaogang He. 2013. "Hostile Attribution Bias and Negative Reciprocity Beliefs Exacerbate Incivility's Effects on Interpersonal Deviance." *Journal of Business Ethics* 120, no. 2 (February): 189–199.

Yang, JungHwan, Hernando Rojas, Magdalena Wojcieszak, Toril Aalberg, Sharon Coen, James Curran, Kaori Hayashi et al. 2016. "Why Are 'Others' So Polarized? Perceived Political Polarization and Media Use in 10 Countries." *Journal of Computer-Mediated Communication* 21 (5): 349–367.

Yon, Daniel. 2019. "Now You See It: Our Brains Predict the Outcomes of Our Actions, Shaping Reality into What We Expect. That's Why We See What We Believe." *Aeon*, July 4.

Yudkin, Daniel, Stephen Hawkins, and Tim Dixon. 2019. *The Perception Gap: How False Impressions Are Pulling Americans Apart*. New York: More in Common.

Zaki, Jamil. 2019. *The War for Kindness: Building Empathy in a Fractured World*. New York: Crown Publishing.

Zell, Ethan, Christopher A. Stockus, and Michael J. Bernstein. 2021. "It's Their Fault: Partisan Attribution Bias and Its Association with Voting Intentions." *Group Processes and Intergroup Relations* 80, 964–981.

Zhang, Yunhao, and David G. Rand. 2021. "Partisan Bias in Non-Political Information Processing." Working paper. Massachusetts Institute of Technology.

Zhou, Shelly, Elizabeth Page-Gould, Arthur Aron, Anne Moyer, and Miles Hewstone. 2019. "The Extended Contact Hypothesis: A Meta-Analysis on 20 Years of Research." *Personality and Social Psychology Review* 23 (2): 132–160.

Zmigrod, Leor, Peter Jason Rentfrow, and Trevor W. Robbins. 2020. "The Partisan Mind: Is Extreme Political Partisanship Related to Cognitive Inflexibility?" *Journal of Experimental Psychology: General* 149 (3): 407.

Zoizner, Alon, Shaul R. Shenhav, Yair Fogel-Dror, and Tamir Sheafer. 2020. "Strategy News Is Good News: How Journalistic Coverage of Politics Reduces Affective Polarization." *Political Communication* 38 (5): 604–623.

Index

Page numbers in italics refer to figures and tables.